Reviews of *The Finest Years*

'Drazin's is a genuinely quixotic enterprise, being both mad and lovably heroic at the same time. These days it is an uphill struggle, surely, even to get people to remember that there once existed a film-maker called Alberto Cavalcanti who fashioned in *Went the Day Well?*, *Champagne Charlie* and the ventriloquist dummy section of *Dead of the Night*, three of the most vibrant and unusual narratives in British cinema... The book is studded with similar unlikely odysseys ... fascinating stories, all of them, narrated with wit, generosity and erudition'   Jonathan Coe, *Guardian*

'The 1940s: were they the finest years of British cinema? Looking back, I suppose they were; but, then, no one knew what would follow. Charles Drazin writes well about that far-off time... Famous and forgotten names are painted perceptively in Drazin's portraits... Two directors stand high above the rest – one celebrated, one unsung: Carol Reed and Robert Hamer... Carol Reed's trilogy – *Odd Man Out*, *The Fallen Idol* and *The Third Man* – places him at the pinnacle of British film-making and Drazin gives full value to his exceptionally sensitive approach'   Moira Shearer, *Daily Telegraph*

'Drazin has not set out to write a straight chronological history... Instead, he has constructed what might be called a biographical mosaic of the period: a series of sketches of some 20 people who contributed to that golden age ... the overall tone is warm and affectionate, since Drazin succeeded in interviewing not only those few of his subjects who survive, but many of those who worked with them, loved and admired them. His own regard is unfailingly appreciative... *The Finest Years* is such a pleasure to read, and so informative, that a mere 250 pages of text seems scanty... With luck, if this book succeeds as it deserves to, Drazin will consider doing a Hollywood-style sequel and giving us *The Finest Years II*'
                    The Tablet

'Gossipy and opinionated, but also informative and fun'
                    Sight and Sound

The Finest Years
British Cinema of the 1940s

Charles Drazin

I.B. TAURIS

LONDON · NEW YORK

Published in 2007 by I.B.Tauris & Co Ltd
6 Salem Road, London W2 4BU
175 Fifth Avenue, New York NY 10010
www.ibtauris.com

In the United States of America and Canada distributed by Palgrave Macmillan
a division of St. Martin's Press, 175 Fifth Avenue, New York NY 10010

First published in 1998 by André Deutsch Ltd
Copyright © Charles Drazin, 1998, 2007

ISBN: 978 1 84511 411 4

A full CIP record for this book is available from the British Library
A full CIP record is available from the Library of Congress

Library of Congress Catalog Card Number: available

Typeset by Derek Doyle & Associates, Mold, Flintshire
Printed and bound in Great Britain by TJ International Ltd, Padstow, Cornwall

For Christopher

Contents

General Editor's Introduction

It is a pleasure and a privilege to be able to include a new edition of Charles Drazin's *The Finest Years: British Cinema of the 1940s* in the Cinema and Society series. When it first appeared in 1998 it signalled the arrival of a major new talent in the field of film history. That talent has been abundantly confirmed in his subsequent books, *In Search of the Third Man* (1999) and *Korda: Britain's Only Movie Mogul* (2002). His work is characterised by painstaking and meticulous scholarship, a mastery of the techniques of oral history, shrewd judgement and a lively, accessible style of writing.

The title of his book *The Finest Years* needs no justification. British cinema during the 1940s reached a level of both audience popularity and critical esteem that it has not equalled since. The peak year of cinema attendance in Britain was 1946, and the industry, galvanised by the war, produced a greater density of cinematic masterpieces than in any decade before or since. Drazin describes his book as 'a group portrait of *individuals*' and the individuals he chooses are mostly those he considers to have been neglected by historians. So he deliberately excludes Michael Powell and Emeric Pressburger, arguably Britain's greatest film-makers, Alexander Korda and Laurence Olivier, all of whom made major contributions to 1940s cinema, on the understandable grounds that all of them had already received extensive scholarly coverage. Instead he brings to life a gallery of talented but unsung figures who formed the creative heart of the revivified film industry.

There are the enterprising but unlikely film tycoons Filippo Del Giudice and Gabriel Pascal, whose flamboyant careers ended – perhaps predictably – in bankruptcy. There is the talented team that made up what one commentator called 'Mr Balcon's Academy for Young Gentlemen': Ealing Studios' Robert Hamer, Angus Macphail and Cavalcanti. There are the 'documentary boys' (Humphrey Jennings, Pat Jackson and Harry Watt) whose films have been retrospectively seen as capturing the true spirit of Britain at war. There are the once popular and successful but critically overlooked directors like Herbert Wilcox and Anthony Asquith. And there is Jack Beddington, head of the films division of the Ministry of Information, who Michael Powell once described as 'one of the most unjustly forgotten men of the war'. It is good to have them all recalled and recognised with the kind of sympathetic understanding that Charles Drazin brings to his analysis.

Jeffrey Richards

Acknowledgements

I would like to express my gratitude to all those people who shared with me their reminiscences of the British cinema of the 1940s. Their memories played an invaluable part in bringing the spirit and atmosphere of that time alive. They are: Alvin Bailey, Roy Baker, Moira Beaty, Martin Benson, Helen Blackburne, Sir Dirk Bogarde, Roy Boulting, Dallas Bower, Betty Box, Guido Coen, Sidney Cole, Jill Craigie, Brenda Danischewsky, Bob Dunbar, Sir Denis Forman, Harry Fowler, Harold French, Sir Alec Guinness, Richard Guyatt, Charles Hassé, Judy Hassé, Sir Anthony Havelock-Allan, John Hawkesworth, Erwin Hillier, Penelope Houston, Bob Huke, Pat Jackson, Stella Jonckheere, David Joyce, Jean Kent, John Krish, Alan Lawson, Nora Lee, Carol Lobb, Bill MacQuitty, John McCallum, Joe Mendoza, John Mitchell, Diana Morgan, C. Pennington-Richards, Peter Pitt, Dilys Powell, Michael Relph, Sir Sydney Samuelson, Charles Saunders, Douglas Slocombe, Julian Spiro, Peter Tanner, Angela Willans, Googie Withers, Geoffrey Wright, Manny Yospa and Freddie Young.

For information, advice, contacts and videos, I wish to thank Sandy Anderson, Kathy Burke, Julian Fox, Douglas Gordon, Sir Nicholas Henderson, Kevin Macdonald, Geoffrey Macnab, Colin Moffat, Caroline Moorehead, David Thomson, as well as the staff of the British Library, the London Library, the Public Record Office, the BBC Written Archives, and in particular the indispensable British Film Institute Library; for introducing me to the members of the BECTU History Project and supplying me with addresses, Roy Fowler; for kindly allowing me to reproduce a Richard Winnington drawing, Nicholas Garland; for providing many of the stills, the BFI Stills, Posters and Designs Department;

for introducing me to the mysteries of wills, marriage and death certificates, as well as other tools of the biographer's trade, Hugo Vickers; for film fan chat, Henrietta Moraes and Francis Wyndham; for arranging publication, Bill Hamilton, Laura Morris, Tom Rosenthal, David Wilson and Louise Dixon; for giving this book a second life in paperback, Philippa Brewster; for getting me started, Alan Ross.

Chief among the enthusiasts were Kevin Brownlow and Peter Hopkinson, who both provided unwavering encouragement and endless practical help; David Sherwin, who was full of insight and inspiration; and Dinah Drazin, who was a better editor than I could possibly have hoped for.

This book owes more than I can say to the example of Lindsay Anderson, who set me on the road and whose death in 1994 deprived me of the wisdom and generosity that he extended as a matter of course to so many other people. I have no doubt that he would have been an uncompromising critic of its failings, but I think he would also have seen its point.

Preface

When I began to research the original edition of this book more than ten years ago, my rather loose method – more intuitive than intellectual – was to scrawl on a sheet of A3 paper pinned above my desk the names of people who haphazardly popped into my head as somehow seeming significant to the period. As these names quickly grew into a sprawling constellation, I realized that to try to write about them all risked reducing them to shadowy ciphers, when what intrigued me most about them was detail, mood, character and motivation.

My decision to focus on some characters to the detriment of writing a more comprehensive history resulted in a relatively small number of individuals emerging from the greater mass. Indeed, my desire to illuminate the shadows sometimes meant including rather unknown figures at the expense of conventionally important ones. I nevertheless still hoped that the resultant group portrait would capture the essence of the British cinema of the 1940s in which they all played a part.

An important unifying principle lies behind what may at first seem to be a disparate collection of profiles. Attuned in its biographical approach to overlapping experience and shared affinity, *The Finest Years* explores the complex dynamics of creative collaboration. As significant as the lives of the people I write about are the various ways in which their paths crossed. Their individual portraits make up only a part of the story; of equal importance is the nature of the creative network to which they belonged. It may seem an odd kind of book that omits detailed accounts of such unquestionably major figures of the period as Sir Alexander Korda, Michael Powell and Emeric Pressburger, but includes a profile of such a comparatively unknown one as, say, Olwen Vaughan, the cinephile proprietress of a private club where many film makers used to gather. Yet, such figures – despite their lack of obvious consequence in the form of production credits – nonetheless provided a critical framework of support and inspiration for the wider film community.

The Finest Years is an attempt to give a sense not only of this community, but also of the nature of the interaction between its constituent parts. The film historian Thomas Schatz borrowed a phrase, 'the genius of the system', from the French film critic André Bazin to suggest the true nature of classical Hollywood. The British cinema I write about was far more fluid and muddled than its Hollywood counterpart, but even if it was too chaotic and financially fragile in its nature ever to amount to a credible system of lasting duration, it did display – to a marked degree – what we might call 'the genius of the team'. Such creative affinity is the main subject of *The Finest Years*, for it explains how a group of individuals worked together to achieve extraordinary feats they could not have accomplished alone. Indeed, to the extent that *The Finest Years* can be said to take an overt stance, it is – through suggesting the complex, organic and highly varied nature of collaboration in the cinema – to encourage readers to resist the simplistic, if often complexly expressed, notions of authorship that have tended to dog the study of film.

A notable development since this book first appeared is the far more positive climate of critical appreciation that the British cinema now enjoys. Little evident ten years ago, this new readiness to celebrate and to understand the British cinema is expressed in the proliferation of websites, university courses and the publication of several new books; the most notable of those that concern the 1940s have been added to the select bibliography. The other significant development is the DVD revolution, which has not only made most of the films I write about in this book easy to see, but also encouraged research into the circumstances of their production. If I have one final hope for this new edition, it is that it will encourage readers to return to the films, which remain the best tribute of all to the finest years.

Charles Drazin
Summer 2007

Introduction

I don't think it's possible to give a true picture of the people I've chosen to write about without providing an outline of the circumstances in which they worked, and this introductory chapter offers an account of some of the realities of the film business of the time.

The number one reality – then as ever – was Hollywood. In the 1940s about 80 per cent of films exhibited in Britain were American. These films were usually popular with audiences and cheaper for exhibitors to rent than British-made films. The size of the American market was four times that of the British. This basic fact accounted for what has been an eternal dilemma for British film producers: whether to make modest films, which could just make a profit in the home market; or to make more lavish films with the aim of breaking into the lucrative American market.

The very existence of a British film industry only became an economic possibility with the passing of a Quota Act in 1927, which required distributors and exhibitors to handle an annually increasing number of British-made films.* Before that 95 per cent of films on British screens were American. The Hollywood distributors met their obligations under the new Act by paying for films to be made in Britain as cheaply as possible. The infamous 'quota quickies' were the result. Most of these cheaply made films were not worth exhibiting, but they met the legal requirements, and had the added benefit for the American distributors of making their Hollywood product seem even more attractive by comparison. The Act was renewed in 1938, and killed off the

---

* The quota started at 7½ per cent and had risen to 20 per cent by the time the original Act was replaced in 1938.

quota quickie by stipulating a minimum cost for a film to qualify. MGM responded by setting up a production subsidiary in Britain. This endeavour was firmly controlled from Hollywood and the directors were American, but at least it provided 'inward investment' and a chance for British technicians to acquire some much needed expertise.

'In the film business you either want to make money, or else you want to go into production,' commented the producer and ex-banker Richard Norton in a succinct summary of the British film industry.[1] But every now and then a fluke encouraged the illusion that it might be otherwise. In the early 1930s, Norton was making quota quickies for United Artists. He met Alexander Korda and persuaded United Artists to back *The Private Life of Henry VIII*. Made for £94,000, the film broke into the American market and took nearly £200,000 in its first world run. Seduced by its success, the City poured money into British films, and producers embarked on a concerted attempt to capture the American market.

Many of these producers looked on enviously as Korda, in the wake of *Henry VIII*, joined the board of United Artists. But in practice this link with an American distributor amounted to very little. United Artists had no circuit of its own, and as a result it was the small independent exhibitors who booked their British films. The American film critic Richard Griffith commented: 'The audiences which came to these small theatres were city slum-dwellers, small-town proletarians, farmers and cowboys. Even if they could understand the West End accents, which was more than doubtful, they could not understand the films. Some British pictures of the period certainly had ideas, taste and talent. There was only one thing wrong with them. So many of them simply were not films in the sense that American audiences understood films.'[2] But the situation was of course much worse if you didn't have an American distributor. The American circuits were owned by the big Hollywood studios, who naturally regarded British films as unwelcome competition to their own products.

By the beginning of 1937 it was obvious that the British assault on the American market had failed. Isidore Ostrer, chairman of the biggest production concern in Britain, announced that 'unless we can get a bigger return from the American market for British pictures Gaumont-British will be compelled to abandon production'.[3] In March 1937 the company published a loss of £98,000 for the previous year. This was quite modest compared to Korda, who in the same period had run up for his City backers a loss of £330,000. As the year progressed the industry was rocked by a succession of further losses and receiverships.

The City learnt the lesson of the Great Slump and wrote off the film industry as a bad investment. It wasn't really a business. But this was also why the British cinema was so fascinating. Against all reason it always finally refused to die, and those people who sought to be its saviours had to be motivated by something other than money.

'I am in films because of the Holy Spirit,'[4] declared J. Arthur Rank, the flour tycoon and Methodist Sunday school teacher whose fortune took the place of the City millions to build up the most powerful film empire the British cinema had yet seen. By the mid-1940s the Rank Organisation was responsible for over half of British production.* 'I began making religious films for showing in churches. This was a labour of love, but it was a great disappointment. My pictures could not stand up to competition, and I learnt the basic principle that it is no use making films unless you can distribute them and get playing-time for them.'[5] So Rank bought his own distribution company and his own chain of theatres, and as his empire grew British films and Britain became as much a cause as the original one of using the medium to preach a moral message.

'When I first came into this industry I had the slogan "Trade follows the film" well in mind, that, as in the past American trade had expanded through its Hollywood pictures, so would British trade likewise expand if aided by a big British film industry.'[6] Rank committed his resources to financing the efforts of Britain's most ambitious producers, who for a few giddy years enjoyed not only Hollywood budgets but also a freedom they would never have found in Hollywood. 'We are building up an organization which will ensure that these films are shown on a world scale never before seriously contemplated by the British film industry,' declared Rank in 1946. 'And I am going to do it, whatever it costs.' Never before had there been such a breathtaking combination of scale, boldness and idealism.

* In 1948 this amounted to 32 out of 63 first features (36 if one includes the output of Ealing Studios, which the Rank Organisation co-financed). The next largest production company, British Lion, made eight first features. (Source: *The British Film Industry*, Political and Economic Planning, 1952.)

In 1947 Rank wrote a note to Sydney Box, his most important producer, to wish him a merry Christmas. 'May 1948 be a year full of happiness for you all and may you have great success in giving happiness to the millions of cinemagoers. We have a big task in 1948 but I feel we have a united team conscious of its responsibilities and great opportunities and as that sense of vocation spreads right down so shall we achieve our great aim.'[7] It's hard to imagine the chairman of a large public company writing such a note today, and an appreciation of Rank's crusading nature is the key to understanding the nature of the 1940s film revival.

The sympathy and admiration for Britain that the war engendered, as well as the genuine appeal of a more vital and realistic cinema, aided Rank's plans for securing a world market. But once peace returned, it was business – or no business – as usual, with Rank encountering the old resistance of the Americans to British films. Many of these films were admired by the sophisticated New York critics, but with only a very few exceptions – notably *The Red Shoes* and *Henry V* – they failed to attract the mass audiences required to pay back their cost.

It's instructive to read in the trade magazines what American exhibitors at the time thought of films that are now considered to be classics of the British cinema. Powell and Pressburger's *A Matter of Life and Death* – or *Stairway to Heaven* as the Americans preferred to call it – may have been a hit in Manhattan, but Phil Schwartz regretted playing it in his cinema in Connecticut: 'This type might be good for class houses, but they are poison to the guy with the average "thinker". He sits and looks at the screen, gets up, smokes, sits again, kibitzes with his wife, who gets mad because she wants to sleep.'[8] Carol Reed's *Odd Man Out* was hailed by more than one critic as the best film of all time, but this made little practical difference up in Middlebury, Vermont. 'I expected big things of this picture,' wrote Kenneth Goreham, the proprietor of the Town Hall Theatre. 'The college apparently enjoyed it, but the natives do not go much for this type of show.'[9] There was a similar response from George James to Ealing's chiller *Dead of Night*, which he played for one night in his theatre in Ojai, California: 'Special notice was sent out to art groups, friends of culture and English residents in the country. Their attendance was almost 100%, but due to the fact that hardly anyone else came, business was far below average.'[10] One is left with the impression from the exhibitors' reports that often the problem with Rank's prestige films wasn't that they weren't good enough, but that they were *too* good.

During the war cinema attendances were at record levels and confidence in the British film industry had never been higher. But even so in four out of the six years to 1946 the Rank Organisation had recorded sizeable losses on the production side of its business.* Film-making was sustained only by the faith – which few people outside the film industry shared – that with continued investment a viable industry would eventually be established.

In the end Rank's efforts were undone by a spectacular own goal. In August 1947 a sterling crisis led the government to impose a tax of 75 per cent on the import of foreign films. Hollywood responded with an embargo on the export of films to Britain. Rank, regarding it as a 'duty and an opportunity', made plans to produce sixty films a year, but even this was nowhere near enough to make up the shortfall of American films which had occupied 80 per cent of British screentime. The following spring the government agreed a compromise with the American producers and lifted a tax that they realized was unsustainable. A backlog of Hollywood films flooded into the cinemas just as the first of Rank's own hastily produced – and in the circumstances inevitably mediocre – efforts were rolling off the production line. The choice for filmgoers was simple. Hooray for Hollywood.

Rank's troubles quickly coloured attitudes to the industry as a whole. To finance the increase in production the Rank Organisation had arranged a deal whereby the exhibiting side of the group, Odeon Theatres, would buy shares in its production arm, General Cinema Finance. Criticism of the arrangement caused the company to issue a statement revealing its huge production losses, which only served to confirm the City's conviction that film-making was a bad investment. The Rank Organisation may have succeeded in refinancing its own production, but investors took heed of the underlying problems of the industry and steered clear of the smaller independent production companies.

In 1948 the government tried to organize private finance on the independent producers' behalf, and when none was forthcoming

---

* 1940–41: £47,357 (loss); 1941–42: £58,494 (profit); 1942–43: £105,100 (profit); 1943–44: £179,412 (loss); 1944–45: £378,293 (loss); 1945–46: £1,667,070 (loss). (Source: company statement in the *Financial Times*, 12 December 1947.)

reluctantly loaned public money through the National Film Finance Corporation. The biggest recipient was British Lion, under whose umbrella most of the country's independent producers sheltered. By 1953 a £3 million loan had been written off and the insolvent company was taken into public ownership. As for the engine of the British film renaissance, by 1949 the Rank Organisation had run up an overdraft of £16 million and was forced to cut back drastically on production. After it had enjoyed the most charmed years in its history, the reality of the British film industry was once again cruelly exposed: its economic stability lay in exhibiting American films, not making its own.

Sir Anthony Havelock-Allan provided me with by far the most lucid and authoritative summary of the British cinema's fortunes. He came into the industry as an assistant to Richard Norton, making quota quickies in the early 1930s. He produced *In Which We Serve*, whose success in America ushered in a new wave of big-budget British features much as *The Private Life of Henry VIII* had a decade before. He formed Cineguild with David Lean and Ronald Neame, producing – among other films – *Brief Encounter*, *Great Expectations* and *Oliver Twist*. He left to form his own production company, Constellation. His last credit as producer was the Lean epic *Ryan's Daughter* in 1970. Few people could have had more direct experience of the highs and lows of film-making in Britain.

'There's a basic difficulty with the British film industry. We make films in the same language as the Americans. And whereas the Americans, not unnaturally, have free access to the only market in the world that can make really big money, which is America, we don't. And because we make films in the same language, by and large the actors and the directors, the English directors, can get paid much more money in America, and so they go to America. From time to time we're lucky. We've got an immense amount of talent here, latent talent, and from time to time things like *The Crying Game* and *My Beautiful Laundrette* and Puttnam's picture *Chariots of Fire* get made here, and if they're so good, they may, against the general trend, get a showing in America – may get into that market, which is the only market that matters. There are something like ten times as many cinemas in America, and the American people still has the habit of film-going. The English people go, but they go to see American films.'[11]

Anyone familiar with the recurring crisis of the British film industry will find it grimly amusing that the latest wave of producers is being funded by Lottery money. No solution could be more apt.

If the 1940s loosened the natural sway of Hollywood, it was more than anything else because of the war. It gave British producers a subject that American films could not compete with. For once their artifice seemed pallid by comparison with the dramatic realism and urgency of home production.

It's relevant to note that in spite of the Nazi occupation a similar process was occurring on the other side of the Channel. However improbable it might seem, the French cinema was experiencing a renaissance too. These were the years of *Les Visiteurs du soir, Le Corbeau, Les Enfants du Paradis, Les Dames du bois de Boulogne*. It proved easier for French film-makers to resist the ideology of their conquerors than it had been to fight off the commercial domination of Hollywood. Flippant as it may sound, the Occupation, with the complete absence of American films it entailed, felt more like the Liberation for the French film industry. As the director Louis Daquin put it, 'Isolation enabled French film-makers . . . to rediscover a genuine native style.'[12]

Every country in Europe was affected by Hollywood's dominance, but Britain most of all. As by far the largest source of foreign revenue, it attracted the presence of several powerful American distribution companies, and indeed for all practical purposes was part of Hollywood's home market. Given this relationship, it was natural that the British film industry should more closely resemble its American counterpart. In a radio talk the director Cavalcanti, who had worked in both France and Britain, pointed out that 'while in Great Britain production is industrialized and almost completely in the hands of a monopoly, in France, on the contrary, it is independently financed and run almost entirely on a freelance basis. This, of course, encourages individual experiment, and altogether an approach more artistic than commercial.'[13]

By comparison with that of Britain the French cinema was little more than a cottage industry. In 1946, pointed out the critic Georges Sadoul, Marcel Carné's budget of £100,000 for *Les Portes de la Nuit* was 'considered an incredible folly, jeopardizing French production',[14] while at about the same time in England Gabriel

7

Pascal was spending over ten times this much making *Caesar and Cleopatra*. The average cost of production in France was a fraction of that in Britain, and cinema attendances were correspondingly small. At the end of the war the average French person was visiting the cinema eight times a year, the average British person twenty-eight times.[15]

Filmgoing in the 1940s was dominated by three large circuits, ABC, Gaumont and Odeon (the last two both belonging to the Rank Organisation). In 1946 there were 30 million admissions a week in Great Britain. This huge market of regular moviegoers entailed a regular change of programme. A circuit cinema would show a film for two or three days, then the next film, and then the next film.

The routine for film producers was to secure a distribution contract before embarking upon production. Because in this way production was tailored to perceived box-office demands – to repeating past success – the odds were stacked against anything different or original. It was no accident that an exceptional success like *In Which We Serve* should have been made by an independent producer who had at first failed to secure a distribution contract but was brave enough to embark upon production anyway.

The exhibitors and the more serious critics always seemed to be in conflict, but this was understandable. To put it in modern-day terms, if you owned a cinema, and you had a family to support, what would you rather show? The latest Ken Loach or *Independence Day*?

To get an idea of the kinds of obstacle the serious film-maker in Britain faced, it's worth looking at the trade magazines again. The word Entertainment was used, not Art; and the most important phrase of all was 'box office'. Full-page advertisements featured glossy pictures of marching bands and dancing girls with names of films that today hardly anyone has heard of – *Hello, Frisco, Hello* or *Is Everybody Happy?* ('It's the picture with a happy toot!') – but which then audiences went to see in droves.

When Sir Alexander Korda came back from America in 1943 to make films in Britain for MGM, he announced that his first production would be *War and Peace*, and that Orson Welles would direct it. The columnist of the *Daily Film Renter* pointed out to his readers that Welles's two previous ventures (which happened to be *Citizen Kane* and *The Magnificent Ambersons*) were not box-office successes. 'My own opinion is that he's too imaginative.'[16]

Nor did Humphrey Jennings – the man Lindsay Anderson contended was the only real poet the British cinema had produced – cut much ice. His feature-documentary, *Fires Were Started*, may today be considered a masterpiece by the critics, but at the time the big circuits refused to take it without substantial cuts, and even then had to be pressurized by the Ministry of Information into doing so. The Gaumont circuit arranged a preview showing in a cinema in Preston. The circuit's publicity manager reported the consensus to be that 'the film was deplorably slow for the first half-hour (this time was taken up in depicting the boredom of the fireman's daily life – unhappily audiences do not wish to be bored these days).' He ended his report by suggesting that 'the film would make a good second feature, provided a good strong first feature was played with it.'[17]

And the producer Filippo Del Giudice may have been responsible for such classics of cinema as *Henry V* or *Odd Man Out*, but he was routinely ridiculed. His attempts to be innovative were dismissed in the trade magazines as fantastic nonsense. He was laughed at not because he was impractical but because he was trying to give the exhibitors what in the main they did not want: Art.

No less a restraint on the development of an intelligent, adult cinema was the attitude of the censor. It was considered an extraordinary advance when in 1938 Wendy Hiller was allowed to use the word 'bloody' in *Pygmalion*. But over five years later, when the feature-documentary *Western Approaches* was made, the censors still objected to the word's use – on this occasion by merchant seamen, adrift in a lifeboat after their ship had been torpedoed, who would no doubt in practice have used far stronger language. A small ration of bloodies was granted only after energetic lobbying.

The secretary of the British Board of Film Censors, Joseph Brooke Wilkinson, had been in office since its inception in 1912, and continued to serve in this role until his death in 1948. He exerted considerable influence over the four elderly presidents he would advise (the youngest was sixty-six upon appointment) and policy changed little in the thirty-six years of his incumbency.

The Board, which had been set up by the film industry,

reflected the general reluctance to treat the cinema as a medium suitable for serious expression. In making its decisions, it regarded its duty as to protect an audience which was composed largely of young people and families. No effort was made to discriminate. Its decisions, which were characterized by a stifling conservatism, entirely suited a trade that preferred the status quo for the smooth running of its business.

A few producers challenged the censors' general attitude that films should not be controversial, but the pattern of progress was a wearying one of defiance and the Board backing down only after extracting as many concessions as it could. *The Citadel* was a landmark in the British cinema. The film-maker and critic Basil Wright described it as 'virtually the first studio film of social or civic tendency to be made in Britain'.[18] When its scenario was submitted to the Board for approval in 1937, the censor wrote: 'There is so much that is disparaging to doctors in this book, that I consider it unsuitable for production as a film. I think it dangerous to shatter what faith the general public has in the medical profession.'[19] MGM-British went on to make the film anyway, but then had to agree to substantial changes to get a certificate.

Muriel Box was head of the script department at Gainsborough Studios shortly after the war. 'During practically every other film made at Gainsborough,' she remembered, 'we had to fight to prevent the blue-pencilling of our scripts and the mutilation of finished pictures.'[20] And this was equally true of the other studios. Michael Balcon has often been criticized for the reluctance of Ealing's films to deal with sex, but it was as much the common sense of a cautious producer.

It was not just British censors that film-makers had to contend with. Before their films could be shown in America they had to conform with the Production Code of the Motion Picture Association of America. When Ealing wanted to make a film of the children's story *Mistress Masham's Repose*, the Production Code Administration – informally known as the Hays Office – objected to the word 'Mistress' in the title, and the project was cancelled. The script of *Scott of the Antarctic* was at first rejected on the grounds that Oates's sacrificing his life for his comrades was suicide, which was against the teachings of the Catholic Church. The Hays Office was only finally persuaded to relent by the argument – sanctioned by an official of the cardinal at Westminster – that Oates could have been saved from the frozen wilderness by the hand of God. It's easy to mock the censors for what seem like patently absurd rulings, but their conservatism was really no more startling than that of society at large.

When there was a post-war vogue for crime films, the critic C. A. Lejeune was just one voice among many when she commented: 'The films are committing a monstrous blunder in entertaining so many morbid themes, and dwelling so insistently on brutal and savage detail. The sensible film-goer does not want these things. The sensible film-goer is sick to the soul of spivs and murderers, cads and racketeers.'[21]

Then as now few troubled themselves over whether such disturbing scenes – although scarcely disturbing by today's standards – had any artistic justification. So it was nothing remarkable that *They Made Me a Fugitive*, a fine film by the great Brazilian director Alberto Cavalcanti, should have been condemned in a Sunday paper under the headline 'Brutality, Lust, Sadism', and dismissed as an 'offensive spectacle'.[22] Such responses would generally have discouraged the censors from being lenient.

Yet for all the difficulties there was a sense of pride, shared by audiences, critics and film-makers alike, in what the British cinema was achieving in the 1940s. In an account of cinemagoing during the war the journalist Guy Morgan commented that one of the most marked phenomena of the war was 'the genuine and unforced interest in British pictures' that cinema patrons had developed after previous indifference and even antipathy. He made the point that the experience of war had shaped a more discerning and critical audience. 'They are quick to detect the phoney in speech and behaviour. They love to be honestly entertained by films that are glamorous, romantic, tuneful, adventurous, preposterous, and clearly removed from any semblance of everyday life. But they very much resent being fobbed off with pseudo-realistic pictures; films that set up to be realistic and aren't; films that simulate life in a half-hearted manner. Hollywood, 4,000 miles away from the nerve centre of the war, have been slower than our producers to take this new circumstance into account.'[23] Richard Winnington, one of the more exacting critics, echoed this perception: 'British films have come to possess a craftsmanship and freshness above that of the regular flow from Hollywood. By contrast they seem miracles of taste and intelligence.'[24]

And writing in 1947,[25] Michael Balcon, who had struggled through the British film industry's darkest days, commented: 'Nobody of my generation and with my interest in films could possibly envisage a situation in 1919 in which a national daily newspaper with a great circulation could rely on maintaining a reader interest by running a popularity ballot on British films;* no more could be imagined a debate in the Parliament of the time in which an issue is made between the importation of American films and American dried eggs. In other words we emerge from the latest holocaust with at least something in our favour and to our benefit – a virile, flourishing new industry: British film production.'†

Perhaps the ultimate proof of the miraculous new vitality was that even the Americans were taking notice. In 1946 the *March of Time* devoted an episode to the British revival. 'Whatever the outcome of Britain's new challenge to Hollywood, a challenge calling for the best each can produce, the final verdict will be rendered as it always must be by the movie-going public – the people who pay their money to be entertained.' In reality Britain's 'challenge' was like going one round with the Champion, but for a few wonderful months before the edifice came crashing down it seemed a genuine contest.

* The *Daily Mail* inaugurated its National Film Award in 1945, in the words of its organizer, 'to give encouragement and pay tribute to this increasingly important Industry, which possessed the means of spreading British culture and the British way of life through the world'. (Source: *Preview 1948*, World Film Publications, p. 27.)
† The characteristic dissenting voice of Lindsay Anderson was the exception that proved the rule. Motivated by an article that George Stonier (a pseudonym for William Whitebait, the film critic of the *New Statesman*) had written in *Vogue* in praise of British cinema called 'The Ascending Spiral', Anderson replied in *Sequence* with a critical piece called 'The Descending Spiral'.

Filippo Del Giudice

Writing of a new generation of British film-makers who had come to prominence during the war, Thorold Dickinson, one of the most distinguished of their number, commented that they 'were piloted by producer-impresarios, two of whom were outstanding, Michael Balcon of Ealing Studios, and Filippo Del Giudice of Two Cities Films'.[1] The mere fact that Balcon aspired to make good, not just commercial, films was in itself enough to make him remarkable. But as just about anyone who knew him would agree, he was 'conventional', 'middle class', 'suburban', and for many film-makers he could be as much a hindrance as an inspiration. As Michael Powell put it, 'Mickey Balcon was not an exciting leader.'[2] Filippo Del Giudice was not really a leader, but he was exciting.

While Balcon had long been at the heart of the British film industry, Del Giudice – or Del as inevitably his hard-to-pronounce name was shortened – was an outsider; while Balcon was professional, Del was in spirit an amateur; and while Balcon was careful, Del was a gambler. But maybe it was only a gambler's instinct that could have been responsible for *In Which We Serve*, *The Way Ahead*, *The Way to the Stars*, *Odd Man Out*, *Henry V* and *Hamlet* – pretty much the backbone of the 1940s British film renaissance. It was the kind of achievement that usually results in knighthoods and busts and eponymous awards, but Del received no such public recognition, and today is forgotten.

He was born in Trani, southern Italy, in 1892, and was brought up in Rome. He trained as a lawyer, and worked for the Vatican. When in 1933 he fled Fascist Italy, he brought with him to London a portrait of Pope Benedict XV with the pontiff's signature and testimony as to the bearer's *'energia del carattere'*.

Although with hindsight the choice of referee seems characteristic of Del's grandiose conception of things, his early days in London, when he knew nobody and could not speak the language, were spent in poverty in a run-down basement flat off the Cromwell Road. But with his papal reference he soon managed to scratch a living teaching English to the children of Italian waiters, and eventually, when he had managed to learn enough English himself, was able to return to his old profession.

He stumbled into films by chance. In 1936 Warner Brothers had brought an injunction in the English courts to stop Bette Davis making a film in Italy, and the film's producer, Ludovico Toeplitz, turned to Del for advice on Italian law. It is easy to imagine how the crazy, extravagant world of films, with which at that time even the City was flirting, and in which foreigners like Alexander Korda seemed divinely favoured, must have appealed to the flamboyant Del Giudice. He was smitten and, with fellow Italian Mario Zampi, founded the film production company Two Cities, the two cities then being London and Rome, although the latter, unsurprisingly in view of the political situation of the time, would soon be replaced by New York.

The two men persuaded a Major Arthur Sassoon and a Colonel Crossfield to finance the beginning processes of film producing – the buying of rights and the commissioning of scripts. They went on to make a successful film version of *French Without Tears* in 1939 for Paramount, and then, a year later at a time when Germans usually came in only two dimensions, both of them bad, *Freedom Radio*, an admirably intelligent story about a Viennese doctor setting up an anti-Nazi radio station while his wife, blinded by dogma, becomes an important figure in the Party.

But in spite of having made one of the first and best anti-Nazi propaganda films, both Del and Mario Zampi were interned as enemy aliens when Italy came into the war.

It meant the end of Two Cities, Mark 1, but Del, who in his flight from Italy had already experienced such an abrupt reversal of fortune, did not allow himself to be disheartened for long. He appointed himself camp leader, organizing everything from schools to banks. His stay was brief. While the luckless Zampi was interned for the duration, Del – who was a diabetic – was released after only a few months. He returned to London to revive Two Cities.

Del was keen to contribute to the war effort, and doubtless to show his loyalty to his adopted country. His idea was to team up with a famous writer and to produce a film that would command international prestige, rather as Gabriel Pascal had done with Shaw's *Pygmalion*. He settled on Noël Coward. Anthony Havelock-Allan, who had produced a modest wartime thriller for Two Cities called *Unpublished Story*, knew Coward slightly and arranged a meeting. Coward, who was a sea captain *manqué* and never happier than when on board a destroyer, eventually came up with the story of HMS *Kelly*, the ship of his great friend Louis Mountbatten which had recently been sunk off Crete.

As Coward thought the cinema 'a soul-destroying industry in which actors of mediocre talent were publicised and idolised beyond their deserts, and authors, talented or otherwise, were automatically massacred',[3] Del had pulled off something of a coup. 'His English was appalling and his enthusiasm boundless,'[4] Coward wrote of their first meeting. And he would never come to regret the association, remembering in his memoirs with considerable fondness 'the over-exuberant and most lovable Filippo', who 'in spite of all storms and stresses and difficulties, never allowed his faith in me and the picture to be shaken for a moment.'[5]

These 'stresses and difficulties' included opposition to the project from the powerful Ministry of Information, the withdrawal of two distributors who objected to the proposed casting of the film, and sneering articles in the press about the unfitness of Coward to play Mountbatten. Somehow Del kept going when more 'sensible' producers would have lost their nerve, and by the time he held a party at Claridge's in early 1942 to celebrate the formation of the production team that would make *In Which We Serve*, he had found the money.

Even then it could easily have ended in disaster. After all, Coward knew nothing about making films. But Anthony Havelock-Allan managed to persuade David Lean to become Coward's co-director. Lean already had the reputation as the best editor in British films and had turned down Havelock-Allan's invitation to direct quota quickies for him at Pinewood. But *In Which We Serve* at last offered him an opportunity that he considered to be worthy of his talents.[6]

In Which We Serve opened to an avalanche of rave reviews. It was the second most popular film at the British box office in

1943,* and – a rare feat for a British film – impressed on the other side of the Atlantic too, where it grossed $1.8 million (£250,000). The *New York Times* called it 'one of the most eloquent motion pictures of these or any other times',[7] and Coward won a special Oscar for his 'outstanding production achievement'. Del the gambler had won the jackpot.

When I was researching this book, I had the good fortune to meet Guido Coen. At the beginning of the war he and his father were interned as Italian citizens, and met Del on the ship that took them all to the camp on the Isle of Man. In the camp Guido became Del's assistant, and later joined him in London when he was released a year after Del.

The two men worked together closely for seven years, and Guido was able to witness the extraordinary rise of Two Cities from obscurity to being the boldest and most renowned company in British films. He was present when Del, 'scratching his belly' and 'in his pants',† called Noël Coward for the first time, and nearly sixty years later still marvelled that this unknown Italian, with his erratic English, should have persuaded the 'Master' to make a film for him. *In Which We Serve* became the template for Del's future plans, and was, as Guido put it, 'the stepping stone into the big world'.[8]

The next stepping stone was but a short pace away. Competing with *In Which We Serve* for studio space at Denham in early 1942 was another stirring propaganda piece, *The First of the Few*. Its producer-director-star, Leslie Howard, was every bit as patriotic and celebrated as Coward. On the eve of war he had abandoned a comfortable life of movie stardom in America, where he had lived for many years, to return to an embattled Britain. Through the Blitz he had championed the fight against Nazism in broadcasts to America on the BBC, and he had made one of the first propaganda films of the war, *Pimpernel Smith*.

During their tenancy of Denham they exchanged favours. Del played a Fascist Italian mayor in *The First of the Few* and Howard spoke the commentary that opened *In Which We Serve*. They were soon to work together in a more significant way. Two Cities was

* *Random Harvest* with Ronald Colman was the most popular.
† This call was made from Del's flat in Grosvenor House, hence his scanty attire.

producing a small film to promote the Auxiliary Territorial Service. The director Adrian Brunel began shooting at the tiny and poorly equipped Highbury Studios, and the first few days' rushes were unsatisfactory. Brunel regarded it as just a teething problem, but none the less Del suspended the production and asked his new friend Leslie Howard if he would take over. Howard said he liked the idea but wanted to do it in his own way, and so the little picture became a big picture.

The hapless Brunel recalled the experience bitterly. 'I was *not even consulted* – I, the director – and the decision seemed to be in the hands of another who had only a limited technical knowledge and no technical experience – he had not witnessed any of our difficulties.'[9] Del is not mentioned by name, but there is little doubt that he was the 'another' responsible for the decision. He was not a naturally cautious man, and the trouble with the rushes seems more like a pretext. He wanted to entice the powerful and influential Leslie Howard into the fold.*

The two were well matched. Both behaved like crusaders on a mission, and found in the war a cause. From the very outset a major partnership was envisaged. At about the same time as Howard took over the production of *The Gentle Sex*, he also joined the Board of Two Cities.

At the meeting which appointed him, he declared: 'I have seen my friend Del Giudice at work for many months and I think he has got the great gifts which we absolutely need, and those particularly which people like myself are unable to supply. He is able, for instance, to discuss with expert knowledge with people on the difficult and complicated distribution and financial aspects of the business, and hold his own against them. He is definitely a man of whom the fullest use should be made and I personally shall rely on his closest collaboration.'[10] Del had these words written down on a sheet of paper to use – much like his signed portrait of the Pope – as a reference.

What Howard really admired in Del was his readiness to dream on the same scale as himself. Del's ability to hold his own in the 'complicated distribution and financial aspects of the

---

* The blow for Brunel was softened by the fact that he would continue to work on the film as Leslie Howard's assistant. The two men were close and had formed a company together in the early 1920s called Minerva Films. The company made comedies and its scenario writer and co-director was A. A. Milne.

business' amounted to treating such dreary details with the disregard that Howard felt they deserved.

Two Cities used to have regular production meetings at Denham, but Guido Coen remembers that Del would never familiarize himself with the costs or query budgets. 'Prices are going up,' he used to say with a resigned shrug. 'Please don't bother me with details of money – we are making a great picture.'[11] Such an attitude was unusual in a chief executive. That it flourished was because of the war. Leslie Howard himself often touched upon the theme in his radio broadcasts. 'I knew that money and the material things are, in these days, being shown up in their true unimportant light as never before. That it did not matter how much property was destroyed, nor how much wealth poured out for our cause, because property and gold had become valueless. I knew what it was to belong to a free nation with a noble motive and that we were headed for ultimate triumph. And as I listened to the enemy sneaking overhead, I knew the real meaning of being an Englishman in Britain in the year 1940.'[12] He carried this attitude into the studio. 'Nobody could persuade Leslie to worry about money,' his daughter Ruth recalled. ' "What is money?" he was heard to say . . . "Nothing must matter except the final excellence and integrity of the film." '[13]

Leslie Howard and Del Giudice were allies in ambition and extravagance, but it didn't matter so long as they were vindicated at the box office, and *The Gentle Sex* was one of the most popular British films of 1943. 'It became a really worthwhile money-maker,' Coen remembers, 'a great success. So immediately Del thought: "I don't want to go with the little guy, it means nothing, I want to go with the names – those are the people that know what to do." And from that moment onwards he had around him the very best. That's what excited him.'[14]

From that moment onwards he also had a generous distribution contract with the Rank Organisation. Arthur Rank who had, as Del put it, written him 'a nice little cheque'* to make *The Gentle Sex*, would write many more for him. Del's productions were central to the Rank Organisation's attempts to break into the American market,†

---

* According to Guido Coen, it was actually Mrs Rank who wrote a cheque for £75,000 – not so little in those days.
† Implicit in the very name Two Cities (London and New York) was the fact that the company's productions had to be successful on both sides of the Atlantic to make a profit. The average cost of a Two Cities film was £200,000 to £300,000, far in excess of what could be recouped at the British box office.

and Two Cities enjoyed a guarantee of costs plus a fifty-fifty share of profits from foreign sales.[15]

No one did more to promote through feature films the vital interests of the country, or to forge the national myth that still shapes our ideas of Britain during the Second World War:* *In Which We Serve* (the Navy) and *The Gentle Sex* (women in military service) were followed by *The Lamp Still Burns* (nursing), *The Demi-Paradise* (Anglo-Soviet relations), *The Way Ahead* (the Army), *This Happy Breed* (Noël Coward's study on what it is to be English), *Henry V* and *The Way to the Stars* (the Royal Air Force).

These films did not come off any production line; they were the expression of individuals. Some were deeply flawed, but they engaged because they were *personal*. Del's revolution was to put his faith in people. 'When he picked on somebody, and had faith in them, he would go along with that person,' said Coen. 'No question of him saying, "Well, I don't think that this is right." '

The industry was astonished when in 1943 Del gave Laurence Olivier responsibility for the most expensive British film ever made up to that time. Michael Powell, who encouraged Olivier to put himself forward as a director, summarized the response: 'Entrust an actor on his first film with £350,000 and let him direct himself! You must be mad, Del!'[16] But it was not just a star of Olivier's stature that Del placed his faith in. When, soon afterwards, Del backed the young Jill Craigie to make the documentary *The Way We Live*, doubtless the response was: 'Entrust a woman to direct a film. You must be mad, Del!' And it must have seemed equally mad to allow a twenty-four-year-old Peter Ustinov to direct *School for Secrets*. But because Del did not seek to impose his own view on these productions, they all had the coherence of a single vision and there was nothing to stop the occasional masterpiece.

'There was not a pennyworth of strategy,' Guido Coen said. 'If we had two or three pictures to make, there's your strategy: we'd got work for well over a year.' But there was an underlying ethos, and some years later, after he had been forced to leave Two Cities, Del would codify that ethos in a document he called his 'Technical Testament':

* Balcon at Ealing was the nearest rival, but was bargain basement by comparison.

I believe that this business has three separate fields: (a) Administration (b) Creation and Craftsmanship (the artistic and technical field) (c) Sales (distribution and exhibition). I do not believe that all these matters can (from an artistic point of view) be carried on successfully by the same man.

I belong to the 'administrative' side and that is the reason why I am not going to call myself a 'Producer' but an 'Administrator'.

The 'Administrator' must have a 'flair' for stories and be able to create an atmosphere in which an artistic product can be brought to life.[17]

The word 'artistic' peppers his credo. 'I am only interested in the Comédie Française and the Old Vic,' he declared of the kind of cinema he wished to encourage. 'I think that the world is going to be, little by little, more inclined to a serious approach to this medium ... There are an enormous amount of people in each country who do not go to the cinema at all: it is for these people I am providing entertainment different from the stereotyped one. To achieve my kind of entertainment for that potential audience – and there are millions – a method of integrity must be adopted.'[18] Del's practice had been to delegate direct responsibility for producing a subject to a subsidiary unit, which would also have had a direct say in the choice of that subject. 'In my concern stories are only decided upon and writers, cast and technicians only engaged by each subsidiary company after discussion between the "Administrator" and the leading personality of the subsidiary company.'[19] And that personality, according to Del, was the director, who must be accorded complete freedom. 'We all know that if you have a very good Director it is useless to interfere with his work. If you interfered it would be like looking over the shoulder of Picasso or Augustus John whilst they are doing their work. Anybody really great could not stand being watched in such a way.'[20]

Del's 'Technical Testament' was an extraordinary document which a Mayer or a Selznick would have regarded as seditious nonsense. Treating film-makers like painters betrayed a dangerous naivety. But for a short while its principles held some sway in Britain, and, as Basil Wright put it, this 'wholly permissive attitude to film-makers (whatever the ultimate financial problems) led to a Golden Age of British films'.[21]

Among Del's strengths were a genuine understanding of, and respect for, the artist's temperament, boundless enthusiasm and a razor-sharp intellect. He was full of extravagant phrases, which to English ears could often sound like shameless flattery but owed more to a natural effusiveness. Dallas Bower, who first approached Two Cities with the idea for a film of *Henry V*, remembered that conversation with him was a matter of interrupting his torrent of words with a 'Shut up, Del!'[22] Then he would listen to what you had to say.

For film-makers who regarded the corruption or dilution of their ideas as a disagreeable but unavoidable fact of life, it was a wonderful surprise to find a man who actually encouraged them to pursue their vision. Del talked their language and shared their values. If you found the great German screenwriter Carl Mayer penniless and starving in the street – as Dallas Bower did – who would you take him to? Del, of course – who found him a job at Two Cities. It was such generosity of spirit on a profligate scale that made him unique in the film business. Del's extravagance proved to be both his triumph and his undoing. 'I want to be the butler to the talented people,' Anthony Havelock-Allan remembered him saying. 'The only thing was that he then began to live in a lifestyle which meant that however much the talented people were making, he clearly was making rather more.'[23] By 1946, when Two Cities had become a part of the Rank Organisation, 'rather more' meant £10,000 as a basic salary, £10,000 for the upkeep of his London house, another £10,000 for his country mansion, £10,000 for travelling expenses, and £10,000 for entertainment, including £3,000 for cigars at 27s 6d apiece.[24] 'I only get leetle money, but the company pay for my comforts,' said Del, modestly summing up the situation.[25]

While most of the nation was enduring austerity and rationing (sacrifices movingly depicted in many Two Cities films), Del did not stint, and there are many witnesses of the grand scale on which he played the role of impresario. Sir Robert Bruce Lockhart, who was negotiating a script contract with Two Cities, recalled a dinner Del invited him to at the Hungaria Restaurant: 'On this occasion there was a party of eighteen or twenty film-stars and directors. I sat next to a beautiful Norwegian blonde and divided my attention between her and the caviar and vodka, the grouse and Mouton Rothschild, and the Courvoisier brandy.'[26]

At Sheepcote, his country house in the Chiltern Hills, Del threw magnificent parties, entertaining 'talents', starlets and cabinet ministers alike. Sir Nicholas Henderson, who was Ernest Bevin's private secretary, recalled an occasion soon after the war: 'Del greeted us with soft, yet demonstrative handshakes and a faint smell of perfume. He was wearing loud-check tweeds and thick-rimmed, dark tortoiseshell glasses. He exuded hospitality. He led us over deep-pile carpets and between enormous bowlfuls of tulips to the drawing-room. The house party were already a bit tight ... Mrs Bevin shouted merrily to me through the ether: "Hello, Henderson, we're having a lovely time." Del, who had just returned from a visit to the USA, produced a box of a hundred cigars and a trousseau of ties, socks and coloured braces, all of which he gave Bevin.'[27] Asked how he could afford such parties, Del would reply, 'Ippity pays.' Ippity was his name for Excess Profits Tax, against which the entertainment costs would be set.[28]

It was impossible to overlook the absurd indulgence of such occasions or Del's own comically fulsome manner. Many of his guests thought he was a buffoon, but others recognized that what he had achieved for the British cinema far outweighed the excesses of Sheepcote. 'You can't judge Filippo like normal people,' commented Sir Stafford Cripps, one of Del's distinguished visitors. 'Creative artists are different.'[29]

Del took a disarming pride in showing off his splendid surroundings. In a magazine profile of the time he can be seen posing in front of a Canaletto,* gazing into the stippled waters of the Grand Canal, and pouring cocktails at the bar in his private cinema; leopard skins and antlers hang from the oak-beamed walls of the converted barn. On a table by the cinema screen stands a model of HMS *Torrin* from *In Which We Serve*.[30]

I don't think Del had any idea of the disapproval that parading such luxuries would provoke. The Italian instinct for display and munificence came up against the puritan streak of the English. Perhaps Del saw himself as a kind of latter-day Duke of Urbino. The splendour was all part of encouraging wonderful work, of creating – as he put it in his 'Technical Testament' – 'an atmosphere in which an artistic product can be brought to life'. Significantly, the first photograph in the

---

* 'I bet it must have been a copy,' commented Guido Coen when I told him about this picture.

magazine article is of Del behind a desk in his tapestry-lined study, with a secretary in attendance. A caption makes the point that 'This is not just his home. It is the headquarters of Two Cities Films.'

Del made no distinction between his work and his private life. They were intermingled, and he was passionate and excessive in both. He was fond of women, and endearingly prone to lose his heart to them. Lacking English discretion, he made little attempt to keep his liaisons secret and his weakness for the opposite sex was widely known. 'There was one girl whom he seemed to love with all his heart,' wrote Sir Robert Bruce Lockhart. 'Assuredly he spoilt her. One day he came in sore distress to a friend of mine. "I have a heavy grief," he said. "*She* has left me." Great tears rolled from his eyes as he came to the crowning tragedy. "You remember that lovely frame with my photograph on the piano? I gave it to her . . ." Then, with a loud sob, he added, "She took the frame, but left my picture." '[31]

Probably the girl was the Norwegian blonde Sir Robert had sat next to in the Hungaria – Del's mistress Greta Gynt, an actress whom he had met through Gabriel Pascal. They seem to have had a fairly stormy relationship of regular break-ups and reconciliations. Guido Coen remembers Del tearfully confessing on one occasion that he lacked the strength to keep his resolution never to see Greta again. 'Have pity on me!' he sobbed before ringing to ask her to come back. It was a lacrimose and typically operatic display, but also showed that Del possessed a touching recognition of his own failings, even if he was incapable of correcting them. He was so besotted with Greta that long after she had left him he would go out only with women who looked like her.

People like Del are one of the reasons why sensible parents through the ages have warned their daughters against going into the acting profession. He certainly seems to have taken every advantage of the access to young and beautiful women that his position as a leading film producer afforded him. No one else I have written about in this book has been remembered with quite so much admiration and affection, nor with so many warnings of 'For God's sake, don't use this story!'

Del's amorous adventures were not in themselves exceptional, but they help to complete the picture of a warm, generous-hearted man with a zest for life and an appetite for glamour and excitement. With an Italian feel for the stylish and heroic, he devoted himself to eluding the commonplace. 'We'll have a banquet!' he would say even if it was just an ordinary meal.[32]

Whether it was winning the war or building the new society, Del sought to take up the great causes, but he did so with an Italian pragmatism: as circumstances changed, he made sure to keep in with the most exalted circles and to cultivate whoever happened to be the most influential people of the time. In an industry which was so heavily dependent on government support this was particularly important. In the election of 1945 he effortlessly changed horses. 'Let's face it, Guido, I've always been a socialist deep down,' he said to Coen when the Labour Party won, although he had previously been friends with the other side.

'I think you should go into politics and represent the film industry, and have a voice there,' he told the socialist Jill Craigie, who added: 'I was very useful to have around when he had politicians at his table.'[33] Ernest Bevin and Sir Stafford Cripps were frequent visitors. When the health-conscious and vegetarian Sir Stafford came, Del ate spinach only. Perhaps, as a diabetic himself, he could offer some special sympathy for a Chancellor who suffered such poor health: on one occasion he managed to persuade Cripps to travel to Switzerland with him for a lavage.[34]

Jill Craigie thought Del was apolitical, but at the same time he was a natural – if opportunistic – idealist. This idealism presented itself most obviously in his attitude towards films. He never compromised the principles he outlined in his Technical Testament, even though it set him in open conflict with the way the industry was run. He could reach a *modus vivendi* with politicians of whatever persuasion, but not with the distributors and money-men of Wardour Street.

The crusader in Del would of course have appealed to Arthur Rank, the Sunday school teacher turned film mogul. But if he was on the whole inclined to be generous as far as the likeable Italian was concerned, his chief executive and right-hand man John Davis gave no quarter.

It was Davis who had brought to an end the agreement with Two Cities whereby the Rank Organisation took on all the risk but received only half of the profits (if there were any). A clause in that agreement gave the Rank Organisation script approval. It had never been exercised before, but Davis turned to it when Two

Cities embarked on its most ambitious project, *Henry V*.

However fulsomely everyone would speak of the film after its huge success, when it was actually being made 'nobody believed in it', Guido Coen remembered. 'I can't say that the Rank Organisation really wanted *Henry V*.' The very expensive and risky production provided a perfect pretext to intervene. In return for script approval, Del was forced to yield a controlling interest in Two Cities. He lost his independence for this reason alone, maintained Coen, not because of the cost of the film.[35]

But Coen maintains with equal conviction that the 'overheads of Two Cities were out of all proportion' and that its eventual collapse – or, as happened, absorption – was inevitable. *Henry V* may have turned out against all expectation to be a success, but it could not offset the failures that would follow, like Thorold Dickinson's *Men of Two Worlds*.

Dickinson's film tells the story of a Westernized African musician who returns to his village in Tanganyika and persuades his people to reject the superstitious practices of a witch doctor in favour of modern medicine. It was intelligent, ambitious, slightly dull and even more expensive than *Henry V*. Shot on location in Africa with out-of-date Technicolor stock left over from *Henry V*, it had to be reshot in Denham. It ended up costing £600,000.[36] So far from the mere 'gamble' of *Henry V*, everything about *Men of Two Worlds* seemed to make box-office disaster a certainty: the colossal expenditure, a story set in an obscure colony, no 'love interest', and a leading role played by an unheard-of African actor. That the first public performance should have been in Dar es Salaam, at Thorold Dickinson's insistence, was in keeping with the heroic madness of the venture.

Del liked to think of himself as 'an administrator of talents'. *Men of Two Worlds* exposed his major failing in this role. He could give artists full rein, but did not know how to steer them back in the right direction when they went off course. The idea for the film had been sold to Two Cities by the Films Division of the MOI. It had begun life as a story outline called 'White Ants' written by one of the Division's officers, Mrs Arnot Robinson. Del chose Thorold Dickinson as the director. Dickinson then went to Africa and wrote a script, which the Films Division greeted with dismay. 'I think this script is a rather distressing compilation,' wrote their adviser, Angus Macphail, the highly experienced scenario editor of Ealing Studios. He went on:

To my mind it's so inferior to 'White Ants' that it affords no basis for discussion or compromise. If Mr Del Giudice has stated that he would like to produce 'White Ants', I suggest he should again be offered the opportunity of doing so. He could start by throwing 'Men of Two Worlds' into the dustbin.

I think Thorold Dickinson is a first rate director, one of the very best in this country. But I don't think he's a good writer. If he's summoned here to discuss the matter, I bet you he'll defend his script till the cows come home and no progress will be made by anybody.[37]

This was the sort of situation where the constructive intervention of a hands-on producer like Korda or Balcon might have made a difference. Del, indulgent to a fault, did not know how to save Thorold Dickinson from himself, and at the same time save unnecessary expense – which was much more important as far the Rank Organisation was concerned.

In addition to the huge cost of *Men of Two Worlds* there were several expensive projects which never even reached the screen: £50,000 for the film rights of Winston Churchill's *Life of Marlborough*; £50,000 for the rights of Somerset Maugham's *Then and Now*, abandoned after nearly another £100,000 had been spent on it; and plans for a bio-pic of *Talleyrand* which never came to fruition. Once Two Cities had become part of Rank, it was inevitable that sooner or later the man Del scathingly dubbed 'il contabile' (the accountant) would seek to eliminate an unnecessary risk.

Del 'represented the one thing that made John Davis think that films were an unacceptable business to be in,' said Anthony Havelock-Allan, 'which was that sooner or later people began to spend money like water. It's a business where, no matter how much you try to control, sooner or later you find that they were not spending £300,000 on making a film but £600,000.'[38]

In 1946 the Rank Organisation found itself responsible for some spectacularly huge expenditure with no obvious return. Quite apart from Two Cities, there were the prestigious but costly films of the Powell and Pressburger company the Archers and of Cineguild under the umbrella of the Independent Producers; then there was over a million spent on Gabriel Pascal's breathtakingly dull Shaw epic *Caesar and Cleopatra*, and another million on *London Town*, a dud musical starring the comedian Sid Field and directed in Technicolor by the colour-blind American director Wesley Ruggles. Such lavish films could only be justified by success in the American market, which had proved elusive.

Something had to be done to staunch the flow and Two Cities was an obvious target. In deciding to get rid of its guiding spirit, Davis was certainly the prime mover, but many others in the organization had also lost confidence in Del by this time. Richard Norton, who had at Rank's suggestion tried to talk him out of his wilder ideas, could discern 'no return whatsoever except politics and political intrigue'.[39]

By far Del's wildest idea was that the cinema could be an art the equal of any other. Believing in the quality of his own films, he wanted them to be exploited in a special way, with long runs of at least a year in selected theatres before being given a general release. Word-of-mouth publicity, he believed, would then help to ensure their success. This attitude challenged the whole set-up of an industry which, as Del put it himself, was geared to 'routine products with a quick turnover'.[40] The producer Bill MacQuitty was in a good position to see both sides. He had produced Jill Craigie's documentary *The Way We Live* for Two Cities and had also worked closely with Sydney Box, who from 1946, as production chief at Gainsborough, was at the heart of Rank's growing determination to produce economical but popular films. MacQuitty recalled a climate in which films were little less ephemeral than dramas on television today. The cinema manager 'put on a black tie and stood at the door, and ushered the people in to four shows a week. He had a different one on Sunday, and then two days for the others. So even if he got an absolute smash hit on Monday, it went off on Tuesday. It just had the Monday and Tuesday. Then another film came in . . . Del's great fight was to let the thing run for a year if it would.' But this required a degree of individual care and attention that an assembly-line system could not easily provide, and, as MacQuitty put it, 'buggered up the whole of the financial mechanics of running a circuit'.

Del had argued vigorously for such individual exploitation, and was convinced that with his prestige films he could change the public's 'movie habit'. But once he had failed to win this argument within the Rank Organisation, the single most important force in British films, there was even less chance of him swaying the industry when he was outside. Guido Coen believed that Del did not want to leave Rank, but the fundamental difference of approach left him no alternative.

In the spring of 1947 Del sold his shares in Two Cities, as anxious to escape an impossible situation as the Rank Organisation was to get rid of him. He set up a new company, which with typical *élan* he called Pilgrim Pictures. The name was a statement of intent: to conduct a crusade on behalf of the prestige British picture, to pioneer a system of production and exhibition inspired by the needs of 'humanity' (Del was not afraid to use such lofty terms) rather than commerce. Pilgrim would be less a company than a mission. Had it not already been appropriated, the motto 'Ars gratia artis' would have been ideal.

An indefatigable scribbler of notes, memoranda and policy documents, Del would later set down his view of the Rank years in an account that captures the wearying struggle that individualists within a corporation, more often than not, have to face:

I had to accept the invitation of [the Rank Organisation] in 1942 to enter first into a distribution contract with their distributing concern, and later on, in 1943, whilst I was facing the greatest difficulty inherent to the production – unwanted by them – of *Henry V*, I had to join them altogether . . .

They never dared to oppose me in connection with the choice of stories and talents. But something new and unexpected happened to me. The huge organisation had by then selected as one of their leading chiefs a gentleman only competent in accountancy and exhibition. There was not yet enough power in him to stop me doing the many films which in the words of the Manchester *Guardian* 'brought most honour to the British Screen'. But still they wanted to prove that I was not only 'extravagant' but altogether 'wrong' in the selection of stories and talent, which according to their opinion, was not giving to them films of commercial value ('box-office entertainment' as they call them). In order to prove that they were right the method of 'general exploitation' was applied to my films . . .

I had fought all the time for my 'special method of exploitation', winning only in respect of *Henry V*, whose entire cost was not paid to me before one year after the great triumph of that film. Meanwhile over-powered by debts and commercial weakness I had to subjugate myself to the commercial wealth of the organisation, and I lost my independence altogether and was compelled to increase my fight and my crusade for films of 'quality', nearly exhausting my strength in this fight, until the moment I thought that it was wiser to re-acquire my complete independence . . .

There is no possibility of selecting stories and talents if the people controlling distribution and cinemas have to supply the finance and studio space for production. If one organiser of production depends on them, he must either subject himself to their interferences and influence, or, if he has enough strength and ability, go on fighting all the time. But in either case he will never be able to control the exploitation of his films.[41]

At Pilgrim, Del renounced the distribution guarantee – conventionally regarded as the *sine qua non* of production – as a point of principle and sought finance from outside the film industry. In his wishful thinking he thought he might achieve the best of all possible worlds, producing a film without interference and then selling it in his own way.

In an interview with the *Leader* magazine soon after he had set up Pilgrim he declared, 'If I were an exhibitor or a distributor, I also would look after business instead of art. People of great responsibility give the public not what they want but what they need. Publicans simply supply their customers with whisky and beer. Worrying about people's health isn't good for pubs.'[42] Such a mixture of piety, forthrightness and arrogance would have won him few friends in an industry where, after all, most people were exhibitors or distributors.

A letter Del wrote to one of his 'talents', Bernard Miles, conveys the mood of defiance with which he set up Pilgrim.[43] In its florid, colourful style it suggests a man who had all the fondness of his native land for grand opera, with its plots and intrigues and high emotions from revenge to *l'amour fou*. The occasion was the considerable success in America of Miles's film *Tawny Pipit* (1944) after it had been shelved there for three years. At the Rank Organisation Del had been criticized for backing this wartime story of a village's efforts to protect a rare bird's nest from an assortment of predators ranging from schoolboys to army tanks. He was convinced that its release in England had been so contrived as to make the film appear to be a flop; and he was equally certain that the adoption of his 'special method of exploitation' for the release in America, where the film played for longer than usual runs in art houses, was only because John Davis thought it would fail and so discredit him.

In the letter Del gloats at the backfire of the scheme: 'This film was shown in the hope that all my theory could be smashed by example. They hoped that *Tawny Pipit* would have done the trick, but Providence has silenced my enemies, and the triumphal praise of the intelligent American critics has given them an unforgettable lesson.' He then eggs Miles on to make the most of the situation. 'It is time, my dear Bernie, for you to write about it. Don't let us give time to these mercantile people who are trying to kill the very roots of this new expression of a British art.' With echoes of Blake exhorting the New Jerusalem, he asks, 'Where is your master pen, which is pungent and sharp as a sword?' and offers an accompanying assurance. 'You have nothing to fear. There is going to be Pilgrim, which is going to give all chances to the real talents, and in time, as soon as I have enough space, there is a greater chance for you. Let us fight for these ideals. We shall enjoy life much more than any money can ever offer in pride and fun.' Here is Del the crusader, the gambler and, not least, the intriguer.

But he was too excitable and impulsive to make a truly effective Machiavelli, and often ended up foiling his own schemes. The newspaperman and film critic Ernest Betts was briefly Del's public relations adviser. It was a hopeless task, for, as Betts recalled, Del loved gossip and was notoriously bad at keeping secrets. The news that Pilgrim had been promised £1 million by the City was far too irresistible for Del to keep quiet for long. Without waiting for Betts's advice, he gave an interview to the London *Evening Standard* in which he revealed that one of the backers was Sir John Ellerman, then reputedly Britain's wealthiest man. As Betts would have told his boss if he had been consulted, Sir John had a hatred of publicity amounting to an obsession. Soon after the *Standard* article appeared the offer of financial support was withdrawn. Many similar indiscretions would follow. 'It is not fanciful to say that he talked himself into pictures and he talked himself out of them,' observed Betts.[44]

With its connotations of going into the Promised Land, Pilgrim evoked the spirit of the times as a new government embarked on the struggle to win the peace and build a more equal society. And Del, who had so solicitously entertained Bevin and Cripps, must have hoped to strike a chord with a socialist government, which – as competition from Hollywood redoubled in the aftermath of the war – was considering major intervention in support of British feature films.

The first films he made at Pilgrim were notably progressive and campaigning in nature. The Boulting brothers' *The Guinea Pig* (1948) told the story of a tobacconist's son who wins a scholarship to a public school and the struggle he has to overcome class prejudice. Bernard Miles's *A Chance of a Lifetime* (1950) was about a factory owner who, fed up with strikes, challenges his workers to try to run the factory themselves.

The themes of these films were echoed by Del's own desire to challenge the status quo in the film business. The slogan he cheerfully repeated at every opportunity was 'Divorce Production from Sales'. As favourite a pastime of his as antagonizing the denizens of Wardour Street was lobbying the government to introduce radical reform of the industry. When in 1949 Harold Wilson, President of the Board of Trade, set up a committee of inquiry to look into distribution and exhibition, Del wrote to its chairman, Lord Portal, with a number of recommendations:

> In view of the increasing number of 'fictional films', 'mass production' or 'merchandise' which is coming out of British studios, there is no doubt that the reputation of the British film all over the world is losing its grip.
>
> The only way to correct this unfortunate state of affairs is for your committee to recommend to the Government and then to the House of Commons that a law be passed in order to prevent any person or body controlling large chains of theatres and distributing concerns from financing production.
>
> Production in the studio must be financed by a body which is only concerned with the 'quality' of the British film. The finance for 'mass production' ought to remain with those private sources which like to use money in that fashion.[45]

Del suggested that quality film production should be financed by a tax on ticket sales and that a law should be passed to prevent any individual from owning more than fifty to sixty cinemas. It was not only a direct attack on his old friend Rank, whose 600 cinemas were his only hope of keeping afloat in the face of huge production losses, but also on the Rank Organisation's rival, the Associated British Picture Corporation, which had over 400 of its own cinemas.[46]

Among the people who ran the British film industry in the late 1940s there was probably no person more *non grata* than Del. The sadness was that not even the government listened to him. If Del had hoped that a new progressive administration would have sympathy for his record as the most adventurous producer in British films, he was to find that in practice this counted against him.

The government wanted to do what it could to put the film industry on a sound footing, and in particular to help independent producers for whom financial backing was increasingly difficult to find. But it was afraid of the political controversy that would result from state involvement in such a business, and wanted to keep any assistance at arm's length. Rather than give support direct to the producers themselves, it chose to operate through a distribution company.

In early 1948 the Board of Trade formulated an ambitious scheme to attract private capital into British Lion – a distribution company – which it was envisaged would then assist independent producers working under its umbrella. Del was encouraged to associate Pilgrim Pictures with this 'instrument of national policy', as British Lion came increasingly to be called in government memos.

It was an unpalatable development for Del not only because of his objection to dependence on distributors, but because he had already fallen out with the two leading figures in the company, Sir Alexander Korda and Sir Arthur Jarratt. He had approached them in November 1947 when he was seeking finance for Pilgrim Pictures' first feature, *The Guinea Pig*.

It's worth following Del's confrontation with Korda in some detail, because it marked the turning point in his fortunes. It also illustrated his quixotic nature and – in a revealing contrast – Korda's calculation and cunning.

In dispute were Pilgrim's overheads, as well as the script and Korda's suggestion that the actor Kieron Moore should play the lead in the film. A heated argument ensued and the meeting ended in an impasse. After having stormed out in a huff, the next month Del wrote a conciliatory letter to Korda:

It is impossible to explain in a short letter the many reasons for my silence. You have every right to be upset with me for I ought to have written to you before. Since I saw you last many many things have happened which have absorbed all my time. One day I will tell you all. This letter is only to apologise for my silence.

You are a genius. I am a very modest business man and a 'Manager of Talents'. After careful consideration and discussion my talents and I came to the conclusion that it was no use for our work to have any more distribution contracts. None of my talents, who trust me on the administration side, would be prepared to discuss with anyone except me either their stories or cast. I came to the conclusion that it was useless to continue discussing matters even with you in view of the necessity of depending on the head of your distribution or Casting Manager.

But believe me, Alex, when I say that apart from the great admiration which I have for you as a matter of this art I have a great affection and imperishable gratitude for all your kindness and patience and for all the valuable time you have given to me during the last attempts to find a way to conciliate the creed of the distributors with the creed of the creators.

I am sure that if I succeed in financing production without any link with distribution you will be one of those who will appreciate my efforts most, for you belong to creation more than commerce.

In any case do believe in my devoted friendship apart from any business consideration for I shall always have an unwavering admiration for your great powers of creation.[47]

Del had decided to go his own way, and this letter didn't really need a reply. Nor did it get one until four months later, in April 1948, when Pilgrim Pictures was in close touch with the Board of Trade, lobbying for separate financial assistance. On 8 April, Pilgrim's private backer, William Riley, lunched with Wilfrid Eady of the Treasury and then visited Del at Grosvenor House to report on the meeting. By a piece of timing which seems too extraordinary a coincidence not to have been by design, a note arrived by messenger from Korda that very afternoon. 'My dear Del,' he wrote, 'I find that, by a silly oversight, a letter which I wrote to you on the 15th December in answer to yours of the 14th was not sent to you. I am very sorry about this, as it leaves the record of our conversations not clear. Please forgive me for the oversight. I send you the letter now as it was written on the 15th December.' The letter read as follows:[48]

My dear Del,

Many thanks for your kind and unexpected letter. There are several mis-statements in it which I wish to correct.

One, you are giving me too fullsome compliments that I am a genius. I have to defend myself against this accusation very strongly.

The other mis-statement is in the subject matter of your letter which I hasten to correct. It is not a fact that at any time during our conversation anybody has expressed the idea that you have to 'depend' on the head of our distribution or Casting Manager. The truth is quite the contrary. You have asked the help of our Casting Manager which was freely promised to you.

Also I want to clarify another statement of yours. You say you made 'the last attempts to find a way to conciliate the creed of the distributors with the creed of the creators'. Whatever this may mean it was never for a second the subject of our conversation. You were told all the time that neither I nor Sir Arthur Jarratt wished to exercise any opinions on your production policy. I as a matter of fact reiterated often that I did not even wish any discussion with any of the people who you call your 'talents'. The only difference between us was your personal and other overheads which myself and my friends found out of proportion.

Apart from this I am sure you will remember well I even agreed to your request to give you a guarantee for a loan from the Bank.

I write you this letter because I do not wish any misunderstandings to cloud our friendly relations and as a proverb says in your beautiful native language, 'Clara Pacta Boni Amici'.

I hope as I know how close contact you have with your 'talents' and a copy of your lettter goes to them that you give the benefit of the same publicity to this letter of mine.

Yours

Alex

For good measure Korda reiterated his point about overheads in the final paragraph of his accompanying note: 'Our conversations came to a dead end solely on the ground that you asked for 100 per cent guarantee plus 10 per cent for your personal overheads. We thought that our financial friends would not agree to that. I must say also, in all frankness, that neither I nor Sir Arthur Jarratt thought that these conditions were reasonable.'

Both letter and note may have been addressed to Del, but it's hard to resist the conclusion that their message was intended much more for Harold Wilson and the officials at the Board of Trade, whom Korda would have made sure got a copy. The fact that the 'missing' letter was purportedly written back in December 1947 but dated 15 December 1948 only arouses one's suspicions further. The timing was delicate, as Korda was about to deliver to the Board of Trade a long memorandum showing how a bolstered British Lion was indeed the ideal vehicle for supporting independent producers. Any suggestion that independent producers were not free at British Lion would have been compromising.

Korda had carefully chosen his words to capitalize on the popular conception of Del as wayward and extravagant. By contrast, *he* was the safe pair of hands who had the confidence and support of the trade.

Del was incensed by Korda's intervention and it scotched Riley's attempts to persuade him to accept what seemed the only practical option in view of the government's position – namely an association with British Lion. Reporting back to Eady a few days later, Riley wrote of the affair: 'I must say that it left me with the impression that we were faced with an unrepentant situation, the kind which you and I would have resolved behind the Cricket Pavilion before leaving our prep school.'[49] He also took the opportunity to clarify the particularly contentious matter of Del's overheads: 'In contradiction to the last paragraph of Korda's letter: 10 per cent is not, and never was, required for Del's personal overheads but to cover the whole of the general overheads of the company.'

The government persevered with the British Lion plan. But it wanted Del to be accommodated if possible, and in July 1948 received an undertaking from Korda that Pilgrim Pictures would be welcome to join British Lion on the same terms as any other producer. Korda pointed out that this would require Del to renounce his views on the divorce between production and distribution. But there was a more fundamental reason why the two could never work together: it would be like trying to get two artists to paint the same picture, explained Del.[50]

Del's dealings with British Lion and the government in 1948 were perhaps the most foolhardy yet admirable chapter in his extraordinary career. With some vanity, but more with a firm belief in a heroic cause, he turned his back on the certain finance that an association with British Lion would have offered.

In August 1948 Del sent a letter to Harold Wilson that was lament, warning and proposal all in one.[51] 'Although broken-hearted, disappointed and exhausted,' he wrote, 'I have stood with courage and determination and bull-dog tenacity and have prevented my company going into liquidation as, at a moment of physical and mental exhaustion I had decided to do, when I saw your scheme would not work for the kind of films I make for Britain.' He described the British Lion plan as 'an uncomfortable one, for it is evident that the City does not trust British Lion for they know the position of the company is anything but solid.' He then suggested that if the government really wanted to help independent production, it should act as a guarantor of a possible loss: that way it would not actually have to lend money to producers, who would be able to raise money themselves on the strength of the guarantee.

This letter was taken no more seriously than all his other communications with the Board of Trade, but it was prescient. The government was unable to secure any private finance for British Lion and, through the newly formed National Film Finance Corporation, ended up lending it £3 million of public money. A series of heavy losses ate up this sum, and finally, in 1954, the company went into receivership.

Contrary to the government's original intention when it first decided to organize financial support for the film industry, the NFFC would in the event lend money directly to producers as well as to distributors. But Del received nothing. The 'prestige' films he made, with their large budgets, were considered inappropriate investments for taxpayers' money.

With support from Lloyds Bank Del struggled on, but he had staked everything on government intervention and unwisely failed to hedge his bets. Having been so forthright in his condemnation of the distribution and exhibition system, he could hardly expect any favours when it came to promoting his own films. In 1950 *A Chance of a Lifetime* became a *cause célèbre* when the three big circuits refused to book it on the grounds that it was not entertainment. The Board of Trade intervened and, exercising its authority for the first time under the 1948 Films Act, ordered the film to be shown. Reviewers, almost without exception, admired the film for its realism and thought it far better than the escapist fare that the circuits preferred to serve up week after week. Its vice, of course, as far as the exhibitors were concerned, was precisely this – that it had dared to be intelligent.

Milton Shulman in the London *Evening Standard* accurately summed up the mindset that the film had offended. Wardour Street's concept of entertainment, he wrote, had

> nothing to do with the mind, the intellect, the spirit or any of the other ennobling attributes which man fondly believes distinguish him from the animal state. In the holy name of entertainment, the cinema has been converted into a giggle emporium offering convenient facilities for the cuddling of adolescents and the licking of ice-cream. In the sacred name of entertainment, the cinema has consistently been thwarted from developing into a mature art-form capable of making the same kind of significant contribution that literature, the theatre, music and painting make to human happiness.[52]

A Chance of a Lifetime symbolized the battle that Del had been fighting for his entire career in films. Sadly it was his last stand. By the end of 1949 Pilgrim Pictures had been liquidated, and its chief assets – the three films that Del had produced in the course of the company's very short history – were in the hands of Lloyds Bank. Sheepcote, which Del had mortgaged to finance *A Chance of a Lifetime*, was sold off, and after nearly twenty years in Britain he returned to Italy to lick his wounds. 'It is useless for me to waste time when the influence of "J. D." is exercised with power over the entire industry,' he wrote to Bernard Miles.[53] As for Rank, in Del's estimate he was 'a good man but a weak one and blindly follows J. D.'[54]

A particularly galling measure of J. D.'s influence was the fact that Two Cities, the company responsible for Del's greatest triumphs, had been reduced to a shell churning out bland, formulaic productions. And in charge was a salesman! Earl St John had once been an exhibitor for Paramount, and was famously John Davis's man. The story goes that when the writer/producer Eric Ambler found him drunk in the Dorchester Hotel, he put him in a taxi and attached a board to his neck with the words: 'Return to John Davis with compliments.'[55]

Holed up in the Excelsior Hotel in Rapallo on the Italian riviera – in what does not seem to have been such an uncomfortable exile for a man who had just lost his fortune – Del entertained for a while hopes of being able to win back control of the three Pilgrim films. When these faded, he set up a company called Tigullio Films (named after the Gulf of Tigullio), which was intended – as he told *Il Popolo*, a Milan newspaper, in an article rather optimistically called 'Hollywood on the Tigullio' – to carry on 'his battle for the victory of the artistic product'.[56]

'Filippo Del Giudice, Capo Della Produzione' read the logo of the new company in translation of the old Two Cities logo, and Del, in love with his own legend, which he trumpeted at every opportunity, must have hoped that Tigullio would do for the Italian cinema what Two Cities had done for the British.

'My dear Bernie,' he wrote to Miles, using an analogy which had become rather worn by now, 'I feel like a general on the battlefield and I am looking after the great lines of strategy in order to prove to the film world that I am right and . . . when I have been responsible for the first production in Italy, and have proved that all my convictions, ideals and methods, once free from interference of huge concerns of distributors and exhibitors, will be able to pay much more than in the usual way, and when I have proved that the two kinds of film ('habit' and 'non-habit') must be shown in different cinemas and in different ways in order to pay, then everything will be easier for me.'[57]

But Tigullio, whose programme of films had included a

production of *Spartacus* with Errol Flynn in the title role, came to nothing. Del had lost the knack of working miracles.

In a world where the plans for projects that will never be completed vastly outnumber those that are, and where the conduct of everyday business requires a confident belief in the improbable, it is easy for the genius of one year to seem the madman of the next. But to those who had known him during his wartime heyday Del's return to England in 1958 offered a particularly sorry spectacle.

He was penniless and living on the charity of friends, but determined, he told the *Daily Mail*,[58] to make money out of producing films again so that he could pay them all back. He sought to raise money for Olivier's production of *Macbeth*, which had been dropped by the Rank Organisation in an economy drive. He announced a programme of religious epics: *Mary Magdalene*; *Pontius Pilate*, with Alec Guinness in the title role; *Father Damien*, about a leper missionary; and a film about six saints. Even at a time when biblical epics like *The Ten Commandments* and *Ben-Hur* were huge box-office successes, this list must have seemed oddly single-minded, and a considerable departure from his previous films which had been so distinctly British in subject matter. But Del, who had already shown himself capable of boundless faith as a film producer, was suddenly filled with the divine kind too – not on the road to Damascus like St Paul, whose story he wanted to bring to the screen, but in a hotel in Miami in 1951.

It had happened like this.[59] A priest knocked on his door and asked if he could chat to him about God. After they had had a talk and Del still did not believe, the priest said, 'I can see you're a clever man. May I send to you next Sunday a brother who is cleverer than I am?' Next Sunday this priest came, but he lacked spiritual warmth and he too failed to convince Del. Then on the third Sunday Del developed a great hunger for spaghetti. He cooked some himself as there was no one to make it for him on a Sunday. But when he tried to drain it he discovered that his sink was blocked, and he called a plumber. 'I watched him as he worked. Suddenly he turned round to look at me. His eyes burned into mine like great headlamps. I was alone. He was a big strong man with a wrench in his hand.' Del thought he was about to be attacked, but before he was able to shout or run, the plumber said three times: 'Do you believe in God, sir?' Then he went away, leaving Del with his sink unblocked and his eyes open to the mysteries of God. 'I had an appointment with a lady at three o'clock. I telephoned her and cancelled it.' Two days later he went to church and declared himself converted.

With stories like this it's easy to understand why the newspapers could not resist him – even if the financiers showed few signs of yielding to his charms – and headlines like 'Tycoon Saint' or 'Tycoon with a Cross on His Desk' greeted his second coming to Britain's shores. Of his Sheepcote days Del told a reporter, 'Now I will not live any more in that way. Now I have the outlook of religion. This gives me greater happiness than all the money in the world. That old way of life was stupid. Stupid, wasteful and immoral from every point of view.'[60] One wonders what the devout Arthur Rank made of such pronouncements. If Del had hoped for a rapturous welcome to a prodigal son, and perhaps another 'nice little cheque' in support of his production plans, he was to be disappointed – John Davis, the hard-working son who had never left home, ran the estate now and was impervious to such unbusinesslike sentiment.

Nor did Del impress Her Majesty's government, which churlishly – considering the contribution he had made to the nation in the past – refused to grant him a permit of permanent residence unless he could produce a signed film contract. But they had their reasons. In the previous decade he had sought naturalization, but been turned down when Home Office investigations revealed that he had fled Italy not as an anti-Fascist, but because he was wanted on criminal charges for embezzlement.[61]

Somehow learning this only made me feel more fond of Del: it was another example of his *'energia del carattere'*. I was sure that whatever scheme had occasioned the financial irregularity would have bestowed upon Italy some priceless cultural benefit – which of course the Fascists wouldn't have understood.

His last weeks in England were spent in a Benedictine monastery in Gloucestershire. 'Perhaps someone will remember all that I have done in the film world,' he told the reporter from the *Daily Sketch* who found him there,[62] but now there was no more talk of his fabulous production plans and at last he had resigned himself to the fact that he would never make another film. He showed his journalist visitor around his temporary home with as much care as he had once boasted the well-appointed features of Sheepcote. 'We went into a nine-by-six-foot room with a single window. On the pale green walls hung a single picture of The Crucifixion. A metal-framed bed stood in the corner. A tiny wardrobe, a desk and one small armchair were the only other furnishings.' Del rose at 5.30 in the morning and attended five services a day. His only daily luxury was one cigar.

Even in the days of Two Cities the flamboyant Italian had always been regarded with a certain amount of disbelief and amusement. 'They looked upon him as a bit of a clown,' said Guido Coen, 'ready to lick his boots when necessary, but then smirk behind his back.' But now he was an object of pity even to his friends. Coen remembered visiting him and being appalled by the vulgar, gaudy display of religious objects, and Del's behaviour seemed to him not a true turning to God but a kind of religious mania. 'It became embarrassingly evident that he had gone a bit soft in the head.'

The achievements of the past were just a memory, and for some not even that. If he had once seemed to be a kind of Henry V of the British cinema, now – as he wandered from sanctuary to sanctuary a homeless mendicant reliant on charity, faintly ridiculous and spurned by people who had once found it convenient to sing his praises – this elderly man who walked with a stick and was blind in one eye seemed more like a King Lear. Del returned to Italy. He died five years later in Fiesole near Florence on New Year's Eve, 1962.

After the debacle of Pilgrim Pictures, the crashing of the dream, Peter Ustinov wrote to Del: 'Italy's gift is that of discovery; Britain's gift is that of consolidation. It is not your fault if you have made discoveries without being followed, nor is it your fault if Britain has consolidated false discoveries. You have lost no ideals, others have had no ideals to lose.'[63] But Del would have prospered better if he had made more of an effort to accommodate the ways of his adopted country. Perhaps he was deceived by the exceptional circumstances of war, and then the sea-change in politics that occurred with the election of a Labour government, into thinking that Britain was more capable of radical action than it actually was. In spite of the nationalization of coal and the railways or the creation of the NHS, the British tendency was to respect vested interests and to prop up existing systems.

The kind of cinema Del was fighting for would have been a

revolution, but he was too much of a romantic to settle for anything else. To an extent he had fallen in love with his own legend, according to which anything was possible and reverses would be followed by glorious triumphs.

John Davis

In November 1971 the trade magazine *Today's Cinema* set aside a whole issue to mark the knighthood and sixty-fifth birthday of John Davis, then chairman and chief executive of the Rank Organisation.[1] 'We wish him health and happiness and hope that the Motion Picture Industry continues to enjoy the privilege of his dynamic statesmanship for many years to come,' declared the directors of EMI, the Rank Organisation's chief rivals, in a message that was typical of the advertisements, many of them full page, which filled the magazine, from film distributors, exhibitors and producers, as well as the confectioners and ice-cream makers who sold their products in the Rank Organisation's cinemas. They were all paying court, like the vassals of a feudal lord, to the man who was the most powerful, and feared, figure in British pictures. He was also the most detested.

His reputation for ruthlessness was an inescapable part of the admiration he received, a fact that the profile of Davis in *Today's Cinema* did not seek to disguise. 'John Davis, I think, would accept the fact that he is known as a bastard. It's probably the most respectful compliment that is paid to him. He is respected for being a bastard mainly because you know where *he* stands and where *you* stand with him when you are dealing with him. That's what being a bastard means.'

He ruled the Rank Organisation virtually single-handed for thirty years. He had sacked so many members of the board that they formed a club called the Rank Outsiders. When one evening the ousted directors invited him to a dinner and asked him to speak afterwards, he said, 'I know why you've invited me. You're afraid you'll run out of new members. Have no worries, there'll be plenty more.'[2] His attitude was: 'When I want your opinion, I'll give it to you.'

If in the 1950s the British cinema largely meant a diet of stilted dramas and inane comedies, it was because John Davis had wanted it this way. He made his own contribution to the *Today's Cinema* tribute, called 'Business', which is notable for not once mentioning the words 'film' or 'cinema'. The piece could as easily have been about sugar puffs or ball bearings.

'Marketing,' wrote Davis, 'with all that the word implies, was the Rank Organisation's vital weapon in building the powerful industrial and service complex that is the Rank Organisation today. The marketing approach as I see it is basically an analytical one. The problem it sets itself is that of achieving the most profitable compromise between the desires of the potential customer and the ideas and abilities of the designer and manufacturer.'

British cinema fare in the 50s was the result of such thinking – 'the most profitable compromise'. However much Rank's films may have been despised by the critics – who didn't much matter in any case, as the films certainly weren't made for them – they made excellent business sense, an established and popular brand that satisfied the businessman's hankering for the predictable. Davis's lieutenant in charge of production from 1947 was Earl St John. 'His outlook was absolutely early 1930s run-of-the-mill production-line product,' remembered the director Roy Baker. 'Ford did very well with the motor cars, so we can do just the same with the films and stars.'[3] Off the Rank production line rolled the Lockwood or the Bogarde (Mark 1), cheap, dependable family saloons instead of handmade sports cars that were a challenge to handle.

John Davis was a *businessman* who had found himself in one of the most precarious business environments, the British film industry. He single-mindedly set about doing the sorts of things that businessmen do – winning new markets, cutting costs, eliminating unnecessary risks. However much the 'creative workers' may have approved of the first activity and grudgingly accepted the second, few could feel happy about the third because in time they would be considered the most unnecessary risk of all.

But it took a little while for this to become apparent. Back in the 40s when box-office receipts were at a record high, when British films seemed on the verge of securing that elusive dream of a firm foothold in the American market, even businessmen were prepared to entertain the idea that British film-making could be an asset.

John Davis

*

John Davis had never particularly wanted to be in the film industry. He had been educated at the City of London School and trained as an accountant. During the 1930s he had examined the books of a diverse range of industrial concerns, including coal and steel companies. Such was the formative experience of a man who as managing director of the Rank Organisation would many years later comment: 'All businesses are fundamentally the same. The engineers, technicians and creative workers look after the product. The accountant co-ordinates the whole on sound lines.'[4]

In 1938 he began his first job in films as chief accountant to the Odeon circuit. He had been up against a man from Price Waterhouse.[5] The cinemas might just as well have been coal mines or chemist shops as far as he was concerned. But whatever he lacked in aesthetic sensibility, he made up for with thoroughness and administrative brilliance. When three years later Odeon's founder, Oscar Deutsch, died and the circuit became part of the Rank empire, Davis quickly came to the attention of his new boss.

J. Arthur Rank, Methodist and flour-miller, knew little more about films than John Davis did. His mentor had been C. M. Woolf, a legendary film distributor and producer, who had been managing director of Gaumont-British until he set up his own distribution company, General Film Distributors, which went into partnership with Rank in 1937. Dynamic and quarrelsome, Woolf had the soul of Wardour Street and, as Ivor Montagu put it, 'always chose to adopt an aggressive attitude of anti-intellect and anti-art'.[6] Montagu had had to re-edit a film for Woolf back in the 1920s. When he made known his objections about a sequence 'obviously intended to be titillating', Woolf waved them aside with the comment: 'Of course, Mr Montagu is a gentleman, he would not understand.'[7] It was no doubt this attitude which made Woolf so popular with exhibitors: they could rely on him not to lumber them with anything too high-falutin.

Woolf's abrasive, hard-nosed manner was at odds with Arthur Rank's courtliness, but the two men formed a 'friendship with real affection'.[8] In 1942 Woolf died suddenly. In his will he left to Arthur Rank his wrist-watch. Perhaps it was a hint as to who would be his most appropriate successor, for certainly Rank could not have found a finer timekeeper than John Davis, who once observed that 'punctuality is being ten minutes early'.[9] The young accountant had, as Richard Norton remarked, 'a characteristic which delighted Arthur Rank, perhaps because Arthur had seen so little of it in the film business – that of arriving at his office at the crack of dawn, and being still at work when other people were shaking out their napkins round the dinner-table'.[10]

John Davis was every bit as tough as Woolf had been, a quality which the genial Arthur Rank (whom Woolf would certainly have called a gentleman) prized all the more for its absence in his own make-up. As Alan Wood observed, Rank's father, whom he venerated, provided an example he could not live up to alone: 'At the head of the flour-milling concern of Ranks Ltd, the twin virtues of ruthless money-making and Christian philanthropy were combined in one and the same person, Joseph Rank. In the Rank film organisation it needed two people to provide the combination between them.' [11]

John Davis moved into an office next to Rank's, and there was an intercommunicating door. They were so close that at first, like a songwriting team, it was often simpler to assume joint authorship than try to work out who was responsible for what, although occasionally there was a glimmer.

In 1945 when Jill Craigie was in Plymouth making the Two Cities documentary *The Way We Live*, she got a call in the middle of shooting telling her to stop the production as the film could not possibly make any money. She went up to London and asked to see Rank. Craigie showed him an enormous folder of publicity that she had attracted and explained how the whole of Plymouth had turned out, grateful that a film was being made about their city. Rank looked through the cuttings and turned to Davis, who as usual was present at the meeting, and said: 'You see, John? We can't stop it, can we?'[12]

But it was just a difference of detail. Broadly they were in accord. Bill MacQuitty, Craigie's producer on *The Way We Live*, described Davis as 'Arthur's *alter ego*'.[13] They were like 'blood brothers, a Yin and a Yang in a symbiotic partnership'.[14] In Michael Powell's memoirs they act in concert, liking or disliking the same films, reaching the same decisions. Powell dubbed them Prince John and King Arthur,[15] although as time went by it seemed more and more appropriate to reverse the titles and to speak of King John. Rank's huge film empire was the product of his evangelistic zeal, but increasingly it was Davis who made the day-to-day decisions and presided over the process of regimentation that became more and more marked as the decade wore on. Rank was 'the father figure', MacQuitty remembered, 'but in all things outside milling flour he was completely dependent on John Davis'.[16]

Rank was so warm and accommodating, Davis so brusque, that when after the war measures were taken to rein in some of the more ambitious film-makers it was easy to assume that Uncle Arthur must have been bewitched – remember Del Giudice's comment after his flight to Italy: 'He is a good man but a weak one and blindly follows J. D.' But Rank shared with Davis what Michael Powell called a 'small-town realism':[17] he was just as conservative and just as concerned to look after the brass.

It was Rank who, before Davis had arrived on the scene, and under the influence of his mentor in the film business C. M. Woolf, refused to finance *In Which We Serve* or the Archers' *One of Our Aircraft is Missing*. When both these films turned out to be successful, he decided to finance the Archers' and Two Cities' future productions. He had avoided risk and attempted to repeat success in a manner typical of the cautious businessman. He had also recognized his own ignorance of film-making and accorded a large measure of autonomy to the leading film-makers he invited to form Independent Producers. The name of this Rank subsidiary turned out to be surprisingly accurate.

Davis claimed to have supported this approach: 'They were ideal film-making conditions and this was the great thing about Arthur Rank: he was convinced this was the way films ought to be made and I think it was right. But the producers didn't play their cards very well and some took Arthur's approach as a sign of weakness, whereas it was giving them adequate facilities and opportunities to be creative.'[18]

The only real difference between the two men in their conduct of business was that Davis was less prone to sentiment and did not mind making himself unpopular. *The Way We Live*, which could only be distributed as a programme filler, would have rankled with a man like Davis. However commendable it may have been as a social exercise, it was needless expense. He had nothing against creativity so long as it could pay its way, but once it was clear that the producers under the umbrella of the Rank Organisation were losing money, he moved in with alacrity. Where Rank might have tolerated the odd failure, or occasionally have been prepared to support a worthwhile venture which was not obviously profitable, Davis expected every penny to account for itself. If Rank was the magnanimous lord of the manor, then Davis was the estate manager tough on poachers and always exceeding his master in zealousness.

It is difficult to warm to John Davis but I think one can feel a sympathy for him. He was surrounded by creative people who were naturally prejudiced against his profession. Direct and taciturn, he would have felt at a disadvantage in the company of people who were on the whole far more amusing and witty than himself. His inability to meet the film-makers on their own level made him doubly determined to cling on to the certainties of the balance sheet. And the sense he must have had that people were ridiculing him behind his back (and Del Giudice apparently laughed at him to his face) would have bred a siege mentality, and a reluctance to trust anyone.

Davis's whole life had involved an effort of discipline and will. As a child he had struggled to master a stammer, he once told Roy Baker,[19] who had been to the same school as him. He was also painfully shy. Another of the very few people in whom he confided was Dirk Bogarde, the Rank Organisation's top box-office star in the Fifties. Davis gave him this example of how timid he had been. If as a young man he came home to find his parents holding a party, he would take off his cycle clips and put them in separate pockets so that they didn't clatter. He vaselined his key so that it would not squeak in the lock, and waited for a crescendo of noise from the parlour before opening the front door. He would then slip in and carry his bike up the stairs. Even many years later, as managing director of the Rank Organisation, he found receptions an ordeal. Although he had the bearing of a powerful, confident man, and gave the impression, as Bogarde put it, 'of a knife sailing through hot butter', inwardly he was terrified. He coped only by making sure he knew exactly where he was going, in relation to two or three people he knew would be present.[20]

Out of his fears grew a neurotic but methodical quest for control. It accounted for the way in which he ran the Rank Organisation, and perhaps also accounted for a disastrous private life, in which he was married several times and accused of cruelty.

Among film people John Davis is usually remembered as a monster, but given his temperament, his career at Rank can actually seem rather brave, for films were about the most difficult of all commodities on which to impose the order he craved. It was impossible to determine the exact cost of the product. There might be a nominal budget, but if the picture had extensive locations, or if the actors and actresses were difficult, or if the director was slow, then the cost could be much more than had been anticipated. One film could come close to ruining a company.

The line on a graph of Rank's production expenditure during the 1940s would inch up not just a few per cent every year, but from a high ridge shoot up in alarmingly steep peaks. Take Powell and Pressburger. *One of Our Aircraft is Missing*, which they made for British National in 1942, cost £70,000;[21] *The Life and Death of Colonel Blimp* (1943), £208,000; *A Matter of Life and Death* (1946), £320,000; *Black Narcissus* (1947), £280,000; *The Red Shoes* (1948), £700,000.[22] By the mid-1940s the Rank Organisation was forking out Hollywood sums but still with no guarantee of access to the American market.

The atmosphere of constant uncertainty where producers rarely delivered what they promised made a mockery of fiscal managment and bred mistrust. Davis's instinct was to be ever vigilant, to impose economies where possible. While Davis would become increasingly sceptical about the viability of Rank's production interests, he had been a key figure in the Rank Organisation's attempts to break into the American market with big-budget prestige films. Michael Powell called him an organizing genius who had helped to establish 'a proud and responsible film industry' on a sound foundation.

But from the mid-1940s onwards it became gradually apparent that a sound foundation meant giving up hope of making any money in America and downscaling budgets accordingly. A particularly brutal shock occurred in August 1947 with the British government's imposition of the 75 per cent import duty on foreign films, which put paid to the Rank Organisation's attempts to get a foothold in the American market.

Davis had to combat the false confidence that had resulted from the wartime success of British films. Critics and filmmakers thought they could take on Hollywood, and production values became more and more grandiose. 'In those days,' remembered Roy Baker, 'if your picture didn't go over schedule it was looked upon as being no good, anyway. That was the attitude of mind.' Having previously made documentaries for the

Army Film Unit, he found himself shocked by the unnecessary delays that swelled the schedule of his first feature film at Denham from eight to thirteen weeks. 'Oh, well, it's only another few bags of flour,' he remembered an assistant director on the production saying.[23]

Davis can seem like the John Birt of his time. To make production viable he had to administer some unpleasant medicine and was reviled for it. Inevitably Filippo Del Giudice of Two Cities, the leading advocate of big-budget productions, was an early target. It was on John Davis's initiative that the company was first absorbed into Rank and then Del himself forced to leave.

The departure of Del was as important for the signal it gave to the other production companies operating under Rank's umbrella as for any saving of resources it represented in itself. The unmistakable message was that the kind of extravagance Del had come to symbolize would no longer be tolerated. Even Guido Coen, Del's colleague almost from Two Cities' earliest days, felt that Davis had no alternative. 'He was tough, but he had to be tough, because if you looked at that spread of producers that he had under his umbrella, the money was being wasted and he had to pull in the reins, there is no question about it, otherwise Rank would have been in very dire trouble.'[24]

The appointment in Del's place of Earl St John in charge of production, a man who belonged to that breed of exhibitors Del so despised, was another pointed lesson that production policy would in future be sales-led. If it was necessary for Davis to dismantle the framework of ambitious film-making that the Rank Organisation had built up, the great pity was that he had nothing imaginative to put in its place. The only guideline now was: what sold.

Michael Powell described Earl St John as John Davis's 'yes-man' and with a characteristic mercilessness wrote of him: 'Earl was like a great St Bernard dog in his desire to please, in his size and shape, in his great, lined face, and in his anxiety to agree with the last speaker. He puzzled artists with whom he had to work. Nobody disliked him, but nobody trusted him either. To put such a man – or such a dog – in charge of creative artists was a joke, or a crime, or both.'[25]

While Del was responsible for many films which didn't quite come off as well as the classics, they were at least true to themselves. The new regime was characterized by shameless and formulaic attempts to repeat past success. *Madness of the Heart* (1949) was a depressing example of the new dispensation. Made under the banner of Two Cities, it had more the feel of Gainsborough melodrama, and appropriately enough featured Gainsborough's top box-office star Margaret Lockwood.

Black Narcissus had proved that nuns could be big box office, and the actress Kathleen Byron had been memorable as the crazed sister who, consumed with passion for David Farrar, in a jealous rage attempts to push Deborah Kerr over a cliff. *Madness of the Heart* took the ingredients and served them up in an inferior and derivative concoction. It was commercial exploitation of the most tawdry if routine kind.

Margaret Lockwood falls in love with a French aristocrat, then goes blind and promptly retires to a nunnery. But the Mother Superior observes, 'The pull of the world is still in your heart', and sends her back into it. The French aristocrat – a ridiculous Continental lover of the kind that became overused in the British cinema with their sudden availability after the war – loves her no less for her disability, proposes to her and sweeps her off to his chateau. Enter Kathleen Byron as the madly jealous ex-girlfriend, Vérité, and the plot degenerates into a repetition of its only sustaining idea: a murderously jealous lover's attempts to kill her rival. Kathleen Byron tries to push Lockwood out of a high window, to make her trip over a kitten at the top of a grand staircase, to drown her when the two go swimming.

It was typical of the 'boardroom' film that became a staple of Rank's output – the executives' idea of what the public wanted to see. In mockery of Del's slogan, the divorce of production and sales, Davis's policy was their *marriage*. 'It is from marketing that all thinking must start, since however good the company's products or services may be, the company will not prosper if it cannot sell them.'[26] John Davis on business again.

The emasculation of Two Cities set the pattern. Rank's other production companies were similarly reined in. The Archers, who had been regarded as a prime weapon for breaking into the American market, were still making *The Red Shoes* when in August 1947 the import duty on American films was imposed, shattering Rank's export ambitions. It was perhaps the worst time to present the company with a film which was both exorbitantly expensive and – just as bad – innovative, and so a gamble at the box office.* Powell recalled that during the interval between the end of main shooting and the press show, the Archers 'were told repeatedly by John Davis . . . that Independent Producers would no longer be allowed to remain so independent'.[27]

When they lost the extraordinary degree of freedom they enjoyed, the film-makers who made up Independent Producers set out, one by one, for the apparent haven of British Lion, where they hoped to receive the encouragement of Alexander Korda, a *real* film man. If Denham seemed a little like the village of Hamlyn after the visit of the Pied Piper, probably Davis was delighted to see the rats go – they had come close to eating the Rank Organisation out of house and home. Spared the pretensions of the artists, he was able to pursue the single-minded business-man's approach: such film-makers as continued to work for Rank were under no illusions that they had to make a product which met the requirements of the salesmen.

So came the *Carry On* films, the *Doctor* films, the Norman Wisdom comedies. They were formulaic, cheap to make and of broad appeal. It was fine for the business, but a pity for those who had hoped that British films could continue to be inspiring.

Reminiscences of the Rank Organisation in the 1950s make it clear that it was a place where any originality or creativity could not possibly thrive. Davis ruled supreme, and tolerated no dissent. 'When he employed people on the board,' Bill MacQuitty remembered, his attiude was: 'Now your job is this job. You've got it for three months. If you make a profit, you can stay on.'[28] Everything was a yes or no situation.

Davis ran a regime of rigid rules and reprimands. Any laxity was frowned upon. When one of his colleagues turned up wearing a shirt with a pronounced stripe, he said: 'I see you were in a hurry this morning, Mr X; you've come here in your pyjamas.'[29] Perhaps it was this kind of pettiness that Powell had in mind when he wrote of 'John Davis's bourgeois tantrums'.[30]

The fear he inspired among his employees was legendary. Bill MacQuitty visited him in his office one Christmas. 'I opened the door and stood in the doorway. He was writing and he looked up and he said, "COME IN!" I remained standing and he looked up again, and he said again, "COME IN!" I said, "I'm frightened!"

* No one at the time could have known that *The Red Shoes* would become the most successful imported film in America, grossing 5 million dollars.

and that shook him. So he said, "None of your Irish blarney. Come in!" So I walked to his desk, about thirty feet away, and I stood in front of him like the little boy in blue, and he said, "OUT WITH IT! WHAT DO YOU WANT?" I said, "I hardly know how to begin." "COME ON! COME ON! WHAT DO YOU WANT?" "I've just come in to wish you a very happy Christmas." So he left the desk, opened the bar and said, "Have a drink." Normally he would have said yes or no. He wouldn't have gone into it. His conversation was, "Can you make a profit?" '[31]

With his charm MacQuitty was one of the very few people able to elicit a warm response from Davis. Perhaps it was a pity that the great producers who worked at Rank in the 1940s had so quickly chosen to dismiss him as an enemy. Guido Coen believes that had Del Giudice tried to reach an accommodation with Davis, rather than fight him at every turn, he might have remained a significant influence in British films. He would certainly have provided a valuable counterweight. As it was, there was no one of any stature to temper Davis's adding-machine tendencies.

Even away from work, Davis prided himself on his ability to make things pay. His idea of relaxation was looking after his own dairy herd. He knew how many gallons each cow could give. 'Whatever happens to post-war agriculture in this country,' he was reported as saying, 'one thing is certain: we can't get fresh milk from overseas.'[32]

Given such broad tastes in business, it was no surprise that he should have searched for other more dependable ways of making money. In 1956 he co-founded with the American Haloid Corporation the photocopying company, Rank Xerox. The deal was a triumph, and it would make the Rank Organisation far more money than making films ever had. And, inevitably, as the years passed, the company's commitment to film production dwindled. Today they don't make any films at all – Davis's legacy. But it took decades for this logic of the market place finally to assert itself.

Vilified and despised, John Davis's chief crime was to try to run a sensible business. He may have been right when he said that all businesses were fundamentally the same, but if so then he must have recognized that making films in Britain wasn't really a business – it was, sooner or later, a way of losing an awful lot of money.

It was a considerable feat to have resisted the siren voices which over a century lured so many others on to the rocks, but a feat of a kind which could only really be acknowledged by shareholders. Rank had survived where many other film empires had foundered but this survival was inglorious. Those who really loved the British cinema had long ago realized that its finest years were born of idealism and recklessness.

David Lean and Carol Reed

Lean and Reed. Like cat and dog they belong together as much for their differences as their similarities, throwing each other into relief with their contrasting natures. By the end of the 1940s they had both enjoyed a string of successes and were Britain's two most prominent directors. It was natural for journalists to write of them together, and then to compare them. In 1950 the *New York Times* described Lean as 'still second to Carol Reed among British directors'.[1] Today, I suppose, in the age of *The English Patient*, it is Lean who is the more in fashion, his epic extravaganzas from *Bridge on the River Kwai* to *A Passage to India* appealing more to the modern taste for the spectacular.

Just as film critics tended to bracket them together, they seemed as natural an association in the minds of the people who worked with them. Eric Ambler wrote the screenplay of *The Way Ahead*. He recalled discussing with Carol Reed his opinions of various film directors: 'He never told me how he felt about David Lean. I once saw them on the lot of Pinewood talking together. David was being boyish and respectful, a new prefect with the head-master.'[2] Even the two directors themselves recognized the rivalry. Lean spoke of it in an interview: 'We'd sort of see one another in those days, Carol and I, and say to the other, "What, you still here? Hasn't a bus hit you yet?"'[3]

Of the two Carol Reed was the more content to drift along with the vagaries of commercial film-making. 'One can try to pick and choose too much before one has established oneself,' he once told film students. 'I have seen many people fail because they have not realized they were being given an opportunity which would probably never come their way again. Don't wait, therefore, for the ideal thing, but take the chance that comes and make sure that you do everything to make a success of it.'[4]

While Reed enjoyed making films, and tried to make them as often as he could, Lean was prepared throughout his career, if necessary, to wait and wait. Even before he was established as a director, quite contrary to the advice Reed gave his film students he single-mindedly held out for 'the ideal thing'. In the 1930s he was one of the country's leading editors. Anthony Havelock-Allan, who was producing quota quickies at Pinewood, had over a period of seven years repeatedly invited Lean to direct a film. Lean's reply was: 'I'm never going to do any film until I know the film has enough money in its budget for it to be made the way I think it should be made.'[5]

Havelock-Allan was at last able to satisfy Lean with the offer to help Noël Coward direct *In Which We Serve*. Coward proposed that Lean should receive the credit 'Assistant to the Director', but Lean, in another demonstration of his uncompromising nature, refused to be involved unless he received a credit as co-director. The triumph of the production instantly pitched him into the top league of directors, but just as importantly he had a powerful team with which to enhance his reputation. With Coward, the cameraman Ronald Neame and Anthony Havelock-Allan, he went on to make *This Happy Breed*, *Blithe Spirit* and *Brief Encounter*. Lean recognized the value of the right collaborators. He understood the industrial process of making films, as well as the kind of compromises that could swamp the unwary; and he guarded carefully against them.

As a *film-maker* Lean was the equal of anyone. Even if he needed a Coward, or a Dickens, or a Bolt to give him a story, his film sense was so total that it has the weight of an authorial presence. *Brief Encounter* (1945) is – as just about everyone must know – a simple story of a middle-class housewife who falls in love with a married man. On the stage it would have been a touching but slight piece; as the film Lean made of it, it takes on an extraordinary intensity. His genius was for rendering emotion on the screen, for knowing its exact currency in celluloid. His use of the medium of film makes us identify completely with the housewife Laura: we are inside her head, we share her thoughts.

Sequence after sequence leaves one speechless with admiration. Take, for example, the scene in the refreshment room at Milford Junction station when the two lovers, Alec and Laura, part for the last time. It is actually shown twice, at the beginning and at the end of the film, and from two different viewpoints – of outward appearances and Laura's inner feelings. It is an effect that could *only* be achieved in the cinema.

The first viewpoint. Alec and Laura's last moments together are interrupted by the arrival of a gossiping acquaintance of Laura. Alec gets up to catch his train, leaving Laura to endure the woman's small talk. The woman goes up to the refreshment room counter to buy a bar of chocolate. Her words to the assistant are drowned by the sound of an express train passing through the station. When she turns away from the counter to walk back to her table, she is momentarily taken aback to find that Laura has disappeared. But Laura soon returns, explaining that she had gone outside to get some fresh air – an unremarkable incident.

Then, towards the end of the film, we have the second viewpoint of Laura's feelings. We see through her mind's eye. The neighbour witters on, but Laura is lost in her own thoughts: the woman's words are just a distant, muffled sound, and Laura's surroundings – the table at which she sits, the refreshment room – are veiled in darkness. The exterior world is shut out. But a bell announcing the express rings intrusively and reawakes external sensations. The neighbour's strident voice sharply rises and the darkness is dispelled. Before the world was shut out, now Laura perceives it in a super-real way. The express train's whistle becomes insistent and maddening in her head. The camera tilts through forty-five degrees, throwing her askew, and, with a cut, she is pitched towards the refreshment-room door and out on to the platform, where she stares helplessly as the express train rattles by, its slipstream dislodging her tight perm and causing an indecorous hank of hair to flop over her eyes.

The sequence is a perfect visual representation of her emotional state, of her losing then regaining control. It is also a succinct visual metaphor of the theme of restraint that runs through the whole film. When Laura returns to the waiting room after *this* brief encounter, her hair is back in place. This example of pure cinema still fills me with wonder. And the emotional impact, it seems to me, has little to do with Noël Coward, everything to do with the film sense of David Lean.

It is this flair for cinema that makes even David Lean's 'bad' films satisfying. *The Passionate Friends* (1948; a film that Lean had not wanted to make) is novelettish nonsense, but Lean's direction lends it an awesome edge. The film was adapted from an H. G. Wells novel, but as one watches it today it seems a rerun of *Brief Encounter*, an obvious cash-in on a previous success.

Trevor Howard returns for a repeat performance as the lover: in *Brief Encounter* he was a doctor, now he is a university don. A brittle, nervy Ann Todd takes on the Celia Johnson role, now upgraded to a banker's wife. The husband of *Brief Encounter*, Fred, an amiable but dull old stick who spends his evenings doing the *Times* crossword, is replaced by the suave Claude Rains, who spends *his* evenings juggling with high finance. While there is no suggestion in *Brief Encounter* that Laura and Fred have ceased to love each other, only that with the years their ardour has dulled, *The Passionate Friends* makes a deeply unconvincing rigmarole out of the notion that Ann Todd and Claude Rains are bonded by a platonic love.

Lean could not make the story ring true, but none the less he fashioned an impressive piece of cinema. His touch is in every frame – a total control of movement and composition; an uncompromising command of atmosphere, in which every scene is planned to the tiniest detail; and an eye for pictorial beauty. It was in the Alpine locations of *Passionate Friends* that Lean first revealed his taste for the breathtaking landscape. The characters may be two-dimensional, but such is his skill at rendering emotions into celluloid that the mesmeric quality of individual scenes briefly makes you forget the ridiculousness of the whole. When Ann Todd stands at an open window and looks out on to an Alpine lake watching Trevor Howard's boat disappear into the distance, for the length of the scene she is the heart-rending essence of misery.

Command and *control* are two particularly apt words for Lean. The reminiscences about him all suggest a firm, authoritative figure who knew what he wanted. He 'never had much consideration for what actors sometimes have to go through,' wrote Ann Todd, 'just a relentless drive for what he wanted for the scene.'[6] The function of the actors was to deliver *his* vision. Ann Todd would become Lean's second wife. It is no surprise to learn that when she met him for the first time he was behind a movie camera. During the making of *Passionate Friends*, she was appearing in a crowd scene set in the Albert Hall but not filmed there – as she wrongly recollected in her memoirs. 'David as the director was in the roof of the hall to film the whole scene. Then on "Action", strapped to the camera crane, he swooped down out of the darkness like Jupiter on Leda into a close-up of me. It was sudden, dramatic and possessive.'[7]

Carol Reed, by contrast, was vague and sometimes maddening to technicians because he so often appeared not to know what he wanted. Michael Redgrave remembered him as 'the gentlest of directors', who was 'able, with infinite pains and care, to bestow on his actors the feeling that everything was up to them and that all he was doing was to make sure that they were seen to their best advantage'.[8] Actors loved him. He understood their problems, had actually been an actor himself.

For Lean there was only one way to play a scene, while for Reed there could be many. Lean's world was a selective and hierarchical one: some characters mattered more than others. His camera, beautifully in keeping with the star system, dwelt on just a very few people, filling their lives with meaning, while the supporting players seem to exist to do no more than that – to *support* the stars, to offer contrast and to throw the predicaments of the stars into relief: they have little value in themselves. In *Brief Encounter* Stanley Holloway, the stationmaster, and Joyce Carey, 'the refined lady' behind the counter in the refreshment room, are characters from the lower orders existing only to provide some light relief from the trials of Celia Johnson and Trevor Howard, who somehow exist on a higher plain.

By contrast Carol Reed sought to give his characters, whatever their importance to the story, their full value as human beings. In a film like *The Third Man* (1949) there is no hierarchy. The faces of the people on the Vienna streets are as compelling as those of the stars. The little boy who hangs about Harry Lime's flat, or the old man who sells balloons in the empty night-time Vienna streets, are as memorable as Harry Lime standing in the lit-up doorway.

If making a Lean film seemed a little like pinning down a butterfly, Reed was receptive to life as it presented itself on the set. In a charming book called *A Filmstar in Belgrave Square* the mother of Bobby Henrey – the boy who had played so perfectly the embassy child in *The Fallen Idol* (1948) – provided a revealing portrait of the director at work. A frequent visitor to the set, she had been struck by Reed's pacing up and down, his apparent daydreaming, but later learnt from Reed himself what had been on his mind.

> I had planned certain scenes where Bobby would lean over the banisters, but very soon I noticed that when left to himself he was always getting into the most graceful positions, curling his hands, and this was so much more effective than anything I had imagined, so very much more natural, that I changed the scenes entirely to conform with his mannerisms. A director should plan in advance how a scene is to be played, but he should always be ready to put the camera here instead of there, and change everything at the last moment if he comes across a better way of doing it.
>
> That is why I never ceased watching Bobby when we were on location in Belgrave Square. It was my business to make him do on the screen what he did, without knowing it, in real life. When I had that miles-away look in my eyes, I was watching how he walked, and all his ways of laughing, and crossing the street. With children, it is much the same as with grown-ups. To be any good to a director, an actor or an actress must either be wonderful, or know absolutely nothing about acting. A little knowledge – that's what is bad![9]

Reed's great talent was to draw out performances in which there was no apparent division between the actor and the character he or she played. Indeed, in his films you feel there are no *performances* as such, and the actors don't really have *lines* – they simply *are*. Reed took enormous care to be faithful to life's texture. In *The Fallen Idol*, when it came to the boy's 'costume', it was characteristic that he should have chosen not to rely on the Wardrobe Department, but asked that Bobby should be dressed in the red pullover, navy-blue shorts, white socks and brown shoes he was wearing when they first met. This appreciation of the natural was also evident in Reed's preference for shooting on location whenever he could to avoid the studio look that marred so many films of the period. It was against the usual practice, but something he pressed to do from his earliest days as a director.

Carol Reed had the ability 'to make an actor spread and grow', wrote Stanley Holloway,[10] echoing what most of the actors who had worked with him would have said. According to Michael Korda, the creeper that clung to Reed's house received the same treatment: 'Charmed by the luxuriant thickness of the ivy, Carol refused to cut it back. Instead he encouraged it to grow, with the result that it eventually pulled one whole wall off the house, and brought it crashing onto the garden lawn.'[11] David Lean, one feels, would have trained and clipped such growth into a precise topiary.

Jack Hawkins, who had known Reed when they were both young actors at the Italia Conti school, recalled how Reed once bought a fox in a market which he couldn't bear to see caged and the next day set it free in the country. 'I have a feeling that this idiotic anecdote may be a pointer to Carol's marvellously gentle approach to the actors he now directs in films.'[12] Reed gave actors rein, encouraged them to express their own vitality on the screen.

Both directors were equally exacting in pursuit of their vision, but while Lean was on the whole straightforward Reed tended to rely on craft and cunning to get his way. On *The Young Mr Pitt* (1942), Reed's leisurely style of directing caused the film to fall behind schedule. When the cameraman Freddie Young passed on to him the producer's concerns, Reed told him he would use his infallible method to get more time. He would see the producer and pretend to be upset to the point of tears. The producer would then tell him not to worry and to carry on as before.[13] Years later, when Reed was making *Outcast of the Islands* (1951) in Ceylon, Trevor Howard fell and hurt his leg. A doctor was summoned and said that he had torn a tendon and wouldn't be able to work for a week. 'So Carol,' remembered John Hawkesworth,[14] who was a member of the unit, 'said, "OK, get me another doctor, and I want to speak to him first." Another doctor was whistled up and Carol talked to him first. Trevor was all plastered up and bandaged and able to work the next day.'*

A paradoxical influence on Lean was his Quaker upbringing. As a child he was not allowed to go to the cinema. His parents 'thought the stage was pretty wicked, and the cinema was much worse'. Lean remembered them as 'being keenly aware of the passions and trying to keep them under control'.[15] But although his first illicit visit to the pictures at the age of thirteen or fourteen may have been an act of rebellion, when it came to directing them

---

* The deviousness that Carol Reed displayed in these two examples was just the quality required to convey the cock-eyed world of *The Third Man*.

he was just as concerned as his parents to keep the passions under control. By and large his heroes knuckle under. Celia Johnson and Ann Todd in *Brief Encounter* and *The Passionate Friends* respectively return to their dull husbands, Katharine Hepburn in *Summer Madness* (1955) gives up her Italian lover and goes back to America, even Alec Guinness in *The Bridge on the River Kwai* (1957) does the right thing – if inadvertently – and blows up the bridge in the end.

Perhaps it was with a fortitude instilled by his upbringing that Lean resisted so many previous offers to direct and waited for Noël Coward. The master of deference and knowing your place was a perfect collaborator. They shared the same hierarchical outlook, the same awareness of society's rules. It was this instinct for the conventional that made *Brief Encounter* such an affecting film; so much of its poignancy lies in the picture of a man and woman unable to break free of the middle-class world to which they belong. It was the *Anna Karenina* of the Home Counties – not only an affair but a suicide that never happened. But Coward and Lean, it seems to me, were trapped in those values too, never free enough to give an objective view of the world about them.

They were the epitome of the established virtues and conventional good taste, admired for their discipline and professionalism. Noël Coward expected his actors to arrive on the set on time and to be word-perfect. His decadent image was a misleading one. He was really a hard-working martinet. In spite of the considerable controversy at the time about his playing a Royal Navy captain in *In Which We Serve*, no one could have been more suitable, and he treated the actors in his cast like a ship's crew for whom the first requirement of military life applied: to obey orders.

One reason why *In Which We Serve* works so well is that the gap in attitudes between the makers and what they were portraying is not all that great. David Lean, whom Coward described in his memoirs as 'one hundred per cent efficient',[16] was his able first lieutenant, and soon enjoyed spectacular promotion.

He was a natural commander, a master of logistics and organization, able to deploy large bodies of people to maximum purpose. His films were made according to the military virtues of discipline, authority, precision. This sense of film director as general was at its most spectacularly obvious when he was marshalling the Arabs in the desert of *Lawrence of Arabia* (1962), but I think even a supposedly intimate film like *Brief Encounter* has a military conception to it. Whether housewife, husband, handsome stranger or station staff, the characters all seem to know their place.

Lean's world was a schematic, codified one, in which individualism was subordinated. His characters were types – that theatrical equivalent of rank: there were the leads, the supporting players and the Poor Bloody Extras. He could represent life in broad sweeps, but was not equipped to appreciate its inconsequential detail.

As the illegitimate son of the actor Sir Herbert Beerbohm Tree, Reed must have begun very early on in his life to appreciate the shortcomings of convention. The view his films offer of humanity is largely free of the tacit assumptions about class or status that marred so many other British films. It was Alfred Hitchcock who once catchily said that 'cinema was life with the dull bits left out'. But this, I think, was much more true of Reed's films than it ever was of Hitchcock's.

Reed could animate the most pedestrian of stories. The early films he made as a contract director for Gainsborough and Ealing are a delight for this reason. There was *Penny Paradise* (1938) for example, a musical comedy about a tugboat captain who thinks he has won the pools only to discover that his coupon was never sent. This was a routine assignment, but he breathed life into it. Two-dimensional characters became rounded and credible on the screen. *The Girl in the News* (1940) was a production-line detective thriller, but once again the characters – the minor ones as well as the stars – were portrayed with such a degree of empathy and realism as to be memorable. Reed's whole approach to film-making was based on rendering life with fidelity on the screen. He sought truth of performance, truth of situation, truth of setting, but did so with a faultless sense of drama and mood. It was why Michael Powell described him as 'the best realistic director that England has ever produced'.

Everything Reed did in the 1940s was substantial and significant. Chance, and the most favourable circumstances in his film-making life, afforded him the opportunity to shine. In 1943 he made *The Way Ahead* for that most indulgent of producers Filippo Del Giudice. It would be as definitive a film for the Army as Lean's *In Which We Serve* had been for the Royal Navy.

'*The Way Ahead*, surprisingly, was a first favourite with the Army,' wrote Guy Morgan in a 1948 summary of British wartime filmgoing, 'surprisingly because it was about the Army and nothing but the Army, and there had been little evidence in the past that the fighting Services cared to see themselves dramatized on the screen . . . Somehow, some way, Carol Reed and his colleagues got under the skin of the fighting man and sent him away touched, amused, satisfied.'[17]

The whole country was all too familiar with its theme – the process by which civilians from different walks of life and social backgrounds were conscripted into the Army and forged into a single fighting unit. Even here, at the very outset of their rivalry, the approach of Lean and Reed to similar projects reflected two very different outlooks. While *In Which We Serve* observed a social hierarchy, *The Way Ahead* depicted class divisions being overcome. In tone the one film was clipped and austere, the other full of warmth and humour.

Reed's wartime achievements were considerable, but no one could have predicted the extraordinary run of good fortune he would enjoy with the return of peace. Free to choose his own subject, he settled on a film version of F. L. Green's novel *Odd Man Out*, about a mortally wounded Irish terrorist on the run. The moral ambiguity of a story about 'someone who had done something wrong for the right reasons'[18] appealed to him. It also provided him with a rich seam to exploit. *The Fallen Idol* and *The Third Man*, which followed, were so similar in mood that they seemed to complete a trilogy.

Probably it was the most stunning hat-trick in film history. Skimming through the reviews of *Odd Man Out*, I was struck by the unanimity of the critics' verdict. 'Carol Reed's triumph', 'This will be one of 1947's six best', 'British masterpiece', 'Mason back – in the best film of all time': just a few randomly chosen headlines. But the reception was no less ecstatic when *The Fallen Idol* came out the following year. It was 'a singular masterpiece' according to the *Sunday Chronicle;*[19] 'Carol Reed has directed and produced a flawless picture,' wrote the *Daily Express;*[20] and C. A. Lejeune in the *Observer* – who had previously called *Odd Man Out* a masterpiece – wrote that *The Fallen Idol* was the best thing that Carol Reed had ever done.[21] The litany of praise quickly becomes monotonous, and there is no need to spell out what the critics thought of his next film, *The Third Man*. It was The Third Masterpiece.

Of the three 'great' films, *Odd Man Out* most obviously accorded with the popular conception of what a masterpiece should be, but is flawed by a sense of self-conscious deliberation. It announces itself as an allegory too insistently, and nothing seems left to chance in suggesting – or stipulating – the interpretation that should be placed on Johnny's flight through the streets of Belfast. Everywhere he goes, the visual imagery of the city emphasizes the kind of journey he is on: ominous crosses mark out their pattern in window-frames, in lampposts, in the shadows cast by railings, even in the mortar on the walls of houses. Who in the audience could not realize that Johnny is treading along the path of his own Calvary, that the people he encounters along the way represent his own Stations of the Cross? The meaning is further set in stone by the grandiloquence of William Alwyn's biblical-epic score,* and the presence of the city clock fatefully marking the passage of Johnny's last hours on earth. Too neatly the film ends with Johnny's death at midnight, the last image that of the clock face.

The film was finally much less impressive as parable than it was for the poetic realism with which it observed a city half heedless and half uneasily aware of the drama in its midst. It was in the details *off* the story that Carol Reed was at his best: a stray dog chasing after Johnny as he runs for cover after the bungled raid; the townsfolk drawn to their doors by the commotion; the children playing games in the streets; a tram going by. All just fleeting moments, but the sense of life going on regardless lent an extra pathos to Johnny's fate.

An amusing game is to imagine what Carol Reed's films would have been like had they been directed by David Lean, and vice versa. I think Lean would have ruined *The Fallen Idol* or *The Third Man* – he would not have understood their irony, their humour –

---

* There is evidence that Carol Reed himself regarded the use of music in the film as heavy-handed. In a profile of the director, the critic W. J. Weatherby wrote: 'I remember that when *Odd Man Out* had just been released and was being hailed as a masterpiece, I criticized the sound-track in parts for underlining the drama too heavily. Sir Carol wrote to me that he quite agreed but that, alas, it was too late to do anything about it!'

just as Reed would have failed to exploit the full epic scope of *Lawrence of Arabia*.* But *Odd Man Out* could have been a great David Lean film. His characters so often seem to move on tramlines, along a predetermined path. To this extent Johnny, trapped by fate, was an archetypal Lean character.

In Reed's case – to return to the real world – I think *Odd Man Out* was much more significant as the stepping stone to the perfection he would achieve with his next two films. He found his register. He found the things he could do well – an empathy with children, a feel for urban space, a sense of the unexpected.

The Fallen Idol told the story of an eight-year-old boy, the son of an ambassador, who develops a strong attachment for Baines, the butler in the embassy. Mistakenly believing that the butler has killed his wife, he lies to the police in order to protect him. It was a brilliant evocation of childhood, one of the most poignant and convincing ever to have been put on the screen. We have the benefit of the adult's eye, so can see how Felipe misreads the adult world, but at the same time we share his puzzlement and experience the sheer powerlessness of being a child – wanting to have an effect but not having any effect. We share also his perception of his surroundings. The embassy in which Felipe lives is vast, mysterious, almost alive – the way a child but few grown-ups would see it.

Carol Reed's observation is faultless. There's a scene in which Felipe is taken on an outing to the zoo. The child trails after the adults, passing a row of cockatoos on their perches; as he passes each bird, he tweaks its tail in as idle a child's gesture as kicking gravel. It's a tiny little detail easy to miss – one not to be found in any script – but perfectly captures what children actually do. And there were countless similar moments. Dilys Powell realized what skill had been required to animate the child's character so truthfully. 'In this interplay of character and action a great responsibility is laid on the actors,' she wrote in her review of the film. 'I am not, I hope, belittling the ravishing performance of Bobby Henrey if I say that with this young player Carol Reed has performed a miracle of creative direction. It is not simply that the boy never makes a wrong gesture or uses a wrong intonation; he is never *seen* wrong; the delicate complex of his relations with a confusing world is flawlessly apprehended.'[22]

---

* Just look at *The Agony and the Ecstasy* to see how uncomfortable Reed was with such large-scale films.

The skill with which Reed conveyed the unconscious charm of childhood escaped any easily explicable process of intellect. Perhaps the key was that he had not entirely grown up nor forgotten what it was like to be a child himself. But also the story to some degree echoed his own childhood experience. His father, Sir Herbert, kept two establishments, his wife's and his mistress's. As the child of the mistress, and with his father an infrequent visitor, Reed must have had the same sense as Felipe – for whom Mr and Mrs Baines are surrogate parents – of belonging to two families.

He must also have had an understanding of Baines's predicament – who no longer feels anything for his wife but loves Julie, a member of staff at the embassy. The situation brings to mind that of Alec and Laura in *Brief Encounter*. Indeed, when a tearful Julie meets Baines in a tea shop to discuss their predicament, the scene so closely resembles the farewell in the Milford Junction refreshment room that one wonders whether any conscious allusion was intended.

When Felipe, who has followed after Baines, turns up at the tea shop, he is as unwelcome a presence as Laura's gossiping acquaintance, Dolly Messiter. But while Dolly's sole function is to be irritating, Felipe is a complete character. As the adults conduct their grown-up conversation he feeds his pet slow worm with a scone, rocks back and forth on his chair, and eventually asks Julie if he can have the bun she seems to have no appetite for. The scene is funny, ironic, but also very moving.

While in *Brief Encounter* the characters are subordinated to the overall mood, in *The Fallen Idol* they are fully realized and gloriously true to themselves. In my opinion Carol Reed emerges as immeasurably the greater of the two directors, able to command mood and atmosphere without sacrificing truth of character, and free of the stifling convention that Lean's films never entirely escape.

In *Brief Encounter* there's a sense of things which must not be allowed to happen on screen: respect is paid to a rather oppressive morality which means that Trevor Howard has no choice but to start a new life in South Africa, and Celia Johnson to return to her husband. There is an invisible line beyond which we know the characters cannot cross.

It certainly helped Reed to have found a congenial partnership with Graham Greene, who wrote the script, but this should not make us think of *The Fallen Idol* as any less *his* film. Of 'The

Basement Room', the short story on which *The Fallen Idol* was based, Graham Greene wrote that in his conferences with Reed the subject was 'quietly changed' so that it 'no longer concerned a small boy who unwittingly betrayed his best friend to the police, but dealt instead with a small boy who believed that his friend was a murderer and nearly procured his arrest by telling lies in his defence. I think this, especially with Reed's handling, was a good subject.'[23] The effect of the change was to throw the focus on the psychology of the child. It is a difficult task to work out the separate elements in the alchemy of collaboration, but the compassion and the insights into childhood – as far as it is possible to call anything 'straight' – seem to me to be straight Reed. It should not be controversial to argue – especially in light of the indifferent spectacle that the Boulting brothers made of *Brighton Rock* – that Greene had the more reason of the two to be grateful for the partnership that the film began. He certainly must have felt such gratitude when he dedicated to Carol Reed the book containing the stories of *The Fallen Idol* and *The Third Man* in one volume, and wrote: 'Of one thing about both these films I have complete certainty, that their success is due to Carol Reed, the only director I know with that particular warmth of human sympathy, the extraordinary feeling for the right face for the right part, the exactitude of cutting, and not least important the power of sympathizing with an author's worries and an ability to guide him.'[24] A 'warmth of human sympathy' is frustratingly intangible – it's not a striking motif that you can easily pin down on the screen – but it was why Reed was such a marvellous director.

The Third Man was a providential blending of the unforeseen: without a huge measure of luck the film could have been so much less good than it was. But orchestrating chance came naturally to Reed. 'Carol Reed is the kind of director who'll use any ideas – anything that's going. I had notions for the dialogue, and Carol liked them,' commented Orson Welles:[25] the result, the famous cuckoo clock speech. Then there was Reed's discovery of Anton Karas, for whose zither he would ditch an orchestral score. And perhaps most of all the sublime ending in the Viennese cemetery, which had not been envisaged in Greene's original short story version: 'I watched him striding off on his overgrown legs after the girl. He caught her up and they walked side by side. I don't think he said a word to her: it was like the end of a story except that before they turned out of my sight her hand was through his arm . . .'[26]

Reed disliked this happy ending because he thought the audience, who had just seen Holly Martins kill Harry, the man the girl was in love with, would find it unpleasantly cynical. On the day of shooting the camera began to roll and Alida Valli as Anna began her walk up the cemetery lane. Joseph Cotten, as Holly Martins, waited for her to join him so that they could stroll away happily together.[27] But Valli/Anna just walked past him and on and on. 'Nobody uttered a word. The camera kept rolling. The special effects men from their high perches continued to drop toasted autumn leaves from above. I continued to puff on my cigarette, and began to get quite panic-stricken. Was there more to the scene? Had I gone blank? What was Carol waiting for me to do? I took one more puff, then in exasperation threw the cigarette to the ground, at which point Carol shouted through his laughter the word I had been waiting desperately to hear – *"Cut."* '[28]

It was a delicious subversion of the Hollywood values in accordance with which Anna would almost certainly have stopped for the happy ending. Holly Martins, who is a sort of grown-up Felipe, is notionally the hero but flounders around to little purpose. His attempts to sort out the mystery behind the disappearance of his old friend Harry Lime are the sort of thing one of the heroes in his Western novels – or indeed in Hollywood – might do, but are totally ineffective in the real world. With Reed's ending the abiding tone of *The Third Man* was one of profound disillusionment as Holly and Anna discover the true nature of the man they had both loved. There was some argument over what *The Third Man* should be called. Had the title not already been used, it could just as easily have been called 'The Fallen Idol'.

It is true that Carol Reed never made another film that matched up to *Odd Man Out* or *The Fallen Idol* or *The Third Man*. But the fact that *they* had been made was enough. They came about in an extraordinary decade through a conjunction of circumstances that could not be repeated, and it was in Reed's nature to want to move on. 'If you like making pictures, you've got to go from one to another – within reason. It's like being a boxer – there's no good just sitting down.' If *The Third Man* is a masterpiece, it is so because of a serendipity, because Reed never set out to make a masterpiece.

He tended to look for a subject which was the opposite of what he had just done. And to the predictable question of the modern critic, were there any ideas that constantly interested him, he replied: 'No. It's always the project. I know that there are great directors, like Visconti and Bergman, who have a certain view of life, but I don't think that a director who knows how to put a film together need impose his ideas on the world.'[29]

The brilliance of his best work lay not in putting forward a point of view, but in an intuitive feeling for the way people are and what they do. He was an observer. When he wasn't making films he used to while away the hours watching life go by. He took his son to the Cumberland Hotel, and told him: 'This is where I come to learn to make films. You learn about people and how they move and what they do and you have to guess what they do.'[30] As Reed's gift was one of observation, the subject matter was not important – just as it did not matter which particular person might enter the hotel lobby.

'*Le cas Carol Reed*,' according to Lindsay Anderson, was this. 'Can you be an artist of distinction if you don't care what you make films about, or never manage to find your real subject, or perhaps never find yourself?'[31] But the model the question implied just wasn't relevant. I don't think Reed ever looked for a subject in this way. His approach had more in common with that of the Old Masters. Their work was made up of a variety of standard commissions – a crucifixion maybe, an Adoration, a Visitation. Their art lay not in what they chose to paint but how.

Robert Hamer

'I want to make films about people in dark rooms doing beastly things to each other,' Robert Hamer once said.[1] It was not an attitude that the head of production at Ealing Studios Michael Balcon would have encouraged. He felt that films should be *improving*. So although Hamer was lucky enough to make two films as brilliant and uncompromising as *It Always Rains on Sunday* and *Kind Hearts and Coronets*, his time at Ealing was more notable for what he was not allowed to make. Since he was one of the biggest drunks in British films, it's easy to assume that it was alcohol that ruined his promise as possibly Britain's most talented director. It certainly didn't help, but it was a minor difficulty compared to the other obstacles he had to face. His story is a very British one of a film-maker denied the opportunity to express himself freely.

Robert Hamer was born in 1911 into a prosperous middle-class family which had owned farmland in Wales for generations. His father was a bank manager and, by all accounts, a model of rectitude. The young Hamer went to Rossall School in Lancashire, where his house captain's summary of his school career, written in 1930, provides a succinct portrait of the future film director on the threshold of adulthood: 'His apparent cynicism did not mar an attractive and interesting character, whose fault was a too quick temper and whose merit an ability to recover good humour very quickly.'[2] The words suggest a contrariness that would become more marked with the years.

There's a photograph of Hamer from his schooldays. He's sitting next to a table of trophies. His arms are folded and there's a look of confidence. In his time at Rossall many of those trophies had been his, and he must have felt that in the life ahead of him

71

there was no reason why he should not go on winning prizes. He excelled at sports, and was brilliant academically, in 1930 winning a scholarship to Corpus Christi, Cambridge. Few of Rossall's pupils could have enjoyed such a glittering career, and as he left the school behind there would have been no reason for him not to imagine his future prospects as straightforward as the school motto suggested: Mens agitat molem.*

At Cambridge, according to the college records, he received a first in Part I of the mathematics tripos, and then a third in Part II of the economics tripos. It is difficult to imagine that Hamer, who seems to have spent much of his time at Cambridge writing poetry and contributing to revues, could have been much interested in economics, but what must certainly have contributed to his sharp academic decline – from scholarship to third – was his rustication because of a homosexual affair. The episode shocked his deeply conventional family, who would have been further displeased when in 1934 he began to work in films as a lowly clapper-boy at Gaumont Studios.

Hamer's adult character was forged in the heat of that Cambridge scandal. When I visited the composer Geoffrey Wright, who had written half a dozen songs with Hamer for the Footlights, I told him about the school photograph and how dashing Hamer had looked. That was how he was, Wright remembered, until the scandal changed everything. The year he was forced to take off undermined him and snatched away his confidence.

Geoffrey Wright's account reminded me of an impression that another friend of Hamer had earlier confided to me. Brenda Danischewsky was the wife of the publicity director of Ealing Studios, Monja Danischewsky. She had not known about what had happened at Cambridge, but thought that Hamer must at some point in his life have been badly let down – as now it seemed he had been by the undergraduate he had fallen in love with. Sometime afterwards, Geoffrey Wright remembered, Hamer wrote a song about love not being true. In the years to come that would be the lesson of his life over and over again, and, like the song, most of his films told the same story.

Shortly before the war Hamer married an aspiring actress, Joan Holt. Her considerable beauty won her several screen tests, but

* 'Mind animates matter.'

she achieved little real success. Her frustration with her own career turned into jealousy of her husband's. They were constantly quarrelling, and she, like him, drank heavily. Hamer, who possessed a fine aesthetic sense of his own predicament, likened himself and his wife to Zelda and Scott Fitzgerald. This destructive partnership fizzled out in the 1950s, and Hamer would drift through a succession of equally unsatisfactory relationships with other women, none lasting very long.

It was the screenwriter Diana Morgan who told me this. She was one of Hamer's closest friends, and had known him both at Cambridge and Ealing. In the summer of 1993 I visited her at Denville Hall, the home for retired theatre people. My impression from talking to some of her Ealing colleagues was that maybe she had once been in love with Hamer. Certainly she was the most staunch guardian of his memory. In her room on a high shelf, overlooking us as we spoke, was a bronze bust of Hamer. She told me she had once donated it to the British Film Institute, but they stuck it away to languish unseen in some backroom and so she kidnapped it back. She was concerned now to find a fitting home for it before she died.* No one I spoke to knew Hamer better and I had to agree with her view that probably he would have been happier to live as a homosexual.

Two of his verses capture the change in Hamer. Diana Morgan, who had become blind in her old age, knew them by heart and recited them to me. The first was a song Hamer had written at Cambridge for the Footlights:

> Paint a smile on your face
> Laugh with me
> Tears and frowns have no place
> Can't you see
> A little laugh makes you to forget . . .

The second was this:

> Twisted by birth, further by lust contorted
> Mating cripples must achieve
> In their abnormal nude
> Fresh prodigies of attitude.

* Diana Morgan died on 9 November 1996.

Touching most unlikely spots,
Their very limbs true lover's knots,
They reach with every grasping breath,
The greater in the little death.

These were Hamer's songs of innocence and experience.

The man who in 1940 fetched up as an editor at Ealing was wary and battle-hardened. He is remembered for his warmth and mordant humour, but his abrupt, intense manner contrasted with the more easygoing natures of those about him. The 'apparent cynicism' of his school years had developed into a deep pessimism. 'I think that Robert was disenchanted with the world,' said Brenda Danischewsky. 'He was upset because he found himself in a place where people were horrid to each other.'[3] And the comparative serenity of his upbringing could only have accentuated the shock of this realization. Brenda was struck by his preoccupation with ethics and virtue, especially troubling to him, she felt, because he could never live up to his own high standards.

At Ealing he found his old friend from Cambridge, Diana Morgan, and Angus Macphail, the studio's scenario editor, whom he would have known from his time at Gaumont-British. The three formed a little clique and at lunchtimes were often to be found sitting together in the studio canteen playing 'the Ealing game', whose rules Diana Morgan told me were far too difficult to explain. Probably the actor John McCallum was referring to it when in his memoirs he recalled Hamer on location always insisting 'on playing an academic sort of literary guessing game, which could get very esoteric and convoluted at times'.[4] McCallum also remembered that Hamer could do the *Times* crossword in ten minutes flat.

At Ealing Hamer benefited from Michael Balcon's renowned readiness to give new talent a chance. He was made an associate producer and in 1943 co-wrote *San Demetrio, London*, a true story of the exploits of a wartime crew who bring a crippled tanker safely across the Atlantic. A morale-raising exercise of the stiff-upper-lip school, its chief significance for Hamer was the opportunity it offered to win his spurs; it was very different from the bleak pieces that would follow.

In an introduction to a published extract from the script of *Kind Hearts and Coronets* Hamer wrote of 'an impulse to escape the

74

unshaded characterization which convention tends to enforce on scripts'.[5] With the exception of *It Always Rains on Sunday* and *Kind Hearts and Coronets* all his films have to some degree suffered from conceding to such convention. Although Hamer usually wrote or co-wrote scripts, he could not completely escape from the play or novel on which they were based, or the expectations of the studio. In many of his films there is a sense of his having to tolerate scenes for which he had little interest in order to make the most of those that did appeal to him. The result is an unevenness that is itself almost the mark of a Hamer film: he produced some of the most dazzling curate's eggs in the history of the British cinema.

His first credit as director was for the *Haunted Mirror* episode in *Dead of Night* (1945). A woman gives an old mirror to her fiancé for his birthday. In it he sees the reflection of a room where the mirror's original owner killed his wife in a mad fit of jealousy. The mirror takes an increasing hold on its new master, and, once he has married, poisons him with suspicions of his wife's infidelity. The spell is finally broken when the mirror is smashed.

The *Haunted Mirror* is a gripping depiction of madness and destructive passion, but defused by its supernatural framework. The mirror needs only to be broken for the harmonious existence of the couple to be restored. The conclusion implies an essential reason and order, from which the haunted mirror is a departure. It is hard to imagine that Hamer was much convinced by the happy ending and in his subsequent films it would become clear that he expected to look upon such madness in *any* mirror.

In 1945 Hamer made his first full-length feature, *Pink String and Sealing Wax*. Based on a play by Roland Pertwee, it tells the story of Edward Sutton, a chemist in late Victorian Brighton who crushes his children's aspirations with his puritanical rule. His son, David, forbidden to court the girl he loves, ventures into the local pub to drown his sorrows. There he becomes infatuated with Pearl, the wife of the proprietor. Pearl plans to kill her drunken husband so that she can marry her lover, Dan Powell, and exploits David's passion for her to obtain poison from his father's dispensary.

In an interview Hamer said of *Pink String and Sealing Wax* that he 'enjoyed the melodrama but never felt happy with the domestic charm'.[6] The film is really two films yoked together. One centres on the conflict between father and children in the middle-class Sutton household. It is hard to kindle much interest in the two-dimensional characters or to take seriously the rosy outcome in which the father is chastened and all the children achieve their ambitions. The Suttons are surely an example of what Hamer meant by 'unshaded characterization'.

But the other film, focusing on the low-life characters of the Dolphin pub, is compelling. It has its literary counterpart in the fiction of Patrick Hamilton, whose *Hangover Square* Diana Morgan recalled that Hamer much admired. Portrayed on the screen is the same despairing world of hopeless characters drinking away their lives in seedy saloon bars. Hamer shared Hamilton's acute awareness of malevolence and preyed-upon innocence. His characters are greedy, cruel, callous but exhilaratingly alive and pursue their aims with a chilling and merciless opportunism. For the sake of love Pearl will murder and then attempt to pin the blame on the innocent David Sutton. For the sake of money Dan Powell will direct his affections to whichever woman seems to offer the most favourable prospects. There is no kindness, charity or generosity of spirit at the Dolphin, but we are moved, or awed, by the savagery of feeling, unrestrained by the 'civilized' values of the Suttons. The dramatic highpoint of the film is Pearl's realization that she was never loved, that she murdered for nothing. Her mental turmoil, which drives her to suicide, matters to us far more than any of the Sutton family's fortunes. At the Dolphin, Robert Hamer was in his element making films about people 'doing beastly things to each other'.

He was able to express himself with much more freedom in *It Always Rains on Sunday* (1947), a film based on a novel by Arthur la Bern and set in London's East End. Googie Withers, in her third and final appearance in a Hamer film, plays Rose, a one-time barmaid (like Pearl in *Pink String and Sealing Wax*), who is now married to George Sandigate, a decent but dull man much older than herself. When her ex-lover Tommy Swann escapes from prison and turns up at her Bethnal Green house seeking refuge, her old feelings are rekindled. She smuggles him into her home and spends that day trying to keep his presence secret from her husband and stepdaughters.

Hamer presents a world in which deceit and betrayal are routine. Rose deceives her family for the sake of an impossible love. Tommy encourages her dreams, but when the police close in, rather than stand by her he will even knock her down to escape.

In *It Always Rains on Sunday* the characters' lot is to deceive and be deceived. Passion is stronger than virtue. The desire for money, or freedom, or love, leads the characters to disregard any standard of honour or trust. The bitter taste of reality – for Rose, life without love; for Tommy, life without freedom – drives the two main characters to make separate but failed suicide attempts. Tommy returns to prison, and Rose, in an all-for-the-best *Brief Encounter* ending, returns to her family, which in truth seems no less a prison to her. The film's bleak outlook mirrored Hamer's own personal disenchantment: it was the song again about love not being true. If *Kind Hearts and Coronets* is what he will be most remembered for, *It Always Rains on Sunday*, I think, is more typical of the films he wanted to make – the subjects he proposed at Ealing tended to be contemporary, urban melodramas. The film also provides a corrective for the impression that *Kind Hearts and Coronets* leaves of a literary rather than a visual director. Its finale is one of the most spectacular sequences I can think of in cinema. Tommy Swann is run to ground in a marshalling yard. As he tries hopelessly to elude his pursuers, he skips from track to track, dodging steam-engines which grind into motion as if of their own impulse and close down his remaining avenues of escape. It is a memorable cinematic rendering of fate bearing down.

One reviewer wrote, 'Those people who are not spivs or minor crooks have little else to commend them,' and 'It is, perhaps, a pity that thousands of honest cheerful citizens of Bethnal Green could not have had a stronger representation.'[7] It was the sort of review the wholesome-minded Balcon might have written himself had he been a critic. But if *It Always Rains on Sunday* was hardly the example of good conduct that Balcon favoured, none the less it was Ealing's biggest money-maker of the year. When the following year Hamer began to work on *Kind Hearts and Coronets*, he was already established as one of the most successful and individual directors at the studio.

The idea for *Kind Hearts and Coronets* went back a long way. Before Hamer had even become a director, he had wanted to make a film about Landru, the French mass murderer, and was able to pursue the project when he became an associate producer at Ealing in 1943. The project was abandoned after it was learnt that Chaplin was making a film about the Landru murders, *Monsieur Verdoux*, but a few years later Hamer would find another vehicle with which to treat the same theme of murder in polite society.

Roy Horniman's *Israel Rank*, first published in 1904 and reissued in 1948, was a novel of considerable achievement, containing a deadpan Wildean wit which *Kind Hearts* would brilliantly build upon. Horniman's Israel Rank is a half Jew who murders his way to a title and Horniman emphasizes his alien nature. In *Kind Hearts* he becomes the half-Italian Louis Mazzini (Dennis Price), who is otherwise the perfect English gentleman, possessing poise, charm and an impeccable wit. Louis belongs to the society he preys upon, and *Kind Hearts* satisfies on one level as a devastating satire of the hypocrisy of a class-ridden England. Louis embarks upon his murderous trail because the aristocratic D'Ascoynes disowned his mother for marrying an Italian singer, yet in his bloody progress he too acts as though a coronet were more important than a kind heart. The film is a compendium of snobbery and sham conventions. Louis feels keenly the social disgrace of having to take in lodgers, or of being employed in a job instead of a career, or of living on the wrong side of the park. He is the supreme amoral aesthete.

But the sadness underlying the film's viciously black humour is that Louis starts out as a young gentleman of considerable decency. He simply learns that decency does not pay, and in his subsequent career of deceit and murder adapts to the way of a world which pays lip service but scant regard in practice to kind hearts. His childhood sweetheart, the deliciously wicked Sibella (Joan Greenwood), teaches him an early lesson in cruelty. When he proposes to her, she accepts his passionate embrace with enthusiasm, but then calmly announces her intention to marry the very dull but rich Lionel instead.

Louis and Sibella, who lie, exploit, manipulate and murder to achieve their aims, are typical Hamer characters. Their ruthless expediency recalls Tommy Swann in *It Always Rains on Sunday*; or Dan Powell and Pearl Bond in *Pink String and Sealing Wax*. These people will resort to whatever it takes.

It is easy to dwell too much on the self-destructive elements of Hamer's character and regard him as overly intense and severe. Yet although the familiar themes of disillusionment and betrayal are prominent in *Kind Hearts and Coronets*, the film's wit and exhilarating energy reflect another side of Hamer. For all his brooding, he had an enormous sense of fun. Both Googie Withers and Alec

Guinness stressed this. Actors enjoyed working with him. In Alec Guinness's words, 'He was always sympathetic, encouraging and good-humoured.'[8] *Kind Hearts and Coronets* owes much of its success to the virtuoso performances of its cast. Hamer's sensitivity helped actors to give of their best, but this sensitivity was double-edged, causing him to feel far too keenly the many setbacks in his life that would follow.

No other director at Ealing possessed such a strong sense of what he wanted to do, but this was a handicap in a film-maker who had to work within the framework of a company. The people who attended Ealing's production meetings were not just film-makers, but executives. The successful ones were those who knew how to keep in step with company policy, who didn't hold to a strong personal vision and could turn their hand to a variety of different projects. Hamer's distinctive taste made him a film artist but a poor company man, and in the long run this told against him.

In 1945 Hamer made a promising new friend in Mark Benny, a former criminal turned novelist and academic. Benny proposed a story about a young man who has been falsely accused and tried for murder. He becomes so intoxicated by being in the headlines that he really commits a murder to savour the publicity all over again. To Benny's amazement, in a matter of days Hamer had got Ealing to buy the rights to the three-line idea for a large sum, and he was hired to write the script, which became known as *Soho Melodrama*. It was to have been Hamer's next film after *Kind Hearts and Coronets* but the project ran into censorship difficulties.

Finding a film for Robert Hamer became a major preoccupation of Ealing Studios in 1948. He was at the height of his career, and with *Kind Hearts and Coronets* in the process of making an unsurpassed masterpiece of British cinema, yet one by one all his proposals for what he would do next foundered. Surviving minutes of Ealing's production meetings – known as the 'round table' meetings after the large table in the directors' dining room at which they took place – offer an insight into the gulf between what he wanted to do and what he was allowed to do.

While everyone else had given up on *Soho Melodrama*, Hamer still fought to save it. The minutes for 20 November 1947 record: 'Because of Mr Hamer's confidence in the subject it had been decided not to dispose of it. Mr Montagu said that he would read the latest version.'[9] But the fact that at the same meeting Hamer proposed as a possible alternative *The King at Nightfall*, another Mark Benny idea, showed his realization that *Soho Melodrama* was now unlikely ever to get off the ground. Balcon approved the purchase of *The King at Nightfall* and Benny's services as a scriptwriter, but two months later had turned against the idea. The minutes for February 1948 record: 'Mr Balcon expressed his lack of faith in the subject but before writing it off agreed to wait for the new Mark Benny version.' The unfortunate phrasing hardly suggested that Balcon would reassess the project with an open mind, and Hamer made sure to attend the next meeting with yet another idea.

The play *A Pin to See the Peepshow* by F. Tennyson Jesse, which was based on the famous Thompson-Bywater case, told the story of Julia Almond, who was wrongly convicted as an accomplice to murder when her lover killed her husband. In prison as she realizes that she never really loved anyone at all, she regrets the foolish dreaming that has brought her to the threshold of death. It's easy to see how this study in disillusionment appealed to Hamer, and it would have made the perfect companion piece to *Pink String and Sealing Wax* and *It Always Rains on Sunday*.

At the April 1948 production meeting Hamer suggested the idea as a vehicle for Margaret Lockwood, a star now available to Ealing through their new association with Rank. The response must have made him hopeful. The minutes recorded: 'Sir Michael felt that this was an excellent suggestion and if Margaret Lockwood liked the idea, it would in all probability be the first picture for 1949.' Maybe Sir Michael's recent knighthood had made him less than usually circumspect, for when the project was raised again at the June meeting, it was reported that there was a 'slight possibility that there would be a decision against making this subject' and 'Mr Hamer should prepare an alternative story', words which now had a familiar ring for Hamer.

They were echoed at the next meeting in July. 'In case of insurmountable obstacles Sir Michael advised Mr Hamer to prepare an alternative subject.' The obstacles are referred to in the minutes as 'legal and censorship problems'. Hamer clearly felt these could be overcome if the company wanted to make the film badly enough, and Balcon found himself having to defend the sincerity of his commitment to the project: 'Sir Michael stated emphatically that he wanted to make this picture and wished it to take the second position in the 1949 programme.'

J. Arthur Rank, the Yorkshire miller who made the finest years possible. Affable, scrupulous and principled, he was the most unlikely of film moguls. In this cartoon by caricaturist and film critic Richard Winnington he looks as if he's only just wiped the flour from his hands. It captures the plain-speaking visionary that he was.

The great Filippo Del Giudice, in his own words 'Butler to the *Tal-ents*' and a one-man cinema renaissance. Among the films for which he was responsible were *In Which We Serve, Henry V, The Way Ahead, Odd Man Out, The Way to the Stars* and *Hamlet*. Del Giudice – or 'Del' as everybody called him – was fabled for his extravagance. In the austerity years of the 1940s when most film moguls were content with one starlet on their arm, Del rarely attended a premiere with less than two – on this occasion Margaret Lockwood and Paulette Goddard.

John Davis, businessman extraordinaire and the nemesis of Filippo Del Giudice. As managing director of the Rank Organisation, he would become the most powerful man in British films. In the late 1940s he would save the British film industry from collapse, but at a cost, adopting that time-honoured practice of film executives: Tough on art, tough on the causes of art.

Michael Balcon, who came closer than anyone else to showing how film production in Britain just might be a sensible business.

Here talking to his long-time friend Angus Macphail, connoisseur of literature, prodigious polymath and inventor of the Macguffin.

Carol Reed, my favourite director. Loved by actors and brilliant with both children ...

... and animals.

Anton Karas, in a smart new suit, playing the zither on Carol Reed's kitchen table. Carol Reed looks on from the sofa in the background.

Alberto de Almeida Cavalcanti, known to his friends in England simply as 'Cav'.

Robert Hamer, the British cinema's poet of disillusionment.

The weird and wonderful Humphrey Jennings during the production of *Fires Were Started*. Two of his amateur actors, William Sansom and Fred Griffiths, look on in baffled admiration.

Jennings and Myra Hess during the making of *A Diary for Timothy*.

The two sides of Harry Watt: the nattily dressed bon viveur ...

... and man of action.

The Hon 'Puffin' Asquith, son of the ex-prime minister, Lord Oxford, timelessly fashionable in the faded blue denim boilersuit he wore when filming. 'It was really an odd contrast,' commented Sophia Loren, who would work with him in the 1960s, 'the gentleman in the worker's clothes. But I've never seen a man so comfortably elegant.'

At the round table meeting in September, *A Pin to See the Peepshow* finally went the way of the other Hamer projects. The Lord Chamberlain banned the stage play, and Balcon, who must have felt that his caution was vindicated, 'pointed out that this ban was ammunition to those who objected to the filming of the subject. He had all along detected a lack of goodwill to the idea and he had not felt that the story was a first-class risk' – this of an idea that only a few short months ago, without any mention of such reservations, he had called 'excellent'.

Such reverses 'caused Hamer to have a very neurotic reaction generally,'[10] remembered Sidney Cole, who was an associate producer at the studio. Quite apart from the irritation of Balcon's inconsistency, he must have felt a sense of overwhelming futility: no matter how hard he worked to find a way through, sooner or later – like Tommy Swann trapped by the engines in the marshalling yard – he would be stopped by yet another objection. On a day-to-day level he would have felt at a disadvantage to his colleagues who were making films on a regular basis – and earning their keep. As he was expected to contribute a film to each year's programme, the pressure to find an acceptable project was huge. His inability to do so eventually led to him taking on an assignment outside Ealing Studios (*The Spider and the Fly*). Of course he could always have agreed to make a project which was acceptable to the consensus. And if his first concern had been to be an effective member of Ealing Studios, this is what he would have done. His choosiness was disrupting the programme, and Balcon, who after all was running a business, had every reason to feel frustrated by his behaviour.

The round table minutes of February 1949 reveal what Hamer might have been doing had he been more reasonable. 'If his present possible outside commitments fell through, he might consider working on the Oscar Slater subject.' Oscar Slater was wrongly convicted of murder and, after a campaign by prominent figures including Sir Arthur Conan Doyle, had his conviction quashed by the Court of Appeal in 1928. Miscarriages of justice would have interested Hamer, but he must have known how difficult it would have been to turn the subject his way. Where he would have found darkness, Balcon wanted light.

As ever cautious, and wishing not to offend, Balcon tried to find out what the official reaction might be to such a film, and, in a letter dated 2 March 1949, sought the advice of the Scottish film critic Forsyth Hardy:

> As we specialize rather successfully in films that are based on real and factual material it has been suggested that it would be a dramatic subject redounding to the credit of British justice to take this very famous case in which a wrong was set right in the end . . .
>
> The positive aspect . . . would be to show all those . . . who explored the facts and finally secured the bringing of them before a court of appeal . . .
>
> But what we are anxious to avoid is proceeding with an enterprise that we view with enthusiasm, because we see interesting possibilities of expressing dramatically the British instinct for justice, and then finding that official sources feel that however well and honestly treated the subject might be, our enthusiasm may have been misplaced.[11]

The letter was an example of the fundamental collision of attitudes between Hamer and his boss: the one had as downbeat a view of the world as the other's was positive. Unable to fall in with Balcon's well-meaning but mildly propagandistic intentions, Hamer was stifled.

In the event his outside commitments did not fall through and he was spared the inevitable struggle with Balcon over the Slater project. But it was only misery deferred. He was still contracted to Ealing, and eventually had to undertake a film he did not want to make, *His Excellency* in 1951, an adaptation of a play by Dorothy and Campbell Christie about a former trade unionist who becomes governor of a British colony. He disliked the film and there was little in the story that could possibly have interested him. Although he was as ever drinking, and spent much of the production incapable, there was really nothing about the film worth remaining sober for.

Michael Balcon wrote in his memoirs that Hamer seemed to be 'engaged on a process of self-destruction'.[12] This is certainly true, but he received ample help from a system which could not accommodate his outlook. 'He was thwarted.' When I visited Diana Morgan, I remember these as the first words she had to say of her close friend.

In 1959 Hamer was one of a number of British directors invited by *Sight and Sound* to describe what film they would make if they had the freedom. He challenged the fancifulness of the notion with words which contained a decade of bitter experience. 'Although the mandate states that this is not intended to be a Utopian exercise, I take certain leave to disagree with the premise. Surely, if the intention of the exercise is to encourage temerity and discourage timorousness on the part of the holders of the purse-strings, a certain Utopian approach is not only desirable but also necessary.'[13]

Maybe it was such a 'Utopian approach' that in spite of all the obstacles accounted for films of an unparalleled autobiographical intensity. The characters he portrayed on the screen amplified the 'small black-and-white image of himself' that according to Mark Benny he kept in the depths of his mind.[14]

He played out his own self-destruction by proxy many times. I doubt that any other film-maker in British cinema can boast such an impressive catalogue of suicide scenes. Googie Withers throws herself off a cliff in *Pink String and Sealing Wax*, then attempts to gas herself in *It Always Rains on Sunday*. In the same film John McCallum, the escaped convict cornered by the police in the marshalling yard, tries to throw himself into the path of an oncoming steam-engine. In *The Long Memory* (1952), faced with exile abroad and the inevitability that she will lose her family, a woman tries to throw herself under a tube train.

Even *Kind Hearts and Coronets*, that jewel of the Ealing comedies, was a suicide note. Some time after it was clear that it was going to be a classic film, Mark Benny pointed out to Hamer 'the Freudian implications of killing off poppa Guinness eight times', but 'Robert rejected this interpretation, and insisted that in his script he had been killing himself.'[15]

'No one can be satisfied with one death,' Hamer told Mark Benny. 'I'd like to die like Charles XII, drowned in a butt of brandy, but I'd also like to die like Stefan George, poisoned by a rose-thorn. Bits of me have already died in these ways.'

Hamer had an artist's appreciation of his own misfortune. He put his suffering to work on the screen, returning again and again to a few themes that haunted him. François Truffaut's assertion that a director only ever made one film seems particularly apt in his case. Just as the cinema allowed Hamer to die over and over again, it allowed him to relive the disillusionment that he first experienced as an undergraduate in Cambridge.

His first five films as a director, from the *Haunted Mirror* episode in *Dead of Night* to *The Spider and the Fly*, all tell versions of that story. *The Spider and the Fly*, the film which in 1949 he left Ealing to make, was the last opportunity he had to indulge a mood of exquisite mournfulness that was becoming increasingly at odds with the commercial requirements of the time.

Philippe De Ledocq is an artist-criminal after the fashion of Louis Mazzini, although safecracking rather than murder is his line. Like Louis in *Kind Hearts and Coronets*, he is a cool opportunist. He takes advantage of a woman's love to use her as an accomplice, sacrifices her to the police when his own safety is threatened, then later turns to her when he needs an alibi. Eventually Philippe, who thought himself not to have a heart, falls in love with the woman only to be betrayed by her in turn. The film ends with Philippe enlisting as a common soldier in a unit bound for Verdun – another suicide of sorts.

Hamer would never again be able to tell his story so freely. In the 1950s he had either to take on meaningless assignments like *His Excellency* and the equally dire *To Paris with Love*, or to compromise more promising material.

Father Brown (1954) was a good-natured comedy thriller. The character of Flambeau, yet another artist-criminal, must have inspired Hamer. He built considerably on the character in G. K. Chesterton's stories, introducing an entirely original quality of melancholy. The scenes in which Father Brown seeks to convert Flambeau to the path of righteousness have a powerful emotional force, but necessitate an awkward readjustment to the lighter, comic elements. The happy ending in which Flambeau renounces his life of crime is unconvincing for the character Hamer has made of him, although it may reflect a degree of rather forlorn wishful thinking in his own life. At the time of *Father Brown*, according to Diana Morgan, Hamer considered becoming a Catholic but was unable to make the final leap of faith.

When Flambeau explains to Father Brown why he steals, Hamer would certainly have identified closely with the sentiments: 'I was trained as a good swordsman, but in a world of guns and bombs it is no longer regarded as an accomplishment to know how to die gracefully at dawn. I ride a horse well, but what use is that in a world of tramlines and petrol fumes? I love beautiful things I cannot afford to buy. So quite simply I take them to decorate my world.' Hamer's 'beautiful things' were the films that very rarely he was allowed to make as he wished. These were so contrary to the reassuring images deemed suitable for Britain's cinema screens that it must have seemed like a kind of theft to get away with them. Like Flambeau, Hamer was a cultivated man who was out of step with his surroundings. Mark Benny thought that his 'spiritual home was in the pages of the *Yellow Book*'. [16]

The kindred spirits that Hamer himself recognized were mostly French. Diana Morgan remembered that he was a keen admirer of the French cinema and a close friend of Cavalcanti, who had been a leading figure of the French avant-garde in the 1920s. In the early days of the war he had briefly worked for Cavalcanti at the GPO Film Unit. Here he edited the soundtrack of *Le journal de guerre*, a series of films, made under the supervision of Jacques Brunius, that chronicled the war against Germany before the Fall of France. When Cavalcanti left the GPO to join Ealing, Hamer was one of the young film-makers he would bring with him.

The influence of Carné and Prévert over Hamer's films is particularly marked. We find the same heightened artifice, the same love of words and the same moody fatalism. In *It Always Rains on Sunday* the bustle of Petticoat Lane resembles the Boulevard du Crime of *Les Enfants du Paradis*; Tommy Swann seeking refuge in Rose's bedroom recalls Jean Gabin holed up in an attic and surrounded by the police in *Le Jour se lève*; and the film's atmosphere of doomed love in a tawdry world, although with rain instead of mist, is reminiscent of *Le Quai des Brumes*. And Louis Mazzini in *Kind Hearts and Coronets* has his counterpart in fellow-murderer and aesthete Lacenaire in *Les Enfants du Paradis*. So attuned are Hamer's films to a French sensibility that one wonders whether his talent might not have prospered in France as surely as it was stifled in England.

Mark Benny remembered that Hamer 'could not easily forgive himself if, during a convivial evening, his own style fell to normal contemporary levels' and 'would avoid you for a week after those rare occasions when you had out-drunk him'.[17] In the 1950s, lacking any meaningful film work, Hamer made the most of this other pastime. Diana Morgan remembered him regularly going off on binges, then ringing up after weeks of silence to announce: 'I've been found.' There were attempts to step back from the abyss – periods of convalescence with his family in Wales or drying out in nursing homes – but alcohol would always reclaim him.

His instinct for self-preservation was undermined by his artist's sense: the spectacle of his own slide was too compelling not to be savoured. 'He had above all a period sense for a conspicuous consumption,' Benny wrote, 'the conspicuous consumption of oneself: he relished the detachment with which he could watch himself, as he thought, going down hill, and his subjective landscape . . . was full of steep declines which, with an exquisite feeling of guilt, he had coasted down.'[18] Hamer's last years had their tragic aspect, as he drowned himself in butts of brandy and much else besides, but it's hard not to admire the bravado and swagger with which he played his part. Like another Welsh drunk, he did not 'go gentle into that good night'.

While the only jobs he could find were bland and unambitious assignments, his true voice was still to be found in the scripts he wrote privately and never succeeded in realizing. One of these was *For Each the Other*, which offers a glimpse of the unsettled existence he was leading in the 1950s. Very loosely based on the French play *L'âme en peine* by Jean-Jacques Bernard, it tells the story of two people who are made for each other but after several near encounters finally meet only in death. Hamer provides a self-portrait of himself in the character of the sophisticated Anthony, a connoisseur of poetry, painting and music, who drifts listlessly from bar to bar, from girl to girl, always a whisky bottle in his pocket.

Diana Morgan showed me a copy of a play that Hamer had written. Set in the eighteenth century, it was called *Time Alone Will Tell*. An elderly dowager duchess determines to introduce her granddaughter to the ways of the world while she is still young enough to recover from the lesson, and pays a young man to break her heart. The same story of betrayal again. And probably there were many other projects which never saw the light of day.

In 1960 Hamer collapsed on the set of *School for Scoundrels* and was nearly sacked from the production. It was the last time he would ever direct a film, as understandably offers of work ceased. The routine of drying out and then lapsing back into drink again had long been a familiar one, but now as his addiction clearly threatened both his life and his livelihood, he must have felt a new sense of desperation. He had finally bumped to the bottom, where his agonies were far too acute for him to consider them with the artist's detachment that Mark Benny had remarked on. But the thought is inescapable that these last years of his life would have made a fine Robert Hamer production. Perhaps occasionally he did find himself dreaming the impossible – that he could make a film of his own death, like the writer in *Sunset Boulevard* telling the story of how he came to be drowned in the star's swimming-pool.*

Unable to find work, and doubtless his 'period taste for consumption' making it difficult for him to adjust to his straitened circumstances, Hamer was declared a bankrupt. At the time he was living with Pamela Wilcox, the daughter of the film producer Herbert Wilcox. She too was out of work. Together they shared one shabby room in Chelsea and, as Pamela Wilcox describes in her book *Between Hell and Charing Cross*, 'fell into a period of alcoholic self-pity, clinging to one another in mutual misery'.[19]

In the imaginary production of his last days I think Hamer would certainly have regarded as an important episode a near encounter between himself and a great American film director. In 1962 his agent Stella Jonckheere – who had been literary editor at Ealing Studios during the 1940s – managed to get him two weeks' work in Madrid on Nicholas Ray's *Fifty-five Days in Peking*. His job was to help the screenwriter Philip Yordan make the dialogue for David Niven's character more British. After a week he cracked up and sent Jonckheere this telegram, which I reproduce here exactly as I saw it, curiously garbled I suppose by a mixture of Hamer's drunken wordplay and the Spanish telegrapher's poor grasp of English:

PHILIP CARE UP CRIPPLED BY EMBARASSNET TO EXPLAIN THAT THE BOSS CLASS HAD ORDRED THAT NICHOLAS RAY AND I SHOULDNT NEET IN CASE WE GOT DRUNIL TOGETHER. YOU MAY PUBLISH TO ALL CONCERNED I WRITE THIS IN CLEAR POUR ENRARGNER LES ROUGEURS DES FACTEURS.

Nicholas Ray himself would collapse on set a few weeks later, and be unable to finish the film. The two men would undoubtedly

---

* One of his cherished projects at this time was to film Malcolm Lowry's chronicle of an alcoholic's last days, *Under the Volcano*.

have admired each other and have had much in common. It seems cruel that they should have been kept apart, if all too typical of the film industry's 'Boss Class'.

Hamer returned from Madrid, and under the supervision of his father and twin sister, Barbara, was sent to a nursing home. His father paid the bills and gave his son an allowance of £12 a week. In his films Hamer had revealed himself to be a master of mood and emotion, but he would have been hard put to match the pathos of his own life now coming so unnaturally full circle – at an age when other men might be expected to be looking after ailing parents, here he was being cared for by them. His father wrote to Stella Jonckheere thanking her for having tried to help Hamer and expressing his incomprehension at how he could have so let her down.

Little more than a year later, on 4 December 1963, Rober Hamer died in St Thomas's Hospital. 'The one thing we all fear is to die grotesquely, in bed,' he had told his friend Mark Benny.[20] With his natural pessimism he would not have been much surprised to find that Fate had so arranged things for him.

Angus Macphail

'Ladies and gentlemen, with your kind attention and permission, I've now the honour to present to you one of the most remarkable men in the world. Every day he commits to memory fifty new facts and remembers every one of them – facts from history, from geography, from newspapers, from scientific textbooks, millions and millions of them down to the smallest detail. Test him, ladies and gentlemen, ask him any question.'

Mr Memory steps forward to make his final fatal appearance. When Richard Hannay asks him what are the thirty-nine steps, he is compelled by his calling to reveal the blueprints that enemy agents have made him learn. An assassin's bullet silences him. 'Am I right, sir?' he asks as he lies dying on the stage.

The Memory Man was an early example of Hitchcock's celebrated Macguffin – the secret the baddies are after. The word was coined by Angus Macphail, the scenario editor at Gaumont-British where *The 39 Steps* was made. When he moved on to Ealing Studios, he took the concept with him. Diana Morgan told me that Macguffins were routine at the studio's script conferences. She also told me that the Memory Man scene in *The 39 Steps* was Macphail's idea. The only scripting contributions mentioned in the titles of *The 39 Steps* are Charles Bennett for the adaptation, and Ian Hay for the dialogue, but such credits were often incomplete, and as Gaumont-British's scenario editor Macphail would have been closely involved in all the studio's productions. So Diana Morgan could well be right.

One wants her to be right because it would have a poetic aptness. The Memory Man seems so much like Angus Macphail himself. It was widely believed that he had seen and remembered every film ever made. 'His filmic knowledge was encyclopaedic and his memory so good that he could find a parallel in almost any suggested story situation,' remembered the screenwriter T. E. B. ('Tibby') Clarke.[1] Several letters from Macphail are to be found among Ivor Montagu's papers in the British Film Institute Library. The two friends had been at school and university together, and would cross paths many times in the course of their working lives. One of these letters was written simply to tell Montagu that in the second half of the eighteenth century the average number of desertions from the British Navy each year was 10,000. 'History is simply crammed with wonderful facts that nobody uses.'[2]

Macphail's end was not quite so sudden, but the story of his time at Ealing Studios has just as tragic an aspect as the Memory Man's helpless compulsion, on being asked, to tell what he had learnt. Tibby Clarke thought that Macphail's prodigious memory 'made him, as a writer, rather too prone to rely on film clichés'.[3] Diana Morgan remembered him as having plenty of good ideas but being unable to write convincing dialogue. They both thought he was a much better editor than he was a writer, with one exception – he had a talent for the Gracie Fields, George Formby and Will Hay comedies. It was a bitter skill for such a cultivated man to have. As Diana Morgan succinctly put it, 'He wanted to write things he couldn't write. And he despised himself for writing the things he could write.'[4]

Poor Angus Macphail had only to look in the mirror to know that fate had dealt him a cruel hand. Brenda Danischewsky remembered that he worried about his appearance. 'He was a very funny-looking chap. Tall and gangling and awkward and short-sighted and great beaky red nose, terrible indigestion, foot trouble constantly, supports in his shoes.'[5] Diana Morgan thought 'he looked like a secretary bird'. And as if this weren't bad enough, he had a very high voice. As an undergraduate he decided that a deep voice would be more becoming of a man, so he just talked in a deep voice, which must have made him seem even more peculiar.[6] Life was one long struggle to overcome natural disadvantages. It was little surprise if by the time he had come to Ealing he was considered an eccentric.

A frequent invalid, he was brought up an only child in a kind of domestic monastery, where he was nursed hand, foot and finger. Shy and a likely victim for bullies, Macphail's response to the harshness of the outside world was to develop a protective carapace of books, games, jokes and drink.

After school at Westminster he went to Cambridge, where he

studied French. Here his closest companion was his old schoolfriend Ivor Montagu, who remembered Macphail as 'a red-haired
and rather gauche Scot from Blackheath'.[7] They both loved music
hall and shared a passion for puns, Donald MacGill postcards, and
unintentionally rude newspaper headlines. They played chess
several times a week, at the same time honing their catchwords
and puns. 'To grasp our full littleness,' wrote Montagu, 'it is necessary to cite one. Whenever either offered a gambit he would say:
"Pawn up, poor hopeless nup."'[8] Playing billiards badly was
another pastime: it took them an hour to reach one hundred and a
break of ten was an 'event'. They were members of an auction
bridge four which played that game as endlessly as the two of
them played chess, eventually exhausting so many combinations
of cards that they became bored and experimented with 'strange
modifications, such as the Minus form'.[9] The other two members
of the four were Arthur Elton and Ian Dalrymple. Two decades
later all four would be prominent figures in British films.

Ivor Montagu and Angus Macphail both contributed to *Granta*,
the university magazine, which Ian Dalrymple edited. Macphail
wrote copious film and book reviews. They were slightly fogeyish
but perceptive, and revealed somebody formidably well versed in
literature and the cinema. They also suggested someone who
recognized but could enjoy the mediocre. Reviewing a play by
Clemence Dane called *The Way Things Happen*, he wrote:
'Impossible to deny that it abounds in sentimentality.
Sentimentality is not a defect in a play which obviously makes no
claim to be other than good second rate.'[10]

But Macphail's chief enthusiasm was for limericks, which he
contributed in vast numbers under such names as 'Uncle Angus'.
In the Lent term of 1925 he treated *Granta* readers to a cycle of
nine, each based on one of the muses:

> That fast-stepping dame called Erato
> Simply laughed at the doctrine of Plato
> She said: '*Damn* this Ideal
> That one can't see or feel!
> I'd sooner caress a potato.'[11]

And so on. The following May he even published a book of *Granta
Limericks*. It is the only work by Angus Macphail listed in the
British Library catalogue.

It's hard to summon up any enthusiasm for all these limericks. They are clever, erudite but childish. They were the sort of thing that an undergraduate might find briefly amusing in Rag Week before moving on to something of more importance. But for Macphail, together with all the other puzzles and games, they were a way of life. He had the mind of a trainspotter, finding comfort in useless information.* He possessed exceptional intelligence but it led nowhere. Delicate and fearful, he was reluctant to venture beyond the protective confines of the nursery or the games room.

While Macphail found a retreat in all these undergraduate games, for his friend Ivor Montagu they were a diversion from an extraordinarily varied and intense level of committed activity. Montagu was something of a phenomenon: a communist, a zoologist and anthropologist, a critic, cineaste and table tennis champion – this is just an abbreviated list of his interests. He was bustling with schemes and initiatives, and possessed a sense of direction (or directions) that Macphail lacked.

After university Angus tagged along after his friend. When Montagu managed to persuade *The Times* to send him over to Berlin to survey the exciting film scene there in the wake of *Caligari*, Macphail asked if he could come too.[12] In the event the article was never written, as with a refreshing honesty Montagu decided that he had merely learnt enough from the visit to know he didn't know enough. But the trip wasn't wasted: apart from several excellent games of chess, Montagu met on the journey back to England the actor Hugh Miller, and together they had the idea of forming the Film Society to show films of intrinsic merit in the hope that, as they put it in a preliminary manifesto, the 'standard of taste and executive ability may be raised and a critical tradition established'.[13] Macphail became a founding member.

The commercial industry, which saw no profit in encouraging people to be intelligent about films, sought to discourage the Film Society. The newspapers were little more enlightened. When Ivor Montagu began to write reviews for the *Observer*, he found his five paragraphs cut down to one and refused to continue a job which the paper regarded as of so little account. Macphail, a more

---

* Anyone familiar with contemporary British cinema can find his type in the collectors and cataloguers and games players that people Peter Greenaway's films.

accommodating mixture of the highbrow and lowbrow, took over at Montagu's recommendation, and watched everything.

The Society's films were subtitled by Adrian Brunel at no. 6 Dansey Yard, between Shaftesbury Avenue and Gerrard Street. Anyone who was interested was allowed to hang around and watch. Under Brunel's benevolent guidance Dansey Yard became a second home for the more enthusiastic members of the Film Society, and an informal film academy. Both Montagu and Macphail, who hung around more than just about anybody else, eventually became staff members.

Brunel initiated Macphail into the craft of screenwriting, setting him on the path that he would follow for the rest of his working life. He remembered him as 'one of the most brilliant, resourceful and entertaining colleagues I have ever had'.[14] Macphail crafted one of his finest puns in Brunel's presence. The two were writing a script together in a hotel in Spain. Macphail took a double dose of an 'aperient', thinking it was fruit salts. He was violently sick. 'There was poor Angus, pale as a sheet, nursing a hot-water bottle to his waist. He looked up at me and, shaking his head sadly, said, "Aperients are deceptive." '[15]

Brunel often worked for Michael Balcon at Gainsborough, and this is probably how Macphail came to join Gainsborough in 1926 as scenario editor. Looking at his early career, he seems never to have actively decided to do anything. He just fell into things. People liked him and were impressed by his cleverness, and he was content to follow along. At Gainsborough Balcon could now provide the sense of direction that Macphail didn't have himself as previously Montagu and Brunel had. Macphail would remain 'a faithful friend and counsellor for more than twenty-five years',[16] as Balcon put it, but really he didn't know how to be anything else.

In his memoir *Almost a Gentleman* Mark Benny gave a revealing description of Macphail's approach to his work:

Every story Angus read fell into that sharp, well-stored mind as a collection of technical scripting problems that had been solved, more or less expertly, in a number of previous movies. It was of course disconcerting, not to say humbling, to find that a story-line one had conceived as distinctly, exquisitely one's own had a film-ancestry reaching back to the industry's earliest days; it was impressive, if just a little degrading, to discover that some problem of mood manipulation or plot transition, over which ... I had laboured for days without success, could be solved if we accepted a device used in an otherwise unremarkable movie made in Czechoslovakia in 1929. The peculiar resources he brought to a conference might often seem, to an ambitious writer or director, to have subtly corrosive effects on the individual vision, but at the same time many a favourite project, seemingly bogged down in insoluble difficulties, had been saved from extinction by a timely suggestion from him.[17]

Here was Macphail, the solver of riddles and puzzles. Sidney Cole remembered that it was an invaluable skill when it came to making Ealing's famous chiller, *Dead of Night*. Although its success would subsequently start a trend, at the time such a portmanteau film was rare. No one was sure how to stitch together the collection of stories that made it up. Macphail's contribution was to weave them seamlessly into a coherent whole. The perfect commercial film script, he used to say, was just like the formula for the perfect wedding: something old, something new, something borrowed and something blue.

Macphail was too clever to be proud of what he did. He regarded Ealing's output as mostly pedestrian, but did not have the confidence to build his own identity as a writer. The fact that he had never really lived in the real world was an enormous handicap, but it was much too late to join it now. The puzzles that he pursued so compulsively no longer offered him any protection. He must sometimes have wished that he had put them away long ago. His unhappiness did not escape his Ealing colleagues. 'He just felt an inadequate sort of person,' said the producer Michael Relph. 'I think he would have liked to have been a serious writer ... He obviously had a self-loathing for his job.'[18]

A creature of routine, at Ealing Macphail embarked upon a path of orderly self-destruction. The director Harry Watt described his day: 'Punctually at nine o'clock every morning he arrived to work extremely quickly and efficiently on such epics as the Will Hay and Gracie Fields comedies. Just as promptly, at six o'clock in the evening, he marched straight over to the Red Lion across the road, and drank doubles until eight. He then started to curse us as sycophants, whores and hypocrites.

Knowing he was cursing himself and loving him very dearly, we used to lead him to the waiting hire-car that took him home.'[19]

Macphail would become great friends with Robert Hamer, Ealing's other great drinker and Cambridge intellectual. They both had a sense of not belonging, and the same bleak outlook on life. They also shared an enthusiasm for literature, in particular for gloomy French writers. An ambition of Macphail's was to translate Jules Renard's *Journal*,[20] a work described by the *Oxford Companion to French Literature* as 'a constant revelation of a bitter dissatisfied character for whom life had few rose-coloured moments', a character it would have been all too easy for Macphail to identify with. He was also an admirer of Henri de Montherlant, and would probably have liked *Les Célibataires*, which the *Oxford Companion* describes as 'a study of three decayed noblemen who live together and have neither two sous nor one pleasant characteristic between them'.

Macphail and Hamer lived together in the same block of flats in Lancaster Terrace, which was fondly known by Ealing people as Lost Weekend Corner or Hangover Towers. It seems to have been a place where they just got even drunker than at whatever pub or club they had been to before. Macphail was able neither mentally nor physically to take such punishment, and was often ill, but he enjoyed the support of his many friends at the studio. During the Blitz he stayed with the Danischewskys. 'He arrived with a straw bag, a clove of garlic, seventy-two bottles of Vichy water and two dozen Scotch,' remembered Brenda Danischewsky, 'all of which were put under the stairs with the pram and the baby in it.'[21] Extremely delicate and obviously not fit to look after himself, he was born to be nursed.

It's hard to imagine Macphail ever having been young. Most of the people with whom he worked at Ealing were in their thirties. Born in 1903, he was nearly a decade older but behaved as if the gap between their ages was even wider. 'His morals, his attitudes and his behaviour were all terribly old-fashioned,' remembered Brenda Danischewsky, and 'we did rather treat him as a decrepit old thing'. I think he must have had a sense of youth passing him by.

His taste in literature seemed old-fashioned to her too: he spoke not of the latest names that everyone else was reading, but of the classics of a past age. It was another way in which he retired from the world. 'Poor dear Angus was, I'm afraid, an intellectual. He enjoyed ideas for the idea, and he was much more literary than visual.'

He was a contradiction: a man who treasured Tolstoy and Chekhov, who had ambitions to translate his favourite works in French literature,[22] but earned his living by making up jokes for Tommy Trinder. His own life had an aspect of absurdity that made him ideal to write the routine comedies he had so little respect for. The puns and jokes marked him out as peculiar, but were also a shy person's way of winning acceptance. He was an outsider, but none the less he wanted to be a part of the team. In as much as he gave script advice, often uncredited, on just about every film to pass through Ealing Studios, he was perhaps *the* team player.

He liked the company of the studio. Brenda Danischewsky remembered he once put up a notice on his office door that read: BRING YOUR SINS AND SORROWS HERE. 'Just an invitation to anybody that would like to come in and have a natter.' It suggested an unhappiness, but also revealed a sympathy and disinterested humanity. And this melancholy camaraderie is captured in Stella Jonckheere's wartime memory of him wearing his Home Guard uniform, whisky bottles sticking out of each pocket of his greatcoat, and playing poker with his fellow fire-watchers on one of the studio's sound stages.

Ealing was Angus Macphail's only real home, but its considerable solace was, finally, not enough. 'I expect, in due course, it happened to happen that he was fed up with life,' said Brenda Danischewsky. He did not stay at the studio until the very end, his alcoholism forcing him in the early 1950s to retire early.

In 1953 Alfred Hitchcock, an old friend from the Gaumont-British days, employed Macphail as a writer on *The Wrong Man*. And so he briefly found himself in Hollywood, for him the most alien of habitats. His co-writer on the film, John Michael Hayes, claimed that he was too drunk to contribute anything to the script. 'All he could do was sit there, shaking with his disease.'[23]

The 50s were twilight and rootless years. Mostly ill and not working, he went to the South of France for a while and then returned to England, where he spent his last years 'convalescing' in an Eastbourne hotel. He passed the time reading voraciously and writing letters to his friends. 'I would like to know why the principal adult characters in *Anna Karenina* habitually blush?

These sophisticated aristocrats? Do adults blush? Did adults ever blush?'[24] This was the sort of detail that delighted his magpie mind. His interest in puns and saucy postcards was as strong as ever, but he also revealed a preoccupation with the translation of Russian classics and attempts to write a novel. 'It draws heavily on what are usually called real-life characters. You are fast pinching the best situations,' he wrote to Ivor Montagu. His correspondence was threaded through with a strong nostalgia. In 1961 he wrote to Stella Jonckheere,[25] musing over the idea of a documentary about the studio during the war:

> Do you remember at Ealing we once had a studio competition for a title for 'Went the Day Well'? There was a little man with a bad cough who used to come in on winter afternoons and do the blackout with a bamboo pole. He was awfully sweet and used to help John Dighton and me with story conferences. His suggestion for this particular title was 'BLACKOUT'. And very good too ... And do you remember that there were square nine-foot-high baffle blocks in front of the corridor entrances to the stages? They were filled with earth. Little Mr Grimshaw had turned them (by permission, he was most correct) into little private gardens for himself since they could be reached and observed only with a ladder ...
>
> Quick, my love, before we all forget all the funny things that happened!

Angus Macphail of all people should not have worried about forgetting. But a year after he wrote this letter, in 1962, Ealing's Memory Man was dead.

When I began to write about him, it seemed to me that Macphail's life was the story of the Ugly Duckling, and rather romantically I hoped to write a happy ending – if a posthumous one – in which he was revealed as a swan. But the film business was just not like that. There's no major film that can be indisputably credited to him, and generally his role as script editor required him to be self-effacing. To the extent that the cinema was a collaborative medium, he was, at 'The Studio with the Team Spirit', the epitome of that process, but its victim too. In implementing the vision of other film-makers he was unable to develop any sense of his own. I don't think it was true, as many people at Ealing seem to have thought, that he was unable to write convincing scenes – it was more that he lacked the self-belief to write the kind of scenes that would have suited him. His failure as a writer was, as much as anything else, to be too accommodating of other people's requirements.

But what would have suited him? On the whole the studio was content to exploit him – and he allowed himself to be exploited – as the Memory Man, with the plotlines of thousands of films at his fingertips and answers to all imaginable scripting problems. Comedies, war propaganda films, thrillers, musicals – Macphail tinkered with them all. He would have regarded few as any more than diverting puzzles. But just occasionally, without his actively seeking it, he would work on a subject that was perfectly in tune with his sensibility.

I think this is true of *It Always Rains on Sunday*, one of Ealing's finest films, whose screenplay according to the credits was written by Angus Macphail, Robert Hamer and Henry Cornelius. As we have seen, this film reflected Robert Hamer's own strong sense of disillusionment, but it was an outlook that Macphail certainly shared, the film's bleak vision bearing all the hallmarks of the man who admired Renard and de Montherlant. It's impossible to know for certain what went on behind the credits, but Hamer and Macphail were close, and common sense suggests that their shared disenchantment would have lent an extra edge to the film. Untidy as it may be to acknowledge, authorship in the cinema is rarely ever as singular as critics tend to assume: each collaboration of individuals has its own character, its own unique chemistry.

There is also more than a glimmer of Macphail in Ealing's neglected masterpiece, *Champagne Charlie* (see pp. 126-30). Again he was listed as one of three writers, so it's not possible to ascertain exactly what he did, but he must have been in his element. This story of the rivalry between two *lions comiques* was about the places he most loved – pubs and music halls – and featured characters who indulged in a favourite pastime of his – drinking. It was set in the 1860s, long before the passing of the licensing laws, perhaps a time in which the old-fashioned Macphail would have felt at home.

The film is one long exuberant exhortation to indulgence, where drink is presented as being, on the whole, the answer to life's problems. It must have been wishful thinking for the resident of Hangover Towers, a dream of how he would have liked the world to be, where inspiration to write would come with two or three pints of ale, the only inconvenience being the occasional hangover the next morning. But it also offered the perfect platform for his talents. Although his Ealing colleagues suggested that he was not good at naturalistic dialogue, here the puns for which he had such relish would have fitted convincingly into the music-hall background. I have no doubt that he played a leading part in making *Champagne Charlie* the triumph of comic invention and wordplay that it is, not that he would have had the necessary self-confidence to appreciate this. The artistry that he lent to the film was inadvertent, as in a way his whole career had been.

Angus Macphail's funeral took place in Eastbourne, where he had spent his last years. All his friends were invited. Ivor Montagu made a valediction full of funny stories which Macphail would have appreciated hugely. In accordance with instructions in his will the guests then repaired to a hotel, where they were greeted by Arthur Elton: 'Come in, Sid. Angus would like to know what you want to drink.' It was like old times.

Michael Balcon

With his smart but sober suit, his neat moustache and receding hairline Mick Balcon looked more like a bank manager than a film producer. It is amusing, for seeming so unlikely, that movie star Daniel Day Lewis should be his grandson. Balcon was a sober presence in a flamboyant industry and did as much as anyone to foster the unlikely notion that making films in Britain could be a sensible business. But he also believed that films should be more than a business, and was remarkable for his combination of judiciousness and idealism.

He was born in Birmingham in 1896, the youngest son of Jewish immigrants. His comfortable middle-class upbringing was disrupted by the start of the First World War. He abandoned his studies for a scholarship to Oxford, and in anticipation of military service joined the Birmingham University Officer Training Corps. Here, barely eighteen, he persuaded his fellow cadets to write letters to the press urging that boys from the same schools, universities and communities should be allowed to continue their friendships and associations by serving in the same battalions. This campaign, whose successful outcome was the 'Pals' Battalions', was an early example of Balcon's crusading zeal, but it was also an apposite foreshadowing of his nature as a film producer. Such a notion of a continuing loyalty, whether conscious or not, was fundamental to his attitude. In his film career the friendships and associations he formed were of a rare permanence.

Balcon began his career in films after the war, forming a company to make commercials with an old schoolfriend, Victor Saville. In 1922 they switched to features, producing *Woman to Woman*. Its success established them as leading British producers, and Balcon went on to form Gainsborough.

Michael Balcon

From a studio built originally by the American company Famous Players-Lasky in a converted power station in Islington, he was responsible for a sizeable and comparatively distinguished tranche of Britain's feature film output. It was here that he encouraged a young Alfred Hitchcock to direct films. The spectacular return on his investment of faith would have encouraged his subsequent readiness to trust in home-grown talent.

The passing of the Quota Act in 1927 ensured a guaranteed market for British films. Seeking to expand and in need of the capital resources that the much larger company could offer, Balcon sought financial support from Gaumont-British, and in 1931, although he effectively lost control of his own company, became head of production of the largest film-making concern in Europe.

At Gaumont Balcon pursued that perennial goal of British film producers – access to the American market. He presided over an expensive production programme geared to its perceived tastes, making regular trips across the Atlantic to hire Hollywood stars.* In due course he had to face the equally constant result: financial disaster. In 1936 the company recorded a large loss on production, and Balcon resigned at the end of the year, unsettled by the inevitable aftermath of increased boardroom interference.

The moral he drew from the experience was: 'If you can't beat them, join them.' He became head of MGM's new British subsidiary, now believing that the future for British films was to forge an Anglo-American film alliance. He explained his reasoning in his memoirs: 'If we could combine the resources of a big Hollywood company, their stars when suitable, their global distribution facilities, their financial backing, with the talent we had developed in our own studios, we could surely count on producing films for a world market.'[1]

---

* In his memoirs Balcon would list as examples Richard Dix, Edmund Lowe, Constance Bennett, Sylvia Sidney, George Arliss, Paul Robeson, Madge Evans and Robert Young. They were hardly top-drawer names. The American film critic Richard Griffith would comment: 'For some years, in the early thirties, American audiences marvelled that the few British films they were permitted to see were often directed and acted by people for whom there was no longer much demand in Hollywood. It seemed to us then, that British producers were wooing the American market by the extraordinary expedient of offering attractions which that market had already repudiated.' Supplement to Paul Rotha, *The Film Till Now* (Vision Press, revised edn 1949), p. 545.

He was to be bitterly disappointed. The relationship seemed to him in practice to amount to British subjugation. After having been one of the leading and most respected figures in the British film industry, he found himself shackled by a coterie of MGM executives and nauseated by the production-line mentality of the largest of the Hollywood dream factories. Worst of all was the man who ran the enterprise. Louis B. Mayer 'was the caricature Hollywood tycoon – a short, stout man enthroned in an enormous, lavishly over-furnished office, ruling his empire with a mixture of ruthlessness and sentimentality'.[2] At the MGM sales conference Balcon attended, the delegates sang in tribute to their boss 'Our L.B' to the tune of 'Yankee Doodle', and then wound up the evening with the house song, 'Let the Lion Roar'.[3] Balcon parted acrimoniously with MGM after the production of only one film – the aptly named *A Yank in Oxford*.

Balcon, who had come to prominence running the film company he had started from scratch, was too independent a spirit to fit easily into any organization of which he was not in charge. Ealing Studios, which he joined as head of production in 1938, was ideal because it was small enough for him to run it without his authority being seriously questioned. The 1930s were Balcon's taste of corporate life, and he moved on to Ealing much as a disillusioned city executive might give up his large salary to open a village shop.

A strong reaction to his experiences of the 1930s determined the kind of producer Balcon became at Ealing. Instead of trying to make films that appealed to the American market, he became an outspoken campaigner for films that reflected British values, and could recoup their cost in Britain. And recoiling from MGM's brand of escapism, he embraced realism. Of the years preceding his brief Hollywood sojourn he wrote, 'Now that events can be seen in their historical perspective, one cannot escape the conclusion that in our own work we could have been more profitably engaged. Hardly a single film of the period reflects the agony of those times.'[4]

This wish for social relevance was an unusual aspiration for a film producer, but Balcon's essential seriousness can be traced back to his earliest days in films. When the Film Society opened in 1924, its co-founder Ivor Montagu remembered, the industry did everything it could to hinder this forum for the serious appreciation of the cinema; but he singled out Balcon as the only producer to support the movement consistently.[5] Then at Gaumont-British he produced Robert Flaherty's *Man of Aran*. The celebrated documentarist was true to his record of defeating any sensible estimate of schedule or budget, and it required a genuine idealism to back a project which in the course of its long production would become known as 'Balcon's Folly'.*

Balcon also had the extraordinary notion for those days that films should be made by educated people. At Gaumont-British he set up an entry scheme for graduates, whom the film industry, in the words of the documentarist Arthur Elton, one of the successful candidates, regarded 'like wild beasts and flattered itself that it parted itself as far as possible from any university education'.[6]

It is a mark of Balcon's difference that he should have taken pride in a 'first-class commercial flop' for putting his realist aspirations into practice. While he was waiting to take over from Basil Dean at Ealing Studios, he produced a film for a small company called Balford, which he had set up with the director Walter Forde. *There Ain't No Justice* was directed by the twenty-six-year-old Penrose Tennyson – great-grandson of the Poet Laureate – who had been a protégé of Balcon at Gaumont-British. A close bond developed between the two men, and in his memoirs Balcon described his 'personal affection' for Tennyson as 'second only to that for my own son'.[7]

Tennyson possessed in Balcon's words 'a preoccupation with social problems'. *There Ain't No Justice* was an exposé of racketeering in the boxing world, with characters who, although they may have been a little crudely two-dimensional, were unusually for the time ordinary working people. Tennyson displayed an impressive sense of atmosphere and a realist's eye for the poetry of the incidental and the drama of the human face. 'Real people – Real problems – a human document,'claimed the advertisement for the film in a slogan that neatly encapsulated what would be Balcon's policy for Ealing Studios.

The next film Tennyson made, this time for Ealing Studios itself, was *The Proud Valley*, a story of a Welsh mining community, which had echoes of Cronin's *The Citadel* and *The Stars Look Down*.

---

* Balcon would cite it in his memoirs as one of the proudest achievements of his career.

The tenor of the original script was that the formation of a co-operative would better serve the miners' interests than if they continued to work for the mine-owners, but the war intervened, and, in the interests of national unity, the script was changed to show workers and mine-owners burying their differences in support of the nation.

Tennyson's final film, *Convoy*, signalled Ealing's switch to wartime subjects. It was a propaganda film about the Navy boasting scenes 'taken at sea under actual wartime conditions'. He then joined the forces, despite Balcon's attempts to persuade him that he could contribute more to the national cause by continuing to make propaganda films at Ealing, and was shortly afterwards killed in a plane crash.

Nothing could have done more to entrench Balcon's commitment to realist cinema – or perhaps more accurately a cinema of public purpose – than the loss of someone to whom he was so close. Penrose Tennyson was Ealing's martyr, and his spirit would linger on at Ealing Studios long after his death.

'I was gradually evolving my own attitude towards the sort of films that should be made. The three films with Tennyson had dealt with problems, in two cases social and one wartime, and so in a sense rendered some public service. They were documentary in their approach, but here I must define the term and establish that "documentary" is not a label to be lightly attached to films of a specific, factual type; it is an attitude of mind toward film-making. I had known at the back of my mind since *Man of Aran* that this was and should be the direction my own work should take.'[8]

The war was an obvious catalyst to such thinking, and in Cavalcanti, the producer at the GPO Film Unit – and a man who in France had had considerable experience of features as well as documentary – Balcon found the perfect ally. In early 1940 he invited him to work at Ealing even while he was still officially with the GPO Film Unit. Both men hoped that the unit would be assigned to Ealing's care. When this plan fell through, Cavalcanti resigned and joined Ealing permanently. He oversaw a programme of documentaries, but just as significantly helped to infuse the whole of the studio's output with the documentary 'attitude of mind' that Balcon wrote of.

Balcon's stance was brave for a commercial film company as it was not one that the exhibitors were naturally attuned to, and greater efforts were required to maintain it as the war progressed. In a New Year's Day issue of the *Daily Film Renter* for 1943 Maurice Ostrer put forward the view that many exhibitors would have shared: 'Their Patrons do not want war films. They want humour, music and light romance. Their patrons have been bombed and gunned time and again. Do they want to sit in a cinema and be harrowed by more bombing – if only screen bombing? Wouldn't they rather relax in their seats and laugh with the comedians in comedy, or lose themselves in the harmonies of musicals?'

In an answering article in the same issue Balcon declared: 'I, for one, do not intend to depart from my policy of making war films as and when these naturally suggest themselves. And that, these days, is five times out of six. At Ealing Studios, I am proud to say, over ninety per cent of our wartime schedule has been devoted to films with a war background, and of these (comedies included) each has contained elements of propaganda in varying degrees.'

He was forthright, but at the same time sought to allay the exhibitors' concerns. 'Is your war film exciting, well made, moving, good entertainment? It will pack them in. Let us at last realize that there are no taboos at the box office except the taboo on bad films.' A robust common sense underpinned his idealism.* With his down-to-earth manner he spoke the exhibitors' language, and had a suitably contrite tone when he went on to suggest that films could be more than just entertainment: 'At the risk of sounding pretentious, I affirm that there is another side to it which (for want of a better word) I shall call the *spiritual* side. Film-making is not a cold-blooded process of manufacture; you cannot make films as you make sausages . . . Apart from the financial and administrative end of it, a group of creative people is involved in each film – writers, directors, actors, cameramen, etc., etc. Their combined influence, in conjunction with the producer, shapes the subject policy of a film company – and they cannot be ignored.'

On the wall of one of the stages at Ealing was painted the legend, THE STUDIO WITH THE TEAM SPIRIT. It went back to the days of the autocratic and – by many – much disliked Basil

* So he could in the early years of the war campaign vigorously against the monopolistic nature of the Rank Organisation, but then in 1944 accept a generous distribution contract from them.

Dean (one of a number of such communist-style slogans exhorting his workers to do this or that), but it accurately summed up the atmosphere of Ealing under Balcon, where production decisions were taken at a committee of associate producers and directors, all of whom, with the single exception of Balcon himself, were film-*makers* rather than film executives, and at these meetings presented film ideas of their own even if they had finally to defer to Balcon.

This team has often been characterized as a kind of family. Balcon built it out of familiar faces. Many of the people who became leading figures at Ealing started their careers with him at Gaumont-British – scenario editor Angus Macphail, art director and producer Michael Relph, directors Charles Frend and Robert Hamer. Balcon gave them their apprenticeships and oversaw their advance to positions of prominence. He operated not according to conventional business principles, bringing in well-known names to direct prestigious projects, but relied as much as possible on his own people. The studio drew its strength from the resulting bond of loyalty and friendship, and the continuity these qualities fostered. 'I don't remember any nasty people in Ealing,' said Brenda Danischewsky, 'and that, I think, was a great deal due to Mick.'[9]

In his memoirs Balcon described himself as having retained some of the influences of his provincial upbringing. He contrasted himself to the legendarily charming Korda, of whom he used the words 'brilliant', 'cosmopolitan', 'sophisticated'.[10] His own qualities of steadfastness and integrity were not nearly as exciting, but were if anything even more remarkable for the film industry. 'He was not the proverbial cigar-smoking tycoon at all,' remembered his daughter Jill. 'He was very strict, moral in the best sense of the word, upright, honest, uncorrupt.'[11] With these values he shaped Ealing Studios, and was responsible for the atmosphere of security that made creative endeavour possible.

But his influence was double-edged. However much he may have respected the views of individual film-makers, and accorded them unusual freedom to initiate their own projects, the output of the studio was inevitably coloured by his own rather unrelenting sense of patriotic duty. Balcon felt that films 'should be socially responsible and that they should be trying to say something which was positive,' remembered Michael Relph, 'and I don't think he would have wanted to make a film which really pulled one of our instititutions to pieces.'[12]

This sense of civic duty was responsible for some very indifferent cinema. In the war years the studio turned out morale-raisers like *The Bells Go Down*, *The Foreman Went to France* and *The Big Blockade*. Most are something of a chore to sit through today, and their two-dimensional characters who display a stiff upper lip and a chilling cheerfulness under the most appalling circumstances are hard to take seriously.

Balcon's belief that films should somehow be improving meant that the darker side of life was neglected at Ealing. In the novel on which *The Loves of Joanna Godden* (1947) was based there was a scene in which the heroine struck her younger sister. 'Ladies don't slap each other's faces!' objected Balcon,[13] and the scene was left out of the film. 'The idea of an anti-hero or anything like that he couldn't understand,' commented the director Charles Crichton. 'At one time I wanted to make Kingsley Amis's *Lucky Jim*. He said, "What do you mean? He burns holes in his bedclothes with his cigarettes. We can't make films about people like that." '[14]

His passion for a rather stolid brand of realism could blind him to more subtle modes of expression. Stella Jonckheere remembered that he tended to disapprove of fantasy. When it was once suggested that Robert Bresson should make a film at the studio about King Arthur, his response was: 'I don't want to make a film about a lot of fairies.' Some blimpish pronouncements in his memoirs confirm the dogmatic outlook that this remark suggests. 'I have little patience with people who produce a certain kind of film and then shelter behind the argument that films must reflect the society in which we live. The flaw in this cliché is that it provides a hypocritical justification for sensationalism, squalor and licence – usually sexual.'[15] This prim stance amounted to a refusal to address a whole area of human conduct.

Ealing was a group of very talented film-makers brought together and presided over by a man who – on the whole – was much less sophisticated than themselves. With hindsight the better Ealing comedies seem like a sign of this friction between film-makers wanting their work to have an edge and Balcon's preference for the upbeat and conventional. They were a safety valve – a way of being critical without giving obvious offence.

He was a curiously contradictory figure, progressive in his politics and with a keen social conscience but none the less reactionary. Many women working in the film industry felt that he had little notion of sexual equality, and that the opportunities he gave to clever young men from the universities were rarely extended to them. In the early 1950s Muriel Box, who with her husband Sydney had won an Oscar for the screenplay of *The Seventh Veil*, was about to make her debut for Rank as a director, but the project was scotched by Balcon who sat on the Rank board. 'Asked his reasons, he explained that he wasn't sure a woman had the qualities necessary to control a large feature unit.'[16]

His saving grace was his fairness. If he was narrow in his views, he was not overbearing in asserting them and he was open to persuasion. A letter that Ivor Montagu wrote to Angus Macphail long before their Ealing days captures this quality. Recommending that Macphail should approach Balcon directly with an idea for a film, Montagu wrote: 'He always listens to you, to *you* I mean, though perhaps not always understanding what you say.'[17]

Balcon possessed an awareness of his own limitations – very unusual for a studio boss – and showed a willingness to compensate for them. If he had little creative flair himself, he recognized and respected it in other people. Hugely to his credit, he gave opportunities to people whose approach to life was very different from his own, and in spite of his conservative instincts he tried to learn from his film-makers. Although his opinion inevitably carried great weight, it was never a simple matter of just saying no; he was prepared to defer to an opposing view if it was put with sufficient conviction.

Balcon's objection to ladies slapping each other may have prevented Googie Withers from hitting Jean Kent in *The Loves of Joanna Godden*, but she was able to inflict considerably more violence on Susan Shaw in *It Always Rains on Sunday* – as Shaw's young stepmother attacking her in one scene with unrestrained fury. Balcon could not have approved of it any more than he had the scene in *Joanna Godden*. The difference, one must speculate, is that Robert Hamer vigorously argued his case – while Charles Frend, the director of *Joanna Godden*, did not – and Balcon respected Hamer's creative vision in spite of his own misgivings. Balcon endorsed the principle that individual film-makers should be allowed to express themselves and, once a production was under way, usually did his best to support them. His conservative influence was more predominant at an earlier stage, when the studio's subjects were being chosen. But even here he was comparatively enlightened for granting his directors and associate producers as large a say in the process as he did. Minutes of the 'round table' meetings provide a snapshot of Balcon's reign in the years after the war.[18] And it *was* a reign, if a benevolent one. His authority over the meeting was total: decisions were reached not through consensus but by winning his approval. Nothing could be done without his say. Although specific ideas were generated by the associate producers and directors who attended, Balcon gave strong direction as to what subjects he would favour and how they should be treated.

In the meeting for December 1947, Ivor Montagu raised the possibility of making a film about life in post-war Germany. The minutes recorded that 'Mr Balcon very much liked the idea as it was the kind of contemporary subject we wanted, but he warned the meeting that it might be a subject fraught with complexities as there must be no hint of blackening the authorities in the British Zone.' In July 1948 a project called 'Man in the Zoo', which had been proposed by Monja Danischewsky, was discussed: 'Sir Michael* told Mr Danischewsky that he would prefer him to make pictures with a more realistic approach. He found it difficult to make a decision about it.' In October 1948 Balcon lectured the meeting on the folly of *Saraband for Dead Lovers*, a lavish costume drama which was expected to make only poor returns at the box office: 'The loss on *Saraband for Dead Lovers* would be so heavy that Sir Michael was not inclined to consider favourably any proposition in relation to Technicolor or period pictures as in his opinion we were a company better suited to the production of a more realistic type of film.'

It is clear from Balcon's interventions that the best way to prosper at Ealing was to choose a subject that was contemporary and uncontroversial. And when people put forward proposals, they naturally stressed these qualities. In the meeting for November 1947 Charles Frend raised Compton Mackenzie's *Whisky Galore!* as a possible comedy subject, and Balcon agreed to read the synopsis.

* Balcon was made a knight bachelor in the New Year's Honours List of 1948.

'Here was a modern Scottish story of the type for which we had been searching,' the minutes recorded. In the next meeting Stella Jonckheere proposed a subject about conscription: 'This, too, was a contemporary problem and might present possibilities for a film.'

The minutes also reveal Balcon's thrift and considerable command of practical, cost-effective film-making. In October 1948 he 'reminded the meeting that in his opinion the top figure that could be got from this country was approximately £180,000 and no picture should cost more than £110,000 (as we always exceeded estimates and never came below them).'* He added that as the studio was top-heavy in personnel in relation to output, it was essential for the associate producers to prepare two films a year, as there were gaps in the programme which were never properly provided for. At the same meeting he was highly critical of the script for *Passport to Pimlico*: from a technical point of view, it was 'too long, uneconomical and overwritten. There had been no regard for economy in the use of artists, crowds and exteriors. It had been a mistake to launch the picture with such a script and costs alone were now in exorbitant excess of the budgeted figure.' The emphasis placed on economical film-making was inevitably a factor in the choice of subject matter. When in the meeting for November 1947 Ivor Montagu suggested Britten's *Peter Grimes* as a possible subject, Balcon 'did not feel that he wanted to tackle it because of the difficult production angles involved'.

And always of course there was an awareness of box office. In the meeting for February 1949, Balcon noted that 'so far the most successful team had certainly been Mr Dearden and Mr Relph'. It was no accident that they would be by far the most prolific producer–director partnership at Ealing Studios.

The biggest casualty of the Ealing system was, as we have seen, Robert Hamer, who had project after project turned down. But in fairness to Balcon, Hamer would probably have had similar difficulties in any film company of the period. One of Hamer's projects, *Soho Melodrama*, got as far as becoming a shooting script and then was dropped because of objections from the Hays Office (the American censors). 'It surprised me a little that these expert

* Good value for the time. A routine budget for a Del Giudice production was £250,000 to £350,000.

gentlemen should not have been able, at least two months earlier, to anticipate the Hays Office comment and save themselves much money,' observed the writer Mark Benny who had had the original idea.[19] Balcon was probably being indulgent in letting it get as far as it did. All Hamer's ideas ran similar kinds of risks, and perhaps the biggest accusation that can be levelled against Balcon was that of encouraging false hope. He wanted to be supportive, but finally his caution prevailed. The films most characteristic of Ealing Studios – like *Scott of the Antarctic, San Demetrio, London* and *The Blue Lamp* – were worthy, very British but not great films. But the atmosphere Balcon fostered and his belief in the 'spiritual side' of film-making made artistic excellence possible, even if that excellence was often contrary to what he might have intended. Ealing's best films may have been the films of subversion – *Went the Day Well?, Champagne Charlie, Kind Hearts and Coronets* and *It Always Rains on Sunday* – but it was Balcon who built the enlightened system that made such films possible.

Cavalcanti

His full name was Alberto de Almeida Cavalcanti, but in film credits like a great magician or circus performer, he was billed as just 'Cavalcanti'. Those he worked with in England would shorten his name even further, to just 'Cav'.

I went to Italy to visit Charles Hassé, who had been a close friend of Cav since the early 1930s. Hassé had worked for him at both the GPO Film Unit and at Ealing. Many years later he and his wife Judy would be neighbours of Cav in Capri, where he had bought a house after the war. As we sat on the veranda overlooking a Tuscan valley, Judy regaled me with stories of Cav's inimitable combination of courtly charm and gentle humour. There was the time when he was going off to Ischia and brought them a farewell present. 'There was a knock and I opened this door, and round the door came a plate with an octopus and a camellia in the middle of it, and a little chuckle from Cav.'[1]

'That came from Cav's house,' said Charles. 'That little figure. He had it on his veranda.' I turned round to see a little *putto* embracing a pole with a mischievous smile. Rude, but comic and joyful – it's a quality you can find in some of his films. It seems appropriate that it should now be in the Hassé house, decorated with a style that made their affinity with Cav obvious.

The house in Capri, where Cav lived for thirty years, was probably the nearest place he had to a home. In his old age he fell on hard times and was forced to leave. 'A friend of ours,' remembered Judy, 'saw him at the corner of the road looking up at his house crying. He'd just sold it.'[2] He lived out his last years in Paris. In spite of his reduced circumstances, he gallantly maintained his sense of style to the last. Judy remembers having lunch with him in his small flat near Montmartre. 'He put on an apron, and he had a French menu written on a slate and a rose by my plate and a vase.'

There's an obvious aptness in Cav, the great wanderer of the cinema, ending his days in such a city of exiles as Paris, but it's the image of him looking tearfully up at his lost home in Capri that I find most affecting – and that finally, I think, is more of a key to the kind of person he was. In the course of a long life Cav would leave more than his fair share of homes, and perhaps for this reason the notion meant a lot to him. Not least among his considerable skills was a flair for feeling at home and making others feel at home. It was why he could settle so comfortably in Britain for fifteen years and, in doing so, become one of the country's most influential producers.

When Cav was working at Ealing Studios, he lived in a not very nice suburban house in Stanmore. One summer a robin flew into the room where he kept his books and started to build a nest in one of the shelves. Cav locked the door and eventually a chick was hatched. He kept the room shut the whole summer so that mother and baby would not be disturbed.[3] It was this instinct for nurture that made him so invaluable to a whole generation of British film-makers.

Cav was born in Brazil in 1897 into an aristocratic family. He was only fifteen when he left his native country for Europe. The circumstances were dramatic, and an example of how the major changes in his life tended to be sudden. At school in Rio de Janeiro one of the subjects he had to study was the philosophy of law. In an exam on the subject he had written an answer so unconventional and placing so little reliance on the standard study materials that the teacher, a Dr Nerval de Gouveia, declared that it didn't deserve any marks at all. When de Gouveia left the room Cav mimicked him, reading out the comments the teacher had written on his paper. De Gouveia returned to catch himself being made fun of in front of the class and, furious, banned the boy from his lessons. Cav's friends went on strike in solidarity, and the protest began to spread through the school. Cav's father decided to withdraw his son before matters got completely out of hand, and, listening to his son's pleas that he should be allowed to study architecture, sent him to the Geneva School of Fine Arts.[4]

Cav's parents would join their son in Switzerland, and when he finished his studies and went to work in Paris, they went with him there too. His father died in Liverpool in the early 1920s, where Cav, after abandoning his career as an architect, worked for a brief time in the Brazilian consulate. His mother continued to live with her son until her own death after the Second World War.

The example of Cav's upbringing was one of a rare family closeness. In later becoming a mentor for so many British film-makers, he was merely passing on the encouragement and cherishing he had received himself from his earliest years.

He entered films as a set decorator for the director Marcel L'Herbier, and became a leading member of the avant-garde movement in Paris – a disparate collection of artists with often conflicting beliefs. He had a particular affinity with the surrealists, but was too independent of mind to belong to any single group. If he was committed to anything, it was perhaps above all a spirit of experimentation.

He came to prominence with *Rien que les heures*, made in 1926, a portrait of the life of a city. It was a film that had come about largely by accident. The negative of his first film, *Le Train sans yeux*, had been confiscated because the producers failed to pay their creditors. Afraid that he would be blamed for its non-appearance, Cav got together a few friends and decided to make another film in its place on the cheap. As they couldn't afford a studio, they shot it in the streets.

Rien que les heures was the first film of its kind and revolutionary for a time when documentaries* were always about faraway and exotic places. 'Nobody had an idea that life in the town in which you lived was interesting,'[5] Cav would later comment. With a surrealist's eye he unpeeled the layers of infinite, simultaneous experience that a city offers, but also displayed a mischievous humour and a taste for the playful conceit that became a distinct feature of his film-making. A bewhiskered man with pince-nez puts a garter on a bare female leg. The camera holds the leg in close-up as the man draws the garter towards the upper thigh. Then a sudden cut to a long shot reveals that the leg belongs to a mannequin, and the man is a clothes-shop assistant.

Cav was far too enquiring to be dogmatic. While most of his fellow film-makers in Paris shunned the arrival of sound as

---

* Although this misleading word had yet to be coined.

114

ushering in the era of the photographed play, Cav welcomed it as an opportunity and did everything he could to experiment with the new technology. In 1929 Paramount hired him to direct French and Portuguese versions of American films at the Billancourt Studios. It was well-paid but menial work, in which he had a say over neither subject matter nor manner of treatment, but crucially it offered him an opportunity to learn about sound.

His avant-garde friends, who showed little understanding of his ulterior motive, accused him of selling out. With the passionate militancy of French farmers of a later generation a band marched on the Paris cinema where one of his sound films was showing, rioted and smashed up the theatre. It cannot have been pleasant to be the object of such misplaced anger, although he would certainly have appreciated the dedication to cinema that their violent protest indicated.

It was with some relief that Cav, having mastered sound, left Paramount to make comedies for an independent production company. These were huge commercial successes, but he soon became bored. 'I was fed up with the talk, talk, talk, talk. And after four or five hits I was starting a sixth, and I really couldn't stand it, so I said I was sick. That is a trick I use quite a lot when I don't want to do something. I go sick.'[6]

So the invalid came to London, where he was already admired by film-makers for *Rien que les heures*, and met John Grierson, the founder of the British Documentary Movement. The nearest British equivalent of the French avant-garde existed among the aspiring film-makers who joined Grierson at the Empire Marketing Board film unit, which from 1933 became the GPO Film Unit. Cav explained that he wanted to make *sound* films rather than talkies, and Grierson, who realized that his young film-makers would benefit enormously from Cav's experience, invited him to join the GPO, where a sound system had only recently been installed.

Cav left the commercial cinema for the same reason as he had originally joined it – the chance to experiment. The GPO Film Unit may have produced few films that deserve to be acclaimed as genuine classics – most have a ragged, untidy quality – but its chief appeal lay in the wonder of discovery and the sense of freedom that made such discovery possible. Its value to British cinema was as a school of gifted, committed individuals who would get a feel for film from Cav, their inspired teacher. But Cav's 'lessons' were rooted in practice, in which he would show the same thirst for the acquisition of knowledge as his charges. On films like *Coalface* and *Night Mail* he was as much a pioneer of sound in the cinema as Griffith or Eisenstein were of the putting together of images.

Night Mail was a landmark for the brilliance with which Cav juggled words, music and sound. There was the finale of the film – probably what most people remember when they think of *Night Mail* – as Auden's verse and Benjamin Britten's music accompanied the rhythmic clatter of the train crossing into Scotland. But there was also the symphony of incidental noises carefully composed throughout the film – the slamming of carriage doors, the tapping of wheels, the clunk of signals as well as the counterpoint of the noise of the train with the commentator's narration. This last furnished the opportunity for a typical touch of Cavalcanti wit: as the engine builds up full steam the narrator has to raise his voice to make himself heard above the racket.

Today it requires some research to realize that Cav was even involved with *Night Mail*. In the reference books Harry Watt and Basil Wright are usually cited as the 'directors' or 'producers' of the film, and Cav is rarely mentioned. His actual credit was for 'sound direction', an unusual notion that it was all too easy to disregard. But it was the key to the film's distinction – in the most successful sequences the montage of sound dictating the logic of the images.

The film was an example of how the conventional hierarchy of credits can travesty the true importance of an individual's contribution – in the course of his career Cav was particularly prone to this sort of neglect, victim of his own elusive subtlety. But it was also an aspect of the innovative spirit of the GPO that no one should have been overly concerned with credits. 'We kept on putting on the names of the young people,' remembered Grierson, 'not the names of the people who were concerned. There were years when Cavalcanti's name never went on a picture. We weren't concerned with that aspect of things.'⁷

Cav's own disregard for credits at the time was probably as much an expression of his distaste for the clumsy and inaccurate pigeon-holing that they represented. So pervasive was his influence that no single label could really sum up all he did. But although he did not worry about such matters at the time, as an old man he would be hurt not to receive his due, in the 1970s for example grumbling to an interviewer about a French encyclopaedia that had not even included his name in its entry on British documentary. 'I could very easily go to them and say, "Who is the person who gave you this information?" I think I have the right to do that, but I just did not care and said, "Oh, well, to hell with it. What I did, I did . . ." '[8]

The neglect was part and parcel of the process of teaching, which entailed a necessary degree of self-effacement. But for all its frustrations it was a role Cav wholeheartedly embraced. He talked about many of the GPO's films as if they were exercises. *Coalface* 'was an experiment for *Night Mail*';[9] *Pett and Pott* was 'not quite a film', but 'a sound lesson'.[10] And he customarily referred to the film-makers with whom he worked in the manner of the dedicated and sensitive schoolmaster: 'I got along very well with certain of the boys, which were brilliant boys.'[11]

His chief qualities as a teacher were enthusiasm, humility and a refreshing absence of preconceptions. He drew out the young film-makers at the GPO in a way that respected their natural talents. There were no rigid rules but only endless and exciting possibilities. In place of precise instruction he offered a flawless sense of what 'worked'. He was patient, kind and gentle, offering any criticisms in an oblique way so as not to hurt people's feelings. 'You have a nice little film, Harry. A little slow, perhaps, but building a house is a slow thing, is it not? But the end, it is so dull!'[12] Occasionally he flew into sudden rages, but these outbursts, which were conducted in a mixture of Portuguese, French and broken English, usually provoked only laughter from the people they were aimed at.

When I met Charles Hassé, I remember being struck by the element of admiration in his voice as he recalled his old friend. 'So *warm-hearted*,' he said. 'He listened to whatever you had to say, and improved what you had to say in a way too. He sort of added something.' Here was another insight into Cav, the teacher. It was a two-way process, from which he seemed to gain as much as he gave. For him to teach called for the same curiosity and engagement with a raw material that he displayed as an artist. He brought a sense of style into every aspect of his life and his dealings with people. 'He produced *us*,' commented Brenda Danischewsky who would get to know him well in his Ealing days. 'He got his mother to put me wise to fancy cooking. He got his mother to get toys that would be inspiring for our children. Living, eating, cooking, talking. He was the nearest thing to genius they had there.'[13] For Cav teaching was a natural extension of life – it was simply being engaged with the people and things about you.

His open-mindedness was in marked contrast to the dogma of many of the people with whom he worked. Grierson and his more zealous adherents believed that the ultimate purpose of documentary was to bring information to the masses, a social rather than an aesthetic endeavour. They tolerated Cav's experimentation to the extent that it was necessary to learn the craft of film-making, but always suspected that he did not share their creed.

In 1937 Grierson left the GPO Film Unit and Cav took over as producer. It was the first visible split in the documentary movement, for which Cav's influence was often cited as chiefly responsible. Some thought that the rot had set in as early as his arrival. 'Looking back on it, it was a great mistake to have Cavalcanti, really, because he didn't understand what documentary was supposed to be doing,' commented John Taylor, Grierson's brother-in-law and a chief acolyte. 'Documentary was supposed to be for the service of people.'[14]

Many others echoed these criticisms. Cav either didn't know what documentary was about or just really wasn't interested in it in the first place. Paul Rotha, a leading documentary film-maker but also influential as a film historian, declared in his *Documentary Diary* that there was 'no doubt' that Cav 'saw his hiring by the GPO Film Unit as a stepping-stone into the British feature film industry'.[15] It was a crude reading of Cav's mind which implied a narrowness quite contrary to his nature. It was a particularly flimsy assertion in view of the fact that in order to work for the GPO he had left feature films in France, where he was earning far more money, and that he had continued to make documentaries even after he had moved to Ealing Studios seven years later.

Of the GPO films made during Cav's period in charge Paul Rotha commented: 'No film told its story clearly . . . They each started with some universal conception and then led nowhere. It was due, perhaps, to Cavalcanti's insistence on good technique at all costs.'[16] Again this was crude criticism, coloured by Rotha's own preconception that documentary should always be an exer-

118

cise in social utility. Films like Len Lye's *N or NW* or Humphrey Jennings's *Spare Time* could only in the most tenuous sense be regarded as 'a service to the people', but they achieved a poetic truth. In pursuit of their narrow, anti-aesthetic purpose many documentarists blinkered themselves to the virtues of these films.

Cav, who knew how parochial the British documentary movement was, resented the attitude of many of Grierson's followers that somehow documentary – the form as much as the word – was their invention and belonged to them. When he made a compilation film for the British Film Institute during the war, he had an opportunity to set the record straight. *Film and Reality* was his discourse on the history of the cinema, in which he made it clear that the documentary form had been around long before Grierson chose to give it a name. Indeed, Cav described Grierson's *Drifters*, which launched the British documentary movement – perhaps somewhat mischievously but accurately – as 'one of the *last* and most publicized silent documentaries'. He also stated with clarity the nature of Grierson's achievement: he began 'a powerful movement to use films for civic education and started a new school of British film production'.*

In their vanity the zealots of documentary tended to assume that because Cav didn't dedicate himself exclusively to *their* purpose, therefore he didn't have any purpose of his own beyond a pursuit of style for its own sake (Rotha's 'good technique at all costs'). In fact he was a film-maker of conviction, and anyone who had seen *Film and Reality*, or read any of his articles on the cinema, should have recognized a passionate realist who, however, knew that realism could take many forms.

In *Film and Reality* Cav argued that it was the peculiar property of film to put us in contact with reality. Good cinema, whether depicting truth or fiction, exploited this relationship; and bad cinema, content to behave like a spectator in the stalls, did not. The realist could have as much admiration for a Western or a musical as for a documentary. Jean Vigo, Cav pointed out, was known for his fictional films but also made documentaries possessing the same poetic quality. He might have said as much

---

* Grierson was only interested in the cinema to the extent that it was a form of mass communication. If he were around today, I have no doubt that he would be far more excited by the Internet. He was much more an educationalist than he was a film-maker.

of himself. *Rien que les heures*, for example, had blended actors' performances with the direct recording of a day in the life of a city. *Film and Reality* was a challenge to the conventional categories that dominated British cinema.

Unsurprisingly Cav preferred the expression 'realist films' to 'documentary', which he felt smelt of 'dust and boredom'.[17] A man of deep sophistication, he must often have found the unequivocal nature of his British colleagues very trying – the impoverishing requirement that you must belong in one camp or another, when the stuff of cinema that he was looking for – realism – was to be found in both. For Cav, the wish to make a feature film was entirely natural and no great departure from the kind of film-making he pursued in the documentary field.

Indeed, soon after he arrived in London to work with Grierson at the GPO he had plans to make a feature film. Charles Hassé, who was to have been the producer, remembers that it was about a milk-woman and a post-woman who love, and live with, the same man. A studio had been booked and a cast engaged, but when the script was submitted to the censor Cav 'got the most rude letter back saying only foreigners with names like yours would dare to present a subject like that to the British public'.[18] It was no credit to the British cinema of the time that what the censor had said was probably true.

In April 1940 the GPO Film Unit was assigned to the newly formed Ministry of Information, which at first had little idea what should be done with it. In the absence of any coherent instructions Cav sent the film-makers out into the streets of London to film the preparations that were being made for the onset of war: the digging of trenches in the parks, barrage balloons lumbering into the sky, children crowding the concourses of the stations as they waited to be evacuated. There was no script, no production plan, no official sanction: it was a spontaneous act which would result in the film *The First Days*. The film was as much an 'accident' as *Rien que les heures* had been. In the face of obstacles, this time bureaucratic paralysis, Cav's instinct was once again to take the cameras on to the street and just film whatever might happen. *The First Days* and *Rien que les heures* are really companion pieces. Both chronicle the life of a city, with a keen sense for its random and often surreal activity. 'Cities differ from one another only in their statues, the joys and sorrows of mankind are everywhere the same,' a title in *Rien que les heures* had read.

Whatever doubts the Ministry of Information had about the future of the GPO Film Unit, Cav certainly had his own plans when in the spring of 1940 he took advantage of a term in his contract to leave the unit temporarily to work for Ealing Studios. Soon afterwards – in collusion with Cav – Michael Balcon made it known that he would be interested in some kind of a tie-up with the unit. Then on 1 August he sent a long and rather premature letter to Jack Beddington, the new director of the MoI's Films Division, outlining a detailed programme of films that he had worked out for the unit in conjunction with Cav.[19]

Beddington's reply of 2 August put a dampener on Balcon's ambitions: 'Am I right in understanding that your suggestion in regard to the GPO Film Unit is that you wish to take it over completely? If this is so, I am afraid we have no alternative but to carry on as we are, or make some other arrangement. We are, as it were, trustees of this unit for the GPO and have undertaken to hand it back to them in good order at the end of the war. It could not possibly, therefore, be disbanded, even if we wanted to.'[20]

Within days of Beddington's reply to Balcon's letter Cav resigned as producer of the unit. Forced to make a choice, he chose to work at Ealing, where he would have more freedom than he could have expected in government service, more money and also the opportunity to work in features again.

Asked why he had left, in an interview in 1972 he said: 'My situation at the GPO became very difficult. I was a foreigner. The GPO people wanted me to become a naturalized British subject in order that I could carry on wartime propaganda work. It was very silly on their part. I had been practically in charge at the GPO and they put someone in my place.'[21] This was far from the truth. Maybe there was pressure in some quarters, but the official papers, to be found in the Public Record Office, suggest a consensus that every effort should be made to keep him. In late July 1940 the general manager of the GPO Film Unit, S. J. Fletcher, wrote a memorandum on its future for the MoI:

> The whole matter largely revolves around the responsibilities and the personality of the Producer (Mr Cavalcanti).
> In my view and in the view of many other people both inside and outside the Unit, Mr Cavalcanti is without doubt

the best Producer in the country and it is vital that the Film Unit should continue to have the use of his services. If only on account of his outstanding artistic abilities, however, he is not a great organizer, and studio organization should no longer be his responsibility. He should work only in the production capacity in which he is irreplaceable and his energies must not be wasted on studio organization and routines which can be placed in more capable hands. In other words, it must be put to him kindly but firmly (and this can be done) that whilst he will have complete liberty of action in his own particular sphere, he and all Film Unit personnel will be subject to strict business control.[22]

It was a perceptive appraisal of Cav's strengths and weaknesses, and of the most effective way in which his talents could be utilized. In the event the role that the memorandum envisaged for Cav did become a reality, but at Ealing not the GPO Film Unit.

Cav may have left the unit, but he cast a long shadow behind him. One of the great films to be made there after his departure was Humphrey Jennings's *Listen to Britain*, a breathtaking symphony of contrasting images and sounds of Britain at war. 'It all goes back to Cavalcanti really,' declared the assistant director on the film, Joe Mendoza, when I asked him about it. 'Cavalcanti was the most marvellous film-maker I've ever known in my life, and Cav really trained people to think like that, to think of relationships.'[23] Joe was still a teenager when he joined the film unit at the beginning of the war. Cav would be there for only a few months longer but that short time left a deep impression. 'Nobody realizes how important Cavalcanti was. Don't forget I was just a boy sitting at the back of the theatre. But I used to listen like crazy and Cav would look at a cutting copy and say, "It is not any good. The first three minutes is fine, the last minute is very good, but it is the middle! It doesn't have any shape. We must think of some movement to give it some shape." Cav got people to think analytically about what was on the screen and the succession of images and why it went flat there and nothing happened and why it got better there. That was the way Cav trained people.'

For a man like Cav who believed in no firm division between features and documentaries, Ealing offered an ideal set-up: a commercial features studio run by a producer who – extraordinarily in a business where the attitude was more usually one of contempt – possessed a deep admiration for documentary. The beginning of the war and the fact that Balcon himself had not been at the studio for long created an atmosphere of huge energy. Even before Cav's arrival, Balcon had clearly signalled his wish to make realist films. As we have seen, *The Proud Valley*, about the plight of the miners, and *There Ain't No Justice*, a story with a working-class background about corruption in the world of boxing, were modest productions but distinguished by their readiness to tackle contemporary issues.

Although the two men were in many ways opposites, they were crucially of one mind in believing in the importance of a team, and together they built the legendary Ealing 'family'. Cav had actually already suggested the lines on which Ealing would work long before he joined the studio. An admirer of the early American film comedians, he wrote in an article in 1938 that their great strength 'was that they worked not as individuals but as units'.[24] This was a secret he felt that their British counterparts had yet to learn. 'They are given a director and a close schedule and sent down to the set to work. No one would dream of sending them all off to a country house for a fortnight before turning a foot, so as to get acquainted with one another. Yet this is very much how the early units, like Harold Lloyd's, used to work. The whole group lived in one place. Everybody knew everybody; everybody made suggestions for gags, and the thing went with a swing. If the British companies could get some of this all-one-big-happy-family idea into their productions, they might easily make something worth while.'[25] No doubt his experience at the GPO was foremost in his mind when he wrote these words.

Cav took responsibility for Ealing's wartime programme of documentaries, but also oversaw its output of features. A studio which had previously been best known for its Gracie Fields musicals and George Formby comedies was transformed. 'It was Cavalcanti's close association with me which provided the force from which emerged what are now thought of *en bloc* . . . as the Ealing films,' Balcon would write in his memoirs.[26] Balcon was the business half of the partnership, the person who would read a script and decide whether in commercial terms it would make a good picture, while Cav acted as the artistic director for the studio. Typically, he does not seem to have bothered about such matters as status. While he had a general artistic responsibility for

123

all the films that came out of the studio, he never had a title that reflected this. And, as before at the GPO, he routinely made contributions to films without receiving acknowledgement.

If he could ever be said to have had anything so deliberate as a method, then it depended more on suggestion than overt instruction. Full of ideas and enthusiasms, he was a discreet catalyst. 'Did you ever hear anyone talk about Cav's murmur?' Brenda Danischewsky asked me. It was the few words that he might whisper into a director's ear that would provide the missing inspiration for a scene. 'Something magical happened in the studio,' the Ealing cameraman Douglas Slocombe remembered. 'Sometimes not by a direct idea, but somehow setting people off in a positive direction ... Even a writer like Tibby Clarke often came out of a meeting with Cav and sometimes just one word from Cav would set him off on writing a whole script.'

Cav's enthusiasm for the process of film-making was such that he took an interest in everything, however routine it might have been. Fascinated by the incidental and the random nature of life, he believed that the thing of value could be found anywhere, that *anything* might have some potential. It was an attitude particularly apparent in the editing process. This was Joe Mendoza's memory of Cav at the GPO Film Unit. 'Cav would say in the rushes there was a shot where the camera fell over, but before the camera fell over there was something, something, something. Find me that ... Cav had this fantastic memory. He could remember all the rushes long after the cameraman and the director had forgotten them.' It was the same at Ealing. 'A picture was run and he'd call in to see it,' remembered Douglas Slocombe, and right away he would suggest a whole series of new ideas to put into it that would somehow make a real difference between a film being just rather ordinary or something special happening to it. It was astonishing.'[27]

Cav's very brilliance as a teacher was to some extent a handicap in that it made people ill-prepared to accept him as anything else. He was expected to help the young film-makers, but comparatively little thought was given to what he might want to achieve as a film-maker himself. His talent as a director was largely unappreciated. Balcon himself in one interview asserted frankly that he had 'always thought that Cavalcanti was better producer material than he was director material'.[28] Elaborating, he suggested that Cav's lack of fluency in English was a handicap. 'There must be some difficulties in directing English actors for anybody who hasn't complete mastery of the language. From the visual side he'd always be all right. Whether he was equally good in the direction of actors is a matter for discussion.'*

Balcon was really judging Cav by his own conventional ideas of what a director should be, and Cav was anything but conventional. However progressive Ealing Studios may have been by the standards of the British film industry, Cav had still to contend with a stifling narrowness.

In seven years at Ealing he made only three full-length features. Of these the first, *Went the Day Well?* (1942), has attained the status of a rather oddball classic, and it is his most well-known British film. Based on a Graham Greene short story, it describes the capture of an idyllic English village by an advance party of German soldiers and the attempts of the villagers to summon help from outside. It is a chilling film, which conveys the texture of violence with an accuracy rare for the time. The uncomfortable truth that the members of 'our side' are as likely to be bumped off as the enemy is presented with an unrestrained relish. The vicar is summarily despatched by the German invaders while tolling his church bells to raise the alarm, and the lady of the manor is blown up with a hand grenade. The film has a subversive quality, showing the English villagers to be as susceptible to the bloodlust of war as their adversaries. When the village postmistress overcomes her captor she does so with a naked savagery. In a surreal finale the villagers rally together in the mansion and fight off the Germans' last-ditch attack. They go about their killing with gusto, picking off their victims like targets in a shooting gallery. 'People of the kindest character, such as the people in that small English village, as soon as war touches them, become absolute monsters,' commented Cav. In his later years he would refer to *Went the Day Well?* as a pacifist film. Whether or not he really thought this at the time, the idea of making an anti-war film in wartime would have appealed to his sense of irony.

One of the charms of *Went the Day Well?* is that it does not fit into any easy category. It is hard to know quite what to make of

* Cav wrote a tribute to Balcon in a book published to celebrate his twenty-five years in films. It was perhaps with some sense of irony that he called the piece 'A Film Director Contributes . . .' It was evidence of how he liked to think of himself.

it. Probably Balcon and most other people at Ealing thought of it as a propaganda film warning of the dangers of invasion and the need for vigilance. But watching it today the abiding impression is of a sardonic playfulness. The film is full of quirky detail: a message for help written on an egg (eventually crushed); the tragi-comic way in which the Home Guard are mown down on their bicycles – rarely could a military force have seemed less effective; dead Germans sploshing into the lily pond of an otherwise tranquil English garden. Cav's vision is of life eluding any neat pattern and shot through with the inexplicable. There is a moral ambiguity. Beneath the village's appearance of civilization there lies a barbarity – the villagers who, in repelling their attackers, find that killing can be fun.

'What Cav did to Ealing was to Frenchify it,' Joe Mendoza told me. I think this is right. There is nothing obvious in British cinema to which *Went the Day Well?* can be compared. It seems to me to have much more in common with a film like *La Règle du jeu** – the same sense of dark forces lurking behind a veneer of civilization, even the central setting of a manor house.

During the post-production of the film Balcon wrote a memo criticizing the lack of tension and suggesting that further editing was needed to restore 'the mood of urgency'.[29] He clearly expected an adventure story, with all the ingredients of suspense that his old protégé Hitchcock would have exploited so expertly. But it was Cav's instinct to linger, and to dwell on details. He was less interested in the conventional requirements of a plot than on how human beings behaved in extraordinary circumstances. Really Cav and Balcon wanted to make two different kinds of film. Whether or not Balcon had any sense of such a conflict of principle, or just thought that Cav wasn't quite up to it, I think this was the root of his prejudice against him as a director.

Went the Day Well? is a rather untidy film probably because of this tension between what Ealing was expecting and what Cav wanted to make of it. He was working too much against the grain for it to be completely satisfying. His next feature-length film for Ealing, *Champagne Charlie* (1944), is by contrast a brilliant team

* Back in the 1920s Jean Renoir and Cav collaborated on more than one occasion, although it was a relationship in which they were as much rivals as friends. Cav directed Renoir's first wife, Catherine Hessling, in five films.

effort in which everyone seemed to be pulling in the same direction. It received mostly good reviews. 'To have any sort of musical, let alone British, maintaining a spontaneous running gaiety and an irresistible tunefulness is a new and blissful experience,' wrote Richard Winnington in the *News Chronicle*.[30] But it didn't announce itself as being important, and if today it does not come to mind as a classic of British cinema this is because no one at the time thought a musical comedy worth taking seriously. It was an example of the sort of intellectual snobbery that Cav detested. He was anti-elitist and treasured cinema as a popular medium. He saw no distinction between art and entertainment, between 'highbrow' and 'lowbrow'. 'If you try to be artistic or thrust forward propaganda, you simply become dull,' he declared. 'If a film has understanding and imagination, then its audience will weep or laugh or thrill with it: and that is the only criterion of a good movie.'[31]

The film tells the story of the rivalry between two *lions comiques* in the period of the Victorian music hall: George Leybourne, otherwise known as Champagne Charlie, tops the bill at the Mogador music hall, while the Great Vance is the star of the Oxford. The film's brilliance lies in the detail and atmosphere with which it brings to life a world. It was an exhilarating mixture of high comedy and realism.

Although George Leybourne and the Great Vance were historical figures, the film made little attempt to provide accurate biographical detail. Cav was more concerned to convey the feel of show business life.* In this respect he did all he could to be faithful to reality. Tommy Trinder, Stanley Holloway and Betty Warren, playing music-hall stars, *were* music-hall stars. Jean Kent, who played the daughter of Miss Bessie Bellwood, the proprietress of the Mogador, had – just like her character – been brought up in a show business family and performed in music hall from an early age.

Victorian music hall was enormously popular in the 1940s, and provided a background for a mini genre of British films. But although it was natural to put *Champagne Charlie* in the same category as films like *Gaiety George*, *I'll Be Your Sweetheart* or *Trottie True*, beyond its setting it had very little in common with them.

---

* Just as *Rien que les heures* was less a portrait of Paris than a reconstruction of everyday urban experience.

The films of Humphrey Jennings, Cav's protégé at the GPO Film Unit, provide a far more revealing comparison.

In the opening scene of *Champagne Charlie* George Leybourne arrives with his brother in London and sings a song in the Elephant and Castle pub. What makes the scene endlessly watchable is the wealth of incident off the storyline: the chance, inexplicable detail. All the bustle of a pub is perfectly captured: the patrons pushing past, the snatches of conversation at the edges of your own, the laughter, somebody humming. There's a lady playing a trumpet. She's on the screen for the briefest of moments and her presence is never explained. Her trumpet can be heard in the background as Leybourne leaves the pub, just one element in the general hubbub.

There's a similar moment in Jennings's *Fires Were Started*. Outside the fire station a street musician plays a pipe. Jennings has the camera dwell on him for a few seconds before cutting to inside the station, the pipe now a distant sound. Both directors had a sense for how such countless moments, briefly impinging themselves on our consciousness, were the stuff of human experience.

When Cav filmed the performances in the Mogador, he provided not just the 'man in the stalls' view of the stage but showed us the reactions of the individuals who make up the audience, the girls washing glasses behind the bar, the backstage staff looking on from the wings, the chairman in front of the orchestra pit, and so on. With each view adding another layer of reality, and synthesized into a brilliant montage by the editor Charles Hassé, he sought to capture the totality of life. Jennings revealed the same humanist eye when he filmed the National Gallery and Flanagan and Allen concerts for *Listen to Britain*: the audience were as important as the stars they had come to see.

The highlight of the film is a singing duel between the two *lions comiques* devoted to the virtues of alcohol. When Trinder sings 'Ale Old Ale', Holloway counters with 'Gin, Gin, Gin', and so on to a finale in which Trinder sings the title song, 'Champagne Charlie'. With the exception of the odd hangover, drink is shown as highly beneficial, the chairman of the Mogador for example needing a few pints to write George Leybourne's songs. Food is consumed with relish too. In scenes which would have seemed like the most abandoned wishful thinking to wartime audiences both the music-hall patrons and the performers feast on steak and kidney puddings, pork pies, stewed eels.

And sex. *Champagne Charlie* is perhaps the only British film of the time to celebrate it as a normal and enjoyable part of life. The double meanings of songs like 'Not in Front of Baby', 'Hunting in the Dark', or 'Give Me Another One Do' (about 'the girl who asked for more') might have eluded the censors but were obvious to just about everybody else.

It is hard to imagine that the famously prudish Balcon would have approved of such licence. The responsible middle-class type he represented was a particular target of satire in the film. But in 1944, after an almost continuous diet of stiff-upper-lip war films, even he felt it was time to give audiences a bit of fun for a change, and a comedy about the music hall of the 1860s must have seemed a tame enough subject.

In the event *Champagne Charlie* amounted to a cheerful subversion of the rather pious attitude, for which Balcon was chiefly responsible, that lay behind much of Ealing's wartime output. On another level, however, it provided a positive and very affectionate portrait of Ealing. The camaraderie of the music hall mirrored that within the studio. The pub crawls and hangovers depicted in *Champagne Charlie* were also a familiar part of the film-makers' lives. Many of them went out together. A favourite haunt was the Players', a cabaret dedicated to recreating the Victorian music hall, where the audience sat at beer tables and sang along to the choruses, just like the patrons of the Mogador.*

'It's so English!' American visitors used to say of the Players', while Europeans, impressed by the café atmosphere, exclaimed: 'But it's so Continental!'[32] The same could be said of *Champagne Charlie* – English in subject matter but Continental in style. It shared the spirit of films like *Le Carrosse d'or* or *French Can-can*. The latter – Jean Renoir's evocation of the Moulin Rouge in the nineteenth century – was a direct equivalent in both style and theme.

With *Champagne Charlie* Cav laid a foundation of wit, irreverence and satire that Ealing's new young directors, who had been brought up under his wing, would later build on. In my opinion it was the first great Ealing comedy, the father of films

* Vida Hope, a regular performer at the Players', would appear in *Champagne Charlie* as the barmaid in the Elephant and Castle pub.

like *Kind Hearts and Coronets*, *Passport to Pimlico* and *Whisky Galore!* It is forgotten today, but deserves to be considered as one of the most important films in the British cinema – even if it was only a musical comedy. 'Only comedies can fight against injustice and at the same time elude the censor,' wrote Cav in 1938. 'In fun we can get nearer to human understanding, nearer to final truth than in all seriousness.'[33]

The following year Cav contributed an episode to Ealing's omnibus film *Dead of Night*. If *Champagne Charlie* conveyed the joys of life on the variety stage, *The Ventriloquist's Dummy* revealed its dangers. As one of the very few film-makers to have thought analytically about his craft, Cav was fascinated by the relationship between art and life, and must have been hugely attracted to this story of a ventriloquist whose personality is split, then taken over, by his dummy. Michael Redgrave's performance as the ventriloquist Maxwell Frere is low-key but powerful. There is the tension of bottled-up rage, of a man about to snap. Frere is a washed-up drunk who has long since ceased to have any enthusiasm for his stage act. It is just a job, a means of survival. Life has nothing to offer him, nothing but the wooden routine of his show, to which, used up as an individual, he easily surrenders. With this little film, shot in low-key lighting in an American film noir style, Cav achieved a chilling gem.

But his readiness to experiment led him from time to time to take on projects which did not suit him. *Nicholas Nickleby* (1947) was one such. Many years later, Cav would confess that he didn't really like Dickens that much, and considered Balzac to be 'a far greater writer ... much more human and much more socially important'.[34] So he was about the last person who should have tackled such a project. He sought to capture the style and atmosphere of Dickens, but the caricature and sentimentality of the writer were alien to him. He would almost certainly have been in sympathy with Oscar Wilde's observation that only a man with a heart of stone could hear of the death of Little Nell and not laugh.

Cav's instinct to range, to create a multi-layered world, was at odds with the material. He sought to encompass the often highly digressive episodes of a very long book rather than cut them back. The film became a series of sketches succeeding each other at breakneck pace with no underlying unity. Dickens's exaggerated portraits needed time to be grounded in a convincing setting.

The qualities required to make a success of Dickens, as David Lean demonstrated at about the same time with his brilliant version of *Great Expectations*, were the discipline to keep a tight rein on diffuse material, a mind attuned to the conventional virtues of a linear plot, and – perhaps most of all – a belief in and sympathy for Dickens. 'It seemed to be quite crazy,' commented Douglas Slocombe. 'He wouldn't have been able to understand Dickens. It was quite a ridiculous thing for him to embark on. But I think he so wanted to direct, to stand behind the camera, that when that subject came along he said he would do it.'[35]

In the last days of the war Cav visited a newly liberated Paris and then travelled on to Germany to supervise location shooting of *The Captive Heart*. The trip had a profound effect on him.[36] In Paris he discovered that German soldiers had moved into his apartment and vandalized his possessions. The whole city seemed brutalized. He heard stories of people he knew who had collaborated with the Nazis, and witnessed the huge disparity in people's fortunes that the Occupation had caused. Some friends he met had been reduced to the brink of starvation, while others treated him to meals of a sumptuousness he had never encountered in England.

His impression was of a country that had been dislodged from its foundations, of a people whose moral worth the Nazis had systematically undermined. The weeks he went on to spend in a defeated Germany served only to deepen his despair. He returned to England haunted by the ease with which evil could undo civilized values and reduce ordinary people to acts of depravity.

This was a troubled time for Cav. His mother, whom he adored, died at the end of the war and the bereavement unsettled him badly. In a fit of petulant anger at the meagre salary he received from Ealing, he demanded to be released from his contract and asked that his name be removed from the credits of *The Captive Heart*. But it would be more accurate to attribute his reason for leaving a place where he had been happy to a kind of general despair. He was fed up and acted on the spur of the moment, as he had done a decade and a half previously when he broke a contract to join the GPO Film Unit.

Away from Ealing he directed a crime drama, *They Made Me a Fugitive* (1947), for Alliance Films. Trevor Howard plays an ex-serviceman who, unable to adjust to civilian life, joins a gang of racketeers. Sent to prison for a murder he didn't commit, he escapes and tracks down the people who framed him. The general response of the critics was to criticize the film's violence but to praise its grim realism. The reviewer of *Reynolds News* wrote: 'In *They Made Me a Fugitive* we have one more British film which will cause an uneasy stir in Hollywood, for it challenges and surpasses it in a field in which it has hitherto reigned supreme – the gangster thriller.'[37]

But to place the film so firmly in such a category – as all the critics did then and have done since – was to misunderstand it. Like *Went the Day Well?*, to which it can be regarded as a dark companion piece,* *They Made Me a Fugitive* worked on a metaphorical level – less a 'spiv' movie than a portrait of society corrupted by the effects of war. Like *Went the Day Well?*, it showed the barbarity that human beings are capable of.

The gang leader Narcy is the personification of evil: all who move in his orbit have to some extent been corrupted. In the film we learn that his name is short for Narcissus, but of course it could equally as well be a form of the word Nazi. The Trevor Howard character Clem Morgan is an ex-RAF pilot 'with a fine war record'. He joins Narcy's gang in a state of moral confusion, disillusioned with humanity and expecting the worst of people. When he is sent to prison, it comes as no surprise at all that his girlfriend should ditch him for Narcy, the man who put him there. With his escape, he embarks on a surreal Candide-like journey through a tainted world. The people he encounters seem caught in a trance, bewitched and oblivious to the moral significance of their actions. A farmer shoots at him, taking little trouble to discern whether he is a threat or not. A woman tries to persuade him to kill her husband, and when he refuses does so herself. A lorry driver thinks nothing of his own small-time fiddling but laments the dishonesty of everyone else: 'You never know who's up to what these days.'

They Made Me a Fugitive is an extraordinarily bleak film, made

* The original title of *Went the Day Well?* was 'They Came in Khaki'. It was changed, Cav explained, because everyone laughed when he told them what film he was making. In his thick accent he pronounced it 'They Came in Tacky'. *They Made Me a Fugitive* went through two name changes in the course of its production – first being called 'A Convict Has Escaped' and then 'Deep End'. It would be apt if the final choice of title was a nod to the earlier film.

by a man whose own view of humanity had just been badly shaken. Clem Morgan's journey is a fictional parallel of Cav's trip to Paris in the aftermath of the Nazi occupation: both discover the depths to which humanity can sink. Cav's subversive, playful touches were as evident as ever, but soured by experience into a bitter poetry: 'She loves me, she loves me not . . .' chants Clem as Narcy's ex-girlfriend removes shotgun pellets from his back.

Two undistinguished films followed. *The First Gentleman* (1948), made for Columbia, was based on a successful stage play about the Prince Regent. The American producers did not allow Cav free rein to produce anything more than a conventional adaptation. *For Them That Trespass* (1948) told the story of a playwright who samples life in a rough part of London in order to find inspiration for his writing. With its theme of the relationship between fiction and reality, the subject was of obvious appeal to Cav, but he was unable to turn the material to his satisfaction. The storyline was too insistent and melodramatic for the characters to seem believable.

Cav would certainly have appreciated a freer hand if he could have found it, and at about this time he tried to produce his own independent feature, as he had done when he first began to work in Britain with the GPO back in the early 1930s. He intended to make a film version of *Sparkenbroke* by Charles Morgan, which he thought a bad novel but 'the best script I ever made'.[38] He sought backing from Rank, but by the late 1940s the era of adventurous film-making in Britain was at an end and he received the sort of response that John Davis would increasingly give to film-makers who showed signs of original thought: the project was way above the heads of the public.

Although for nearly forty years Cav had led the itinerant life of an exile, his family had always been with him. Through all the dislocation they had provided him with a spiritual home. Now with his mother dead, he had lost that sense of home. He had lost too the compensation he might have found in the camaraderie he had known at Ealing and the GPO Film Unit.

Soon after his mother's death, he moved out of the house where the two of them had lived in Stanmore and returned to the Blackheath of his GPO days, where he lived alone in a large house with just a cat and a parrot to keep him company. The move underlined his resolve to start anew, but could not make up for his deeper loss: at this juncture in his life his actions would be dictated as much by a yearning to find a home again as by any considerations of his career. In her last days his mother had often raised the subject of what her son should do after her death. 'Go back to Brazil,' she counselled. 'It's your country.' At the time Cav had paid little attention, but it was a different matter now that she was dead.

In the summer of 1949 the Brazilian ambassador to Britain, Francisco de Assis Chateaubriand, invited Cav to give a series of lectures at the Museum of Art in São Paulo. Back in Brazil for only the second time in thirty-six years, Cav met Franco Zampari, a rich industrialist who was setting up a film company called Vera Cruz. Zampari, who had no previous experience of the film business, offered him a four-year contract to set up the new company's production programme. Cav would have regarded it as not just a timely return to his own country but a marvellous opportunity to pioneer a new school of film-making, as he had done first at the GPO Film Unit and then at Ealing.

In the event his return to Brazil was a nightmare. Zampari's capacity for interference made someone like John Davis seem the soul of reason, and Cav found his plans frustrated at every turn. The bitter irony was that he should have ensnared himself in the very situation he would have been glad to escape in Britain: dependence on people who knew nothing about making films.

Cav bitterly regretted his association with Vera Cruz, but none the less in his short time as head of production he made a huge contribution to Brazilian cinema. Perhaps the most significant achievement was to bring over from Europe a formidable array of film-making talent, whose presence would foster an indigenous cinema in Brazil long after Cav himself had departed from the scene. The British film-makers who joined him included Chick Fowle, the cameraman on several of Humphrey Jennings's films, and Oswald Hafenrichter, who had just finished editing *The Third Man*. In addition, there were technicians from Denmark, Italy, France and Czechoslovakia. Perhaps only Cav could have brought together such an international team. His concern was that no single school of film-making should be allowed to dominate, but this polyglot group was also a reflection of his own cosmopolitan nature.

The cameraman Bob Huke, another of the British technicians who worked for Cav in Brazil, outlined to me the 'absolute tragedy' that became of his efforts to establish a film industry in his homeland, and what might have been if he had had his way. Cav saw in Vera Cruz the opportunity to sidestep the dominance of Hollywood that globally had the effect of suffocating most indigenous film production industries. His idea was that instead of straightaway building an expensive film studio Vera Cruz should use this money to build a small circuit, with a cinema in every big city in Brazil. With its own distribution, the company would have a secure market for its own films.

In this step-by-step approach, as Bob Huke recalled, the plan 'was to start off by making films on location, and then putting a little money into one stage, a sound department and cutting rooms, so that you had the basis for servicing films made on location. And then as the films made on location became successful, and the Brazilian public started to support them, they could now raise capital from the usual investment areas, and build themselves a studio, maybe three or four stages.'[39]

The fourth film Cav oversaw at Vera Cruz was *O Cangaceiro* (1953). Directed by Lima Barreto and photographed by Chick Fowle, it was an international success. In Brazil it was so popular that it ran in the country's cinemas for months, keeping the more usual diet of American films off the screens. 'Of course the word got back to Hollywood like a shot, and they did a bit of research and they realized that here was a film company starting up in Brazil that was going to be a serious threat.'

At the time Brazil was Hollywood's second largest foreign market after Britain, so it was worth fighting for. With a combination of cajolery and blandishments the American film industry exercised its commercial muscle. The Motion Picture Association of America invited Franco Zampari and the Vera Cruz executives to Hollywood, where they were regaled with enticing offers of investment: if Vera Cruz built its studio to certain standards, Hollywood would invest in Brazilian production. 'They came back absolutely full of enthusiasm for this idea,' Huke recalled, 'and they raised money from the Brazilian banks and started to build this enormous studio.' It was a complete rejection of Cav's gradualist approach, and all attempts at compromise proved futile. 'What Zampari said was a *pronunciamento*. He formed his ideas and he didn't want to know what Cav recommended even though he had brought him out there.' A 'Latin blow-up', in Huke's words, ensued between Cav and Zampari – 'Things were

said which would never be forgiven and never be forgotten' –
and, after just one year with Vera Cruz, Cav left.

The technicians he brought out to Brazil stayed with Vera Cruz
on long contracts. Huke remembers going along with Chick
Fowle to inspect the newly built studio. 'We wouldn't even have
had enough power to light one of the stages, let alone the four
they were building. There wasn't enough power available at that
time.' Soon afterwards the company went bankrupt.

Cav never got over the nightmare of his return to his native
country. At a time in his life when he needed a sense of kinship,
he found instead hostility and ingratitude. 'It was a mistake to go
back to Brazil,' he would comment many years later. 'It's a
mistake to send a boy of fifteen away from his country because it's
from fifteen to twenty-five you settle your entourage and choose
your friends.'[40]

Cav's sense of personal betrayal prevented him from taking
much satisfaction in his achievements, which were considerable.
Before his arrival Brazilian cinema had consisted almost entirely
of cheap 'carnival' pictures starring the Carmen Mirandas who
had stayed at home. He brought the conception of the European
quality production to Vera Cruz, and provided a benchmark for
the whole industry. He also brought about an atmosphere in
which a film culture could prosper, helping to found the Brazilian
Film Institute in 1954. For the first time Brazilian films began to
win international recognition. 'They were winning prizes in
Cannes long after we had all gone,' said Bob Huke. 'So the film
industry really had a renaissance due to Cav and it never slipped
back into the old slipshod ways.'

Cav stayed on in Brazil to direct three films: *Simão O Coalha, O
Canto do Mar* – a Brazilian version of *En Rade* – and *Mulher de
Verdade*, but there had been too many bitter experiences for him
ever to feel at home. He would never put down roots in his native
country in the way he had in France or Britain. He returned to
Europe in 1955 to direct Brecht's *Herr Puntila und sein Knecht Matti*
in Austria, and made other films in Romania, Italy, France, Britain
and Israel.

Cav never lost the spirit of a pioneer. This urge to move on, to
try something new, determined the shape of a career in which he
would be a major figure in the cinema of three countries. As a
film-maker he had made documentaries, comedies, musicals,
thrillers – although he would not have approved of such crude

categories. One of the frustrations of writing about Cav is the impossibility of keeping up with him. His very versatility and ubiquity makes it hard to give him his due. It is difficult enough to track down all the films he made in Britain – or before that in France – let alone what he did in the various countries he passed through afterwards. Perhaps there are Brazilian admirers deeply familiar with *O Canto do Mar* or *Mulher de Verdade* who regret not being able to see his French or British films. It is to be hoped that one day someone – someone, I imagine, as international in outlook as Cav was himself – will succeed in putting together the complete jigsaw of his extraordinary life.

Harry Watt

I have a photograph of Harry Watt which must have been taken in the early days of the war. He would have been enjoying his greatest success then. He was the star of the newly named Crown Film Unit. He had made the enormously successful *Target for Tonight*, the first documentary feature of the war to show the RAF fighting back. And – perhaps the surest sign of worldly success – he was in demand by the Americans. The producer Walter Wanger, who had just made Hitchcock's *Foreign Correspondent*, wanted him to make a film about American pilots flying for the British, *Eagle Squadron*.

He looks like a prize-fighter. Somehow it wouldn't seem out of place if he were clutching a heavy metal belt in his fists. A cheerful and pugnacious grin plays on his open features. There's something rugged and robustly proletarian about him: this man *would* call a spade a spade, and not shirk to use one. I suppose that to some extent I must be reading into the image what I later found out, but even so few other photographs seem to me to reveal as much of their subject's character.

Although all his sympathies were with the working class, he was himself the son of a Scottish MP. He went to Edinburgh University, but 'never attended any classes'.[1] After university he joined the crew of a schooner and sailed across the Atlantic. He bummed around in Canada for two years, then returned to Britain. For a short time he was a businessman, running a rubber company in Slough which made beach balls and shoe soles out of old inner tubes. But the venture collapsed, leaving him penniless. He drifted through a series of badly paid jobs. 'The next few months were to be some of the most valuable of my life,' he would later comment, 'because I got to know the poor.'[2]

Such were the class divisions of the time that 'getting to know the poor' required a conscious effort of will. There was Jack, for example, in the East End factory. Watt 'had to box very cagey' to get to know him. 'One hint, one slip that you came from a different milieu, that although your values were the same, you had started out from a different level, and a sudden wall arose that was almost impossible to break down.'[3] It was hard, Watt thought, for most people who had enjoyed a privileged upbringing to understand what it was like 'deep down – to live just to eat, and to be forced, for generations, into monotonous dead-end labour'.[4] He was proud to think that *he* had achieved this feat of empathy.

It meant much for his romantic pride that he had come into the film business not from any middle-class aspiration to pursue a *career* in films, but because of hunger. At least that was the story he chose to tell in his later years. 'I was sitting in a café in Soho wondering where the hell my next meal was coming from when I heard that a Scotsman was starting up a film unit.'[5] So he wrote to John Grierson, the head of the the GPO Film Unit, and got an interview. The elitist Grierson usually looked for academic flair in his recruits. But he had served on minesweepers during the First World War, had come to prominence with a film about the Scottish herring fleet, and his grandfather was a lighthouse keeper. Mad about the sea, he had only to hear of Watt's exploits sailing the Atlantic to give him a job immediately.

'I believe I'm the only one who went into the film business because I wanted to eat. I had no artistic bent whatsoever. All I wanted was a square meal.'[6] However sceptical one may feel about whether that was *all* he wanted, the story does convey the sort of film-maker he would become. In spite of his working-class solidarity, Watt seems more classless. There's something American about him. Sitting hungry in that Soho café, he's the regular but resourceful guy down on his luck that Edward Hopper might have painted, or Howard Hawks made a movie about. John Wayne might have played him. Regular guys doing regular work provided the subjects for Watt's films, whether trawlermen in *North Sea*, an RAF bomber crew in *Target for Tonight*, an army platoon in *Nine Men*, or Australian sheep farmers in *The Overlanders*.

He was tough, extrovert, but also committed. He shared that common goal of documentarists in the 1930s – perhaps one of the few things on which the members of this diffuse movement could all agree – to depict the working class with realism. 'The main thing to remember', he wrote of the GPO Film Unit, 'is not that all the films were gems. They were, many of them, amateur and second-rate, but they were revolutionary because they were putting on the screen for the first time in British films – and very nearly in world films – a working man's face and working man's hands and the way the worker lived and worked.'[7] The great achievement was 'to give the working man, the real man who contributed to the country, a dignity'.[8]

Harry Watt's social conscience did not blunt a fierce personal ambition. 'We weren't concerned with names,'[9] Grierson may have said, but Watt was. He was furious that the only credit he received for *Night Mail* was a joint one as producer with Basil Wright, and was still arguing about it in his memoirs forty years later. 'To my memory ninety-nine per cent of what was actually on the screen was directed by me: that is, I was behind the camera with the cameraman, telling him what to shoot, using the actors, casting the actors, all that kind of thing.'[10] There is no reason to dispute this but, as we have seen, it was the way Cav put together sound and image that made the film special. A more reflective man might have made some mention of this.

Combative and down to earth, Harry Watt pitted himself against the rather lofty atmosphere of erudition that existed at the GPO. He prided himself as the lowbrow of the unit, and sought to make simpler, more direct films. In *Night Mail* he had demonstrated his ability to mix with people and to depict humanity on the screen. It was an obvious next step to turn to character and story.

In 1936 Grierson asked him to make a film about the Post Office Savings Bank. Instead of the usual expositional film describing a real situation with a commentary, he made up a fictional story about a fisherman who needs a new boat and gets the money by saving up. Scarcely more than twenty minutes long, *The Saving of Bill Blewitt* came to be regarded, much to Watt's amusement, as a landmark in the history of the British cinema. 'Such a corny story wouldn't get past the third assistant scenario editor in provincial television,' he wrote, 'and it is astonishing to find it described in Paul Rotha's *The Film Till Now* as "a film that was to influence others in the movement and give a line of development towards the use of story and actors".'[11] Rotha's words suggested an element of deliberation to an approach that had been spontaneous. Watt simply did what seemed natural and obvious.

So the 'story-documentary' was born. It was an approach that Grierson would have regarded as retrograde. He had always conceived of documentary as quite distinct from fiction, and was in any case less interested in film *per se* than in how it might be used to serve a revolution in mass communications. *Bill Blewitt*, not to say the GPO Film Unit itself, probably seemed like a rather parochial distraction for a man who shortly afterwards left the unit with the announced intention of spreading the documentary ideal. According to Grierson's concept that ideal was to use the medium of film as a tool of information and education – a tool that belonged less in the cinemas than in the classroom and the workplace.

His plan to concentrate on non-theatrical distribution marked an inevitable split between the documentary ideologues and the *film*-makers. While the other senior members of the unit flocked to Grierson, Watt and Cavalcanti stayed behind at the GPO, even more determined to develop the story-documentary approach of *The Saving of Bill Blewitt*. 'We were convinced that, unless our films, with their message of the dignity of the ordinary man, could compete with commercial film on its own ground, that is, in the cinemas where people paid to see and enjoy them, we would have failed. This meant, of course, that our films must be entertainment.'[12]

Watt deserves to be remembered as a chief engineer of realism in the cinema – much more so than Grierson, who turned his back on the cinema. *North Sea* (1938) was the first feature-length story-documentary. It was about a trawler in distress during a storm, which is saved by ship-to-shore radio. 'It was sold and people paid to see it. This was our final triumph, that people were happy to pay to see it. It wasn't forced down their necks like some handout.'[13] *North Sea* was based on a true incident and used non-professional actors, but the characters they portrayed were fictional. Its challenge was not just to documentary film-makers but to the whole feature film industry. Its success showed producers that it was possible, in place of the unwavering diet of escapism, to make films about real people in real situations.

Watt broke down the boundaries between documentaries and features even further when on the strength of *North Sea* he was asked by the producer Erich Pommer to direct the storm sequences in Alfred Hitchcock's *Jamaica Inn*. His flashy, ambitious side would have been drawn to the idea of working in the far more glamorous world of features, but he also used the opportunity to proselytize on behalf of the story-documentary.

Julian Spiro, an assistant on the film, was one of his more avid listeners. Spiro had found weeks of working with *Jamaica Inn*'s temperamental but formidably conscientious star Charles Laughton trying. Laughton would come in early in the morning to be made up. He would then pace up and down to a gramophone record to get him in the mood. Then, after keeping everyone waiting an age, he would announce: 'It's no good, Hitch. I can't find the man,' and go home. Days might pass until Laughton, who was then a much more powerful figure than Alfred Hitchcock, finally 'found the man'.[14]

By comparison, Watt's stories of documentary film-making sounded marvellous. The robust style of his memoirs gives us an idea of the sort of thing, having quickly become 'one of the boys', he would have told the crew of *Jamaica Inn*. Anybody who 'talked of "waiting for the mood" or "needing the right atmosphere to create", or any of that sort of crap, would have soon got the old heave-ho.'[15] Spiro instantly said yes when he was invited to come to the GPO Film Unit as Watt's assistant. 'I was very happy to leave that world for the real world of films about real people.'

Ultimately Watt's importance to the British cinema lay far more in his ability to inspire others with the cause of realism than in his own films, which are on the whole rather crude. His strength, as he himself put it, was an 'instinctive talent for dramatic journalism'.[16] His films belonged to their time, and those which have survived best are ironically the ones which were of the moment, and addressed the exigencies of the day.

Few British film-makers failed to find some inspiration in the Second World War, but Watt was more naturally suited to take advantage of it than most. Britain fighting on alone against all odds, London under siege – these were subjects that would have appealed to his front-page mind. When the Ministry of Information commissioned a ten-minute film to show America what it was like for London during the Blitz, the original plan was that it should be made from existing newsreel footage which Harry Watt would put together; but he didn't think the footage was good enough. Instead he suggested that the Crown Film Unit should make a film from scratch. It was definitive Watt behaviour

– to swap the comparative safety of the cutting room for the lethal streets of London.

Even today, over half a century later, *London Can Take It* is a stirring portrayal of a city under assault. How much greater its effect would have been then it is impossible to imagine, but for many of the people who worked on the film it was the most memorable experience in their lives. Shot in the midst of a capital city in flames, at extreme personal risk, it was one of those rare occasions when it could be said that a film had made a difference. The American journalist Quentin Reynolds provided a commentary measured in tone but hugely emotive in its effect. His rather doubtful claim to be a 'neutral reporter' only made his sympathy – and the audience's – for the plight of the bombed city seem all the greater.* In the United States *London Can Take It* was given a nationwide release and, by winning huge sympathy for the British struggle, helped to bring the country into the war.

Its importance was matched by the urgency of its making. The show print had to catch a plane which would take it to America. Everyone worked around the clock, and ten days after the original library footage had been rejected the new film was finished. Joe Mendoza was Harry Watt's assistant on the film. 'We literally did work ten days and nights,' he remembered. ' I've never slept on a cutting-room floor in my life since but I did then.'[17]

Most of those nights Watt and his co-director Humphrey Jennings were on the streets of London filming the Blitz. They were out the night the Café de Paris was bombed and witnessed the carnage. Joe Mendoza had been told to stay in the air-raid shelters at Soho Square, where the unit had its offices, but he remembered Harry Watt's words when he returned: ' "Oh God," he said, "I'd like a bloody good drink and a bloody good fuck now." That was Harry.'

Exhausting effort, constant uncertainty, destruction, death – perhaps never had making a film come so close to fighting a war, and Watt – full of heart and determination – came into his own. 'Insight wasn't Harry's line, but Harry was bold. He was very bold. He went where other people either wouldn't go or didn't

---

* It is interesting to note that in *Foreign Correspondent* Joel McCrea played a Quentin Reynolds kind of character, in view of the fact that the producer of *Foreign Correspondent*, Walter Wanger, later asked Harry Watt to make a film for him.

think of going. Harry would always have a go.' Joe Mendoza remembered that Watt was always pressing to be allowed to go on military operations. His next film for the unit, *Target for Tonight*, offered an excuse for him to go on a couple of bombing raids. Later, he would take part in a commando raid on the Lofoten Islands in Norway. Mendoza remembers that he returned from the experience quite unimpressed. He found the reality dull – too much waiting around, like on a film set.

A notice at the beginning of *Target for Tonight* carried the boast of authenticity which was at the heart of the story-documentary: 'This is the story of a raid on Germany – how it is planned and how it is executed. Each part is played by the actual man or woman who does the job – from commander-in-chief to aircraft hand. In order, however, not to give information to the enemy, all figures indicating strength have been made purposely misleading.' In practice much else besides was misleading, but at the time few people cared.

Target for Tonight was a triumph of wishful thinking, but once more Watt had captured the popular mood. At a time where every week seemed to bring more bad news and victory seemed an impossibility, here was a film which for about the first time in the war showed Britain fighting back. The title became a catchphrase. 'A comedian had only to look at a pretty chorus-girl and say "Target for Tonight" to get a howl of laughter and a round of applause.'[18] The film was a huge success not just in Britain, but in America too, where Walter Winchell coined for it the phrase 'the Direct Hit'.[19]

Nearly sixty years later it's hard to understand why the film so appealed to people. A tribute to cool heroism has become instead a comedy of sang-froid. The RAF officers with their languid upper-class accents seem to have only recently walked off the playing fields of Eton – odd heroes for Watt, given his sense of working-class solidarity. Bizarrely absent from the film is the one thing that we know was there all the time. Death seems as unlikely an outcome as if the crew had spent a day at the office, an encounter on the way home with enemy flak more like a minor traffic accident. When a crew member is injured, a comrade casually dismisses his condition: 'It's the shock, I expect. I had the same when I fell off my bike.'

To appreciate it properly perhaps you had to have lived

through Dunkirk and the summer of 1940, you had to have been caught up in the fleeting, evanescent mood of that time, and – just as importantly – not have known, as we know now, that being in bombers was just about the most deadly occupation in the war. The crew of 'F for Freddie' were all drawn from the same RAF squadron. Their average age was eighteen or nineteen. By the end of the war most of them were dead.

So *Target for Tonight* was really the lie that everybody then wanted to believe. Its chief virtue, Watt realized with his journalist's instinct, was to be opportune. The film 'was a glimmer of hope,' he wrote, 'and the public rose to it. It was the luck of the moment at which it appeared that brought about its stupendous success. I have always said I had more luck than talent.'[20]

Target for Tonight was the high point in Harry Watt's career. It was the perfect example of what he thought documentary should be – a topical message delivered to a mass audience, appealing not to the intellect but the heart and gut – a synthesis of Fleet Street and Wardour Street. But it also marked, as he put it himself, 'the end of the road' for him in documentary.

During the production Cavalcanti resigned as head of the film unit to be replaced by Ian Dalrymple, an editor and screenwriter who had previously worked for Korda's London Films. Dalrymple was the choice of the senior film-makers at the unit – including Watt, who would have regarded the appointment as a promising opportunity to develop the relationship between documentary and features that he so believed in. But the two men did not get on. Dalrymple was quiet, shy and thoughtful, in manner one of the cerebral types Watt scorned. Watt's fondness for action, and the fact that in Cavalcanti he had had a producer who became intimately involved in the day-to-day business of film-making, made it hard for him to understand Dalrymple's detachment. 'I was producer, but I was really, in my view, merely running the show,' said Dalrymple of *Target for Tonight*. 'I kept muffled down as long as I thought things were going fine.'[21] But 'muffling down' was not a concept that Watt could readily appreciate. He wanted a hands-on presence, which Dalrymple declined to give.

Ever direct, Watt made no effort to avert a collision course. He criticized Dalrymple continuously and complained to Jack Beddington, the new director of the Films Division of the Ministry of Information, only for Beddington to take Dalrymple's part.

Watt's natural pride and considerable sense of self-importance would have magnified any resentment he felt. With Cavalcanti he had had a say over the policy of the unit that Dalrymple would not have been inclined to give him. Frozen out, he would come increasingly to regard Dalrymple's arrival – even although he himself was partly responsible for it – as a usurpation.

When he threatened to leave the unit, efforts were made to mollify him. Even Beddington wrote to him:

> I understand your feeling that your long service with the Unit has never had suitable recognition. You must be aware, however, that the films you have directed have spoken for themselves, and that your position with the Unit will obviously be regulated by the evident skill and imagination of your future productions.
>
> Dalrymple is perfectly willing that you should be known officially to us as an Associate Producer of the Unit, not merely as a Director, and to this we are agreeable. In the interests of efficiency, it would be better for you to concentrate on the actual production of films rather than on the routine of office, and obviously we shall continue as a rule to pass the ordinary daily business through Dalrymple. What we would ask of you is definitely to undertake certain productions yourself as Director as well as Associate Producer. There is no one in the Unit with your mature touch and it would be a serious loss to us to be deprived altogether of your skill in that capacity.[22]

But it was not enough. Beddington's suggested arrangement was obviously a sop which would change nothing in practice and, too proud to put up with the situation for long, Watt soon left.

This was the time when he was a nightclub turn, lit up in a spotlight and toasted as 'The Man Who Made *Target for Tonight*'. As the unit's most successful director, he was much in demand, and after making *Eagle Squadron* for Wanger he joined his old colleague Cavalcanti at Ealing Studios. It must have seemed like a considerable step forward, but Watt would later confide that he knew at once that it was a mistake:

> With Cavalcanti I used to resign about once a week, and Cavalcanti just laughed and said, 'Shut up, you stupid idiot. Get on with the work.' And I went back to work. I did this

once too often with Dalrymple, and Dalrymple happily accepted my resignation. I rather regretted it, but Ealing were pressing me to join them, and I thought, 'All right, bugger you, I'll go and join Ealing and join Cav.' But, I mean, the moment I did it, I rather regretted it.[23]

There's a sad, wistful tone to these words, which belong to a man whose actions were spontaneous and headstrong. Perhaps all that had been required to make him stay at Crown was a hearty slap on the back and a round of drinks. But the aloof Dalrymple was about the last person to offer such a gesture, even if he had wanted to. Probably he was glad to be rid of Watt's bullying, vulgar presence.*

At Ealing, Watt's first film, *Nine Men* (1943), about a platoon of soldiers in the North African desert, had a topical relevance, but once the war was over a features studio was just the place to expose his limitations. Made in 1946, *The Overlanders* told the story of an Australian rancher who drives his herd thousands of miles south to escape a threatened invasion from the Japanese. It was yesterday's news, lacking any contemporary significance to redeem its crude characterization and unconvincing dialogue.

Watt may have pioneered a realist approach in features, but it mattered that he had little experience of directing real actors; that he had no natural feel for narrative drama as distinct from the journalist's story. He would describe his time in features as as a 'rat race',[24] and his attempts to get back into documentary in the 1950s was an admission that he had taken a wrong turn.

* Joe Mendoza remembers Cavalcanti once losing his temper with Watt on the phone, and screaming in his thick Brazilian accent: 'In seven years I have taught you how to be a film director, but I can *never* teach you to be a shentleman!'

Humphrey Jennings

Humphrey Jennings was the purest example of an *auteur* that the British cinema – perhaps any cinema – ever had. The transition from thought to image was seamless. 'Why were Humphrey's films like they were?' a woman's voice, sounding rather like that of his one-time colleague Nora Lee, asks at the beginning of Robert Vas's *Omnibus* documentary on Jennings.[1] 'They were *him* exactly,' the voice continues, 'they were actually him. If you look at Humphrey's films, you've got Humphrey, the real Humphrey. That's what he was.'

But his efforts to express himself could involve considerable heartache. ' "*Only connect.*" It is surely no coincidence that Jennings chose for his writer on *A Diary for Timothy* the wise and kindly humanist who had placed that epigraph on the title page of his best novel,'* wrote Lindsay Anderson.[2] *Only connect.* The phrase was certainly apt, but Humphrey Jennings found it hard to live up to this injunction in real life.

He often seemed to be on a higher plain than those around him could easily reach, and in place of the serenity of the people he photographed with such love, he was more often bad-tempered. A poem, written by a member of the Crown Film Unit at the time, conveys the anguish that being Humphrey Jennings could occasion – for himself and everybody else:

---

* According to the producer of the film, Basil Wright, it was actually Jack Beddington, director of the Films Division of the Ministry of Information, who put forward E. M. Forster as one of two possible commentators. The other was Max Beerbohm. 'I often wonder what the film would have been like had the choice gone the other way,' remarked Wright. See Basil Wright, *The Long View*, p. 201.

Humphrey Jennings

Why does Humphrey shout?
What's it all about?

. . .

Why does Humphrey scream
And let off so much steam?

Is Mac to blame
    for losing a frame?
Or is it that Krish the cretin
    isn't yet in?
Has he had bad luck
    with Ken and the truck?
Is it that Dora
keeps talking to Nora?

Just what it is
Is hard to tell,
But the fact remains that
He shouts like hell.[3]

Jennings's tantrums and his biting tongue were notorious within the unit. To be asked to work with him was like being sent to the Russian Front. Too many of his assistants had been driven into nervous breakdowns for such an assignment to be willingly undertaken. In 1941 Joe Mendoza, only nineteen years old, was asked to work with him on a film about the National Gallery concerts because he was the only person in the unit who could follow a score. 'He'll break me!' he pleaded to the unit's production manager, Dora Wright. 'Look, Joe, Humphrey is a bully, nobody has ever stood up to him. If you stand up to him, you'll be all right. You stand up to him and, whatever happens, we *will* support you.'[4]

John Krish was a sixteen-year-old cutting-room assistant on the same film. He remembers taking a moment off for a cup of tea in the studio cafeteria, and Jennings at the door screaming at him in front of the teatime crowd, 'What the *hell* do you think you're doing there!'[5] If you were not their object, these rages could have their funny side. After a night of heavy Blitz in the East End during the shooting of *Fires Were Started*, Jennings came upon a

149

tree with its first blossom. 'The sun was just coming out,' recalled Nora Lee, who was the unit manager on the film. 'Marvellous. A great sign from God for Humphrey. The clapper boy came along. TAKE ONE! Clap. The blossom fell.'[6]

Jennings probably had little idea of the toll he was taking. He focused on his vision to the exclusion of all else. His rages were childlike; he did not understand how he could be thwarted. His self-absorption made contact difficult. 'He was the kind of person who would find it absolutely impossible to go into a shop and buy a pair of socks,' said Nora Lee. 'His choice of words, his erudition, just left the ordinary person completely at sea.'

'Humphrey was awfully strange,' said Joe Mendoza. 'He had green teeth* and his flies were always undone, and flopping fair hair, and this funny sort of manner.' Yet in spite of the weirdness, he could inspire considerable affection. His rages, which were spontaneous, bespoke an honesty. If you could find common ground with him, he was a wonderful, vital presence. He was passionate about what mattered to him, and had no patience for what did not. He was 'arrogant and humble', a shy man and yet at the same time, thought Nora Lee, 'forceful and quite hurtful'.

Partly this must have been his pressure-cooker mind. Painter, poet, essayist, film-maker – seething thoughts constantly straining for one mode of expression or another. 'I am finding more than ever that the chief problem in all times is to fit in all the worlds that exist together,' he wrote in a wartime letter to his wife,[7] who spent the war years with their children in New York. Perpetually switched on and sentient, he didn't have time to be conventionally nice. His letters are striking for their earnestness. They are about grand themes – his art, solidarity with the workers, the future of the nation. No note of levity interrupts their serious tone.

Yet some of the most moving images in Humphrey Jennings's films are of people enjoying simple pleasures, and being ordinary – a WAAF girl at a dance laughing with embarrassment over a photograph, perhaps of her boyfriend; soldiers singing to an

* When I sent Joe Mendoza a draft of this chapter, he wrote back: 'I should let you know that he was always asking me to make appointments for him with his dentist. When I advised him, when we were planning shooting, that he'd be going to the dentist he'd say, "Don't be ridiculous, Joey. I can't possibly go to the dentist in the middle of this . . . make me another appointment." Which I did and the same thing always happened.'

accordion and talking over old times on a train; a Heavy Rescue worker sitting with his mates in a café and explaining over a mug of tea the trajectory of a V2 rocket. These were the kind of fleeting, casual moments that Jennings with his high-octane intellectual life was rarely able to experience himself. Some irony that the film in which he found his voice, made just before the war began, should have been called *Spare Time* – when did Humphrey Jennings ever have any spare time? His films were heartfelt with a vision of what in his highbrowness he could not easily share: the warmth of simple human contact.

His letters show that he was aware of his own solitary nature, and sought to change it. 'Much better at talking to people and seeing their point of view,' he writes in one, 'more tolerant.'[8] The films were landmarks in a personal struggle for maturity. Of *Fires Were Started* he wrote that he was 'really beginning to understand people and not just looking at them'. He thought the experience would make him 'personally more bearable'. Having to deal with people – this was the first time in his life that he had to elicit actors' performances out of a cast – was making him 'much simpler and more human'.[9]

The Silent Village, made in 1942, imagined the obliteration that the Czech town of Lidice had suffered at the hands of the Nazis being visited upon a Welsh mining community. In a radio broadcast Jennings described how his unit 'lived in the miners' cottages and lived with them'.[10] Lived *with* them. The thought that, in spite of their different backgrounds, their different classes, they might have touched each other, meant an awful lot to Jennings. 'I think those people were genuinely sorry to see us go,' he said in his broadcast. The words carried a wistfulness that his listeners could have known nothing of. He was then deeply moved by the miners' favourable reception of the finished film. 'I wonder if they realize what that means to one of the artist tribe – so long, all of us, in ivory towers.'[11]

Because the ivory tower was Jennings's natural abode, his portraits of everyday life and everyday people have all the intensity of an outsider's vision. 'Really beginning to understand people and not just looking at them . . .' But looking was what he did instinctively. *Looking* is a key Jennings word. Entirely apposite that he should have been a founder member of Mass Observation, an organization which defined its purpose as to make a 'survey of the British islanders, their habits, customs and social life'. 'I see London' was the name of a poem he wrote during the war:

> I see a thousand strange sights in the streets of London
> I see the clock on Bow Church burning in daytime
> I see a one-legged man crossing the fire on crutches
> I see three negroes and a woman with white face-powder
>   reading music at half-past three in the morning
> I see an ambulance girl with her arms full of roses
> I see the burnt drums of the Philharmonic
> I see the green leaves of Lincolnshire carried through
> London on the wrecked body of an aircraft . . .[12]

These lines do not seem to me to be all that impressive as verse on the page, but they demand a camera. Whether Jennings thought of it or not, they serve as notes for what might have been a brilliant film-poem. An amusing pastime for any Jennings admirer is to extract other poems he might have written from the images of his films. Some scenes from *Listen to Britain* for example:

> I see a thousand strange sights in the cities and
>   countryside of London
> I see empty picture frames in a gallery
> I see a barrage balloon high above Trafalgar Square
> I see an ambulance girl play a piano in the Old Bailey
> I see a horse pulling a cart past smoking factory chimneys
> I see a field of corn waving in the wind and two Spitfires
>   overhead
> I see tanks rumble past a village tea shop . . .

There was a continuum from his eyes into his poet's mind, into a camera, and then back on to a screen. The ambulance girl playing the piano in the Old Bailey, for example – this is how it came about:

Humphrey and Mac used to walk around in the Blitz all night long, and they saw the ambulance girls in the Old Bailey, and Humphrey said he wanted it in. He said there was this girl playing the piano and singing. It was beautiful. He said, 'What do you think she could sing?' So I said, 'What sort of voice has she got?' He said, 'It's untrained. But it's a very pretty voice.'

152

So I said, 'Do you want something sort of folk-songy? You don't want an aria?' He said, 'No, something very simple, like the folk song.' So I said, 'Do you know "The Ash Grove?" ' He said no. So I sang him 'The Ash Grove'. He said, 'Oh, I like that.' So we had 'The Ash Grove'. It was simple like that.[13]

Lindsay Anderson spoke of an almost 'religious feeling for the individual human being' that Jennings's films conveyed.[14] This is true. Yet we never get to know these human beings as people with their own *individual* traits. Indeed, the religious feeling, I think, stems from *not* knowing them as individuals. Unconcerned with the separate personalities, Jennings was able to focus on the humanity common to them all. His viewpoint was that of a person moved by a sense of fellow feeling in a crowd of strangers. His tendency was to idealize. When she was to appear in *A Diary for Timothy* (1945), the mother of baby Timothy went to a lot of trouble to look glamorous for the film. Jennings was annoyed: 'The average mother of Britain does not look glamorous. You were not meant to be a film star, you are meant to represent the mothers of Britain.'[15] He did not say, 'Be yourself!' as perhaps other documentary film-makers would have done. In many ways the perfect Humphrey Jennings hero was Master Timothy Jenkins, the baby who couldn't talk back.

The religious feeling that Anderson spoke of was magnified by the circumstances in which most of Jennings's films were made: the Second World War. Rarely can there have been such an obvious struggle between good and evil, or a nation that felt so in need of God's support. Good films could only be made in times of disaster, Jennings once told the film critic Richard Winnington.[16] 'One thing,' says Alan the farmer in *A Diary for Timothy*, who increases the yield of his farm by blowing up an old tree, 'if it hadn't been for the war, I don't suppose we would have done it.'

Jennings, decidedly odd, laughed at by many of his colleagues, and too cerebral to communicate easily with ordinary people, can seem like a well-meaning Martian on a mission to Planet Earth. He needed guides to help him with the local customs. He single-mindedly sought them out and made use of their acquaintance with normality. 'He was absolutely brilliant at using people,' said Nora Lee. 'He knew exactly what he wanted out of each person.' As unit manager on *Fires Were Started*, Jennings's only feature-length drama documentary, she had helped to find and look after the cast of non-actors. In her case, she felt, Jennings knew that 'she could talk to almost anybody and get an immediate rapport'.

On *Listen to Britain* Joe Mendoza's contribution was his love and knowledge of music. 'All the music that Humphrey seemed to know or care about was Purcell and Handel.' Mendoza was able to choose more appropriate music for the situations in the film. 'Why don't you get something that's cheerful with a nice tune like Mozart?' he suggested, when Jennings told him that Myra Hess was going to play Bach's 5th Brandenburg. Jennings agreed, as he agreed with Mendoza's other musical suggestions, and what would have been a rather austere sequence became a joyful and memorable one of Olympian serenity.

Remote himself, he was adept at garnering the sensibilities of those around him. They were his contacts with reality. This openness to other people's experiences was a fundamental aspect of his film-making. He was a conduit for what people valued and cherished, whether it was a Mozart concerto or a Spitfire. He favoured familiar images and symbols that drew people together; it was an approach that predisposed him to borrow and allude. 'Humphrey used whatever he wanted,' commented Ken Cameron, Crown's sound recordist.[17] He would ransack old films (his own and anyone else's) for the fitting image. Pat Jackson was miffed to find that shots from his film *Ferry Pilot* had been reused by Jennings in *Words for Battle*. But the images were just the raw material. As Joe Mendoza commented, 'I had to get him the materials, but he made the magic.'

Jennings's most significant collaborator was the editor Stewart McAllister. 'They were much the same sort of person,' Joe Mendoza remembered. 'McAllister was terribly dour and very rude and forthright, but bloody clever and with a great feeling for everything, and he understood Humphrey and Humphrey's thought.'

McAllister shared Jennings's difficulties in getting on with people. 'A Caliban,' Jack Lee called him.[18] A small, plain man, he was always falling madly in love with women who did not return his affection. The need to develop a hard skin made him seem forbidding, but with the longing of someone familiar with rejection he would have responded keenly to Jennings's Utopian images of the world. Their temperaments blended perfectly. McAllister's feel for pattern and structure complemented a sense

Jennings had for separate but parallel lives. This partnership of style and content reached its apogee in *Listen to Britain*. McAllister's huge contribution was acknowledged with the credit of co-director. 'The visual ideas were Humphrey's,' said Joe, 'and I suppose the progression and the musical ideas were Mac's if you've got to try and sort it out.'*

Perhaps most important to Jennings was Ian Dalrymple. A shy man himself and an intellectual, he would have understood Jennings's awkwardness in a way the more down-to-earth members of the unit failed to. In a letter Jennings cited Dalrymple's influence as a reason for his having grown in confidence.[19] Dal gave him stability, showed faith in his talent and offered that rarest of commodities for the film-maker – freedom.

Under someone less in tune Jennings could easily have been stifled. What if Grierson were still around? This was his memorable assessment of Jennings in an interview given shortly before he died: 'Jennings was a very stilted person. He was not a very co-ordinated person physically, and I find his films reflect that. They're not very co-ordinated physically. He's not a beautiful woman walking with a sari; he just doesn't know what walking on the high hills of Poona is like.'[20] Grierson homed in on Jennings's maladroitness with the instinct of the bully that he could sometimes be. 'I think the word is that he didn't have a sense of smell,' he concluded. It is impossible to imagine that Jennings would ever have blossomed had Grierson been in charge of the unit instead of Dalrymple. When they did work together after the war, they fell out badly – perhaps Grierson's words above carry traces of residual resentment – and Jennings would comment crossly in a letter to Dalrymple, 'Grierson's ravings not only muddle – they undermine one's own faith in one's work.'[21]

My favourite Jennings film? Probably *A Diary for Timothy*. It is the most moving, but rough-edged. For formal perfection, for essence of Jennings – albeit extracted by McAllister – probably *Listen to Britain* would be the one to put in the time capsule. It never palls. I must have seen it hundreds of times, but still every time I notice something I hadn't seen before. Somehow it has captured

* See also p. 122 for the importance of Cavalcanti's influence.

life's rhythm and texture. To watch it is to experience life afresh with an awareness that usually eludes us. The tiniest things. The gently reverberating clunk of a railway signal in the near-darkness. Yes, it's just like that. There's the pleasure of recognition, but also I think a revelation of the poetry in the every day. The clunk-clunk-clunking has its own music as surely as Myra Hess's orchestra in the National Gallery. A fleeting view of a truck passing under a railway bridge as a train crosses above – the sort of thing you might see on your way to work without noticing, but caught on celluloid this instant arrests your attention. Why? It can't be pinpointed exactly, but it's something to do with a dynamism, underscored by the music on the soundtrack. There's a bustle about this moment, a sense of being alive. In the time-frame of the film it occurs in the morning, and there's all the freshness and vigour of the morning – people going about their business, in this total war the nation's business. There's a simultaneity – the people on the train, the driver of the truck travel in different directions, to different lives, but come together for this brief instant. So much is encompassed in a chance encounter.

The factory workers attending a Flanagan and Allen concert. The individuals' faces in the audience are as memorable as the performers'. Jennings's eye is egalitarian. A cut from Flanagan and Allen to Myra Hess in the National Gallery, the song fusing into the concerto in the same key. John Krish was in the cutting room when this particular bit of magic took place. He made the join, made it over again for Jennings and McAllister to check. 'They just fell about with delight because it had come off.' In its release of meaning it was the artistic equivalent of splitting the atom. Different people from different classes in different places listening to different music, but in that cut shown to be sharing a common experience. Jennings relished such contrasts and juxtapositions.

> To see a world in a grain of sand
> And a heaven in a wild flower
> Hold infinity in the palm of your hand
> And eternity in an hour . . .

Blake might have been describing a Humphrey Jennings film.

Jennings's idea of a script was a few pages of scribbled notes. *Listen to Britain* started out as one film and became another. That cut from Flanagan and Allen to Mozart: 'It was not in anybody's script or preconceived idea,' John Krish pointed out. 'It was all "Let's try that . . ." ' If so often in Jennings's films beauty seemed to come out of the accidental and unforeseen, then perhaps this was because he appreciated how the accidental and the unforeseen chimed in with the nature of life itself. He was the master of serendipity. My favourite moment in *Listen to Britain* was such a chance thing. Jennings had planned to film a children's music lesson in their classroom, but did not have the necessary lights. Asked what the children could do outdoors, their teacher suggested they dance the clapping polka.

'You'd like another shot, wouldn't you?' said the camera operator after the children had done their dance.

'What on earth for?' asked Jennings.

'Well, one of the girls made a mistake. It looked ever so funny.'

'We don't need another take,' insisted Jennings.[22]

It was a mistake in a scene which itself was only being shot because of an oversight. Most self-respecting professionals would have made the children do the dance again. But the child's half-stumble, with its quality of truth, makes the scene.

This was the sort of thing Lindsay Anderson was thinking of when he cited the Free Cinema slogan, 'Perfection is not an Aim.' Jennings allowed for chaos in his film-making. 'He let things happen in front of the camera,' Joe Mendoza said, 'he was waiting for the unexpected to happen, there would be a strange combination of circumstances or objects.' Such an attitude was an enormous challenge to the conventional film industry, which, like any business with its production plans and forecasts, sought order and predictability. Jennings constantly flouted normal working practice. Establishing shot, medium shot, close-up. Conventional film language, which others took great trouble to learn and regarded as the mark of their competence and experience and professionalism, meant little to him. In this sense he was really an amateur. 'He thought of it all as a painter, as a succession of images,' Mendoza explained.

The following sort of conversation would often happen when Jennings was directing. Someone, inured to the normal practice, would ask, 'Where do you want the close-up from?'

'What close-up?'

'Oh, you must have a close-up.'

'I don't want a close-up. I don't need close-ups.'

His work was exhilaratingly *filmic*, but unlike that of any other film-makers. 'He always had his narrative within a frame,' said Mendoza. 'If you compare *Listen to Britain* with other movies you'll find that there are very few cuts in it, and of course the cuts become much more significant because usually when you cut you come into a new image, not an explanation of what you've just seen.'

Jennings's sense of montage was as keen as Hitchcock's or Eisenstein's, but of a completely different kind. In conversation with Truffaut, Hitchcock cited *Rear Window* as an expression of a cinematic principle outlined by Pudovkin, the 'Kuleshov effect': the same close-up of an actor's face could by selection of a juxtaposed shot be transformed into love, compassion, hunger, fear, anger.[23] A shot of a person laughing could just as easily be a shot of a person crying. In a Jennings film each strip of celluloid had its own intrinsic value. His faith in the texture of reality meant that a person laughing was always that.

In *Listen to Britain* there's a sequence in which a horse clops by on a rainy pavement. It had to be shot at five in the morning. The sound of the horse's hooves could have been recorded separately, but Jennings insisted that it be recorded in synchronization. 'It makes a total world,' he explained. 'You've got the noise of the horse and the wind and the people passing in front of the camera. It's all real.'[24]

If I find *Fires Were Started*, the film that many consider to be Jennings's masterpiece, less satisfying than *Listen to Britain*, I think it's because it doesn't seem quite so real. A full-length story-documentary tracing the course of a fire brigade unit's day during the Blitz, it required Jennings to take a fundamentally different approach. He was no longer the well-meaning but detached observer; he was seeking for the first time to delineate character, to get to know a group of people as individuals. While the eye of *Listen to Britain* (and later *A Diary for Timothy*) was undiscriminating, here he strives to *like* his characters with an intimacy that was alien to him. In one of the most famous scenes of the film, the firemen get into their fire-fighting gear and are introduced each in turn as one of their number plays the tune 'One Man Went to Mow' on a piano. It is a stirring sequence, but entertaining rather than true. It feels staged and lacks the sense of spontaneity that is such a characteristic of Jennings's other films.

Jennings was at his best when he was showing the audience a

Humphrey Jennings

world, and teaching them to see it anew. He seems to me less convincing when he attempts to tell a story. His script for *Fires Were Started* was, as usual for him, little more than a page of notes. I think it shows. The narrative structure is poor, the climax of the film, in which the firemen fight a blaze in a riverside warehouse, overly long. Maybe it's significant that it was the only film on which Jennings and Ian Dalrymple had serious differences. In Jennings's own outraged words, 'Ian of all people suddenly demanded what amounted to a massacre of the film – all this arising out of the criticisms of one or two people in Wardour Street – who had other irons in the fire anyway and fight every inch against us trespassing on what they pretend is their field.'25 In the event a compromise was agreed and Jennings got 'a sort of minimum re-cut which is at least not the massacre it was before'.26

Jennings's reaction seems to me a prima donna's response. I find it hard to believe that Dalrymple, who had always given his film-makers support, would have bowed to pressure from Wardour Street. Far more likely that, as someone who had learnt his trade in features and had considerable experience of the kind of narrative-driven film Jennings was attempting, he himself believed there to be serious dramatic flaws.

A Diary for Timothy was a return to what Jennings did best – a portrait, rather than a narrative, of Britain in the last year of the war. The film is addressed to the baby Timothy, who is born at its start. We can all identify with Timothy in a way we cannot so completely with adults, however much sympathy we might feel – he is not old enough to be a stranger. Helpless and blameless and unformed, he was a tabula rasa on which the audience could project their hopes and dreams. He was a symbol of everyone's potential to amount to something worthwhile, but also of the future for which everyone bore some responsibility. 'Are you going to have greed for money or power ousting decency from the world as they have in the past?' asks the narrator. 'Or are you going to make the world a different place? You and the other babies?' If anything, the film has become even more poignant today now that we know the answers to these questions.

Nothing Jennings did in peacetime compared with his wartime films. The fellow feeling that was such an inspiration to him – the sense of cause and camaraderie – was lost. His early death in 1950 raises the question of whether he would ever have found another theme to inspire him. 'Had he lived, had he reached maturity ...

159

he might have done some wonderful things,' commented Sir Denis Forman, who had worked with him after the war.[27] When he was director of the British Film Institute in the early 1950s, Forman put on an exhibition of British films for the Italian government and showed nothing but Jennings films. 'The Italians were absolutely stunned. They said, "This is neorealism ten years before we invented it." ' Forman believes that Jennings would have built on the dramatic realism of *Fires Were Started*. But it's difficult to imagine who would have backed him.

Towards the end of the war Jennings proposed an idea for a feature about New York and London to Two Cities. 'People have often asked for the fusion of the realistic school of film-making with the fictional,' he wrote in his proposal. 'Here it is. A small group of actors in the foreground and the vast double canvas of the two great cities beyond them.'[28] Jennings was seconded to Two Cities for a few months, but according to Nora Lee the idea eventually foundered because of his inability to finalize a script. 'He couldn't put things down on paper. Everyone would say where's the script and he'd bring up one bit of paper and say this is all I need. That was not good enough for people to put money into it . . . Being clever or being creative didn't matter a damn. You just had to have the nous of being able to put up a front.'

If someone as enlightened and indulgent as Filippo Del Giudice couldn't harness Jennings's talent when the British cinema was enjoying its greatest moments, it's difficult to imagine anyone else doing so when it was in the doldrums ten years later. Many other directors, far less idiosyncratic than Jennings, had been subdued in the decade of Family Entertainment. 'If he had lived he would have become so disillusioned,' commented John Krish, who did work as a director in British features during the 1950s. 'He would have to have done a feature, and he wouldn't have lasted a week.'

Could Jennings have prospered abroad? His sensibility through his entire film-making career was so wedded to English themes that it is difficult to imagine. In any case there were many other pursuits claiming his attention. He is perhaps unusual for a great director in that he was not *in love* with the cinema. He could easily have given up film-making altogether. Outside a relatively small circle of cinephiles the work of Humphrey Jennings is unknown. 'One always hopes – without too much presumption – that one is helping to keep the work alive,' wrote Lindsay

Anderson, perhaps Jennings's most eloquent advocate. 'Yet as the years pass these films, which should be familar to every school-boy and girl in the country, seem to be seen and known by fewer and fewer people.'[29]

Usually it's just a pity when some talented artist is neglected, but in Jennings's case Lindsay Anderson's use of the word *should* seems absolutely appropriate. He painted such a visionary picture of England, an embattled but noble England, an England inspired by generosity and self-sacrifice, that one feels he *should* belong to all of us, as precious a part of our heritage as Keats or Shelley. It would help if his films were shown on television,* but they hardly ever are. Few of the TV executives have even heard of him. He is written about from time to time, but rarely with the sort of sympathetic lucidity that Lindsay Anderson was able to show.

Jennings would certainly have appreciated the poetic resonances of his own death – in the first year of a new decade, in Greece with a copy of Trelawney's *Last Days of Shelley and Byron* in his pocket. 'And I don't think that was coincidence either,' commented his friend Ian Dalrymple. 'I just think that Greece has claimed another poet.'[30] Jennings had gone to Greece to make a film about health for a series commissioned by the European Economic Commission on the theme of 'The Changing Face of Europe'. He slipped from a rock while looking for possible locations. 'It was absolutely typical of him to go like that,' said John Krish. 'I know exactly what he was doing. He was saying, "If we come here – or just *here* a bit . . ." And there was the cliff, and that was it.'

* It's often occurred to me that, shown each year on Christmas Day, *Listen to Britain* would do far more to foster a sense of national togetherness than the Queen's Speech.

Ian Dalrymple

In 1947 Ian Dalrymple spotted a young actor in a small theatre in Notting Hill Gate, and gave him his first part in films. Although *Esther Waters* was a flop, it set Dirk Bogarde on the road. Forty years later he would sum up Dalrymple – or Dal as he was fondly known – in an obituary: 'He was modest, cautious, calm, and in every way a gentle man. A gentleman is how he would best be described but sadly that word is now out of date, perhaps one which he might have thought pretentious. Nevertheless that is what he was.'[1] These words are echoed by everyone I've spoken to who knew Ian Dalrymple. He was a gentleman, and many were surprised that he should have belonged to a profession whose principal thoroughfare was famously known for being shady on both sides.

After Cambridge, where he had been editor of *Granta*, Dal got a job in the mid-1920s with Adrian Brunel, whose cutting rooms in Soho had gained a reputation as a kind of film university. Then he joined Gaumont-British through the graduate entry scheme that Michael Balcon had established and rose to become chief editor of the studios. He was fortunate to have taken the first steps in his film career under the guidance of two enlightened individuals who would have considered his idealism an asset instead of a handicap.

In the 1930s he turned to scriptwriting. His most notable credits were for *South Riding* and *The Citadel*, two films which stood out for a rare social commitment. In their realist tone they had more in common with the story-documentaries of the GPO Film Unit than with the largely escapist fare of the British feature film industry of the late 1930s. So when in the early days of the war Alexander Korda wanted to make a morale-raising propaganda film about the RAF, it was natural that he should have turned to Dal. *The Lion Has Wings* was crude and hastily put together in five weeks, but as much as anything was intended as an experiment to see whether such a drama-documentary approach would appeal to a general audience.

As the GPO Film Unit had for some time been pursuing the same formula – factual films which would have the appeal of entertainment – the box-office success of *The Lion Has Wings* was bound to be of extreme interest to them. When in the summer of 1940 an idea that Michael Balcon should run the unit came to nothing, and at the same time Cavalcanti, who had been the unit's acting producer, left to join Ealing, Dal met the two senior directors at the GPO, Harry Watt and Jack Holmes, and with the approval of the unit's new masters, the Ministry of Information, it was decided that he would become the new producer.

In practical terms it couldn't have been a worse career move. His salary of £900 was a sixth of what he had been earning in features, and, as the Ministry of Information were considering disbanding the unit, he was employed at first on a weekly basis. In taking on such a job, he could only have been motivated by principle. In the event a report commissioned by the Films Division urged the continuance of a reorganized and re-equipped unit, and the Crown Film Unit – a name that Dal himself suggested – was born.[2]

Dal would describe working with the 'fervent enthusiasts' of the unit as an 'honour',[3] and in the director of the Films Division, Jack Beddington, he had a powerful and supportive ally, but the reality of public service was disillusioning. He had to learn the hard lesson that however desirable enterprise and imagination might seem in theory, they were often frowned upon in practice. So far from being pleased by his ambitious plans to build up the unit, the officials in the higher reaches of the Ministry viewed them with disapproval for exceeding the modest effort that they themselves had envisaged. The Director General sent a memo to Jack Beddington to complain:

> I think I should call your attention to the fact that, first of all, your new producer, Mr Dalrymple, seems to be taking the bit between his teeth and doing as he likes. This won't do at all; he must do as he is told; the sooner he is brought under control the better. Secondly, you will remember we said we were not

going in for long films. There would therefore be little prospect surely of this Unit doing 12–15 three-reel films in a year? The whole thing is getting out of hand once more and becoming just an absurdity.

I asked that you should consider what was the minimum effective output for this Unit to keep it in existence, and to provide a staff to secure this minimum. Upon this we could build if we wanted to, but only if we wanted to. To the extent of this minimum we would undertake to keep them in work. This aspect of the problem does not seem to have been considered.[4]

In his reply Beddington defended Dal robustly, and also sought to seize back the initiative: 'I cannot tell you what is a minimum effective output for this Unit. We want good films more and more and it is impossible to say long beforehand exactly what kind of film we want.'[5] This tack would become the precedent for extracting funds from an always reluctant Treasury, as under Dal the Crown Film Unit embarked upon an adventurous programme of film-making.

In his tussles with bureaucracy Dal would write many memos to the various government departments. They are notable for their attention to detail, their close and reasoned argument and, perhaps most of all, their compassion. In one memo he would complain: 'The salaries paid to the Unit not only bear not the remotest resemblance to parallel commercial salaries: but are against Trades Union understandings and every principle of equity.'[6] And many more memos followed as he fought to rectify the injustice. When the unit was moved to Denham Studios, Treasury rules required that the staff be issued with a formal notice of dismissal and then re-employed. Dal asked if he could send out a covering letter to soften the effect of the notification. It was an example of rare thoughtfulness.

But in his communications there was often a note of irritation too. Aware of how much *he* had been prepared to sacrifice, he took to heart other people's mean-spiritedness. During the making of *Target for Tonight*, he was furious when the Treasury refused to allow him to spend any money towards the comfort of the RAF personnel who featured in the film. 'If I am to be forbidden this discretion,' he wrote testily in a memo, 'then (having already surrendered five-sixths of my income) I suppose I shall have to pay for these additional items myself out of what I have been reduced to in a desire to serve the State.'⁷ And doubtless he would have done so had the Treasury not had a change of heart.

Dal's attitude was to supervise the overall running of the unit but not to interfere in the day-to-day work of film-makers whom he felt knew far more about making documentaries than he did – an aloofness that, as we have seen, maddened Harry Watt and led to his leaving the unit. But if Dal's style was to stand back, he none the less actively encouraged the development of those people in his charge. John Krish was sixteen when he joined Crown in 1941. He remembers Dal talking to him for a long time to find out what his interests were. When Dal discovered that the new recruit had a passion for model theatres, he sent him to work with the unit's art director Edward Carrick. When that turned out not to be suitable after all, he was moved to the sound department, and then to the cutting rooms. 'The wonderful thing about it was because they thought there was something there, they wanted to make sure that I learnt as much as possible in the shortest possible time.'⁸

Nora Lee, who had been working in the film library of London Films, joined the Crown Film Unit when it moved to Denham Studios in early 1941. She was 'a fairly unserious young woman', who spent much of her time flirting with members of the unit. Dal recognized in her 'an intelligent person frittering away her time' and put her to work with Humphrey Jennings.⁹ The experience pulled her up short. Jennings was difficult and temperamental, but she was in tune with his outlook and experienced an intellectual fulfilment she had never known before: 'It was an amazing revelation.' Dal had given her this chance in life.

Such individual stories may not seem of enough significance for the film histories, but they indicated in Dalrymple a sensitivity and a quiet discernment which, however intangibly, forged the wartime character of the Crown Film Unit. 'He was low-profile,' commented Sir Denis Forman, who would get to know Dal after the war, 'but I think he had command, he knew what was happening, and he recognized talent very quickly.'¹⁰

The leading talent was Humphrey Jennings. He went to visit the Dalrymples at their house in Chorleywood for the weekend and stayed for two and a half years. As we have seen, the closeness of that relationship – the faith Dal showed in Jennings – was an important factor in bringing about the brilliant sequence of films that Jennings made during the war.

In the late 1940s Forman, then films officer at the COI, witnessed this relationship at first hand when Jennings made *Family Portrait* for Dal's production company, Wessex. Jennings spent little time in philosophical discussions with Dal, 'but he regarded him as a touchstone of good judgement and common sense. Was this idea too wild? Refer it to Dal. Did this sequence work or didn't it? Refer it to Dal ... And Dal on his side was generous, easy and never proprietorial in respect of Humphrey, which he might well have been since he was his producer throughout the formative years at Crown.'

'I think one of the reasons why he has never really been acknowledged for his incredible contribution to that era', commented Nora Lee, 'was because he was not pushy himself.' In place of the tiresome tendency of figures in authority to try to appear all-knowing, Dal did not feel that he had to intervene in order to be doing his job. His approach was to facilitate rather than to stipulate. Because such non-intervention was by its nature undramatic, it was easy to overlook the battles he fought to give his film-makers a sense of freedom in an activity where the expense, the numbers of people involved, the myriad organizational difficulties, all contribute to clogging up artistic endeavour.

Another person in charge would probably have clamped down on some of the more unconventional behaviour of the unit. A producer of less sensitivity would have found it hard to put up with Humphrey Jennings – his tendency to embark on expensive shooting with only scraps of notes for a script; or to change the whole conception of a film in the middle of shooting, as he did in the case of *Listen to Britain*. Another producer would probably not have supported such a risky venture as *Western Approaches* (1944) – shooting a feature in a tiny lifeboat in the Irish Sea with an expensive Technicolor camera, one of only three in the country at that time; and entrusting such a difficult project to Pat Jackson, a young director who had never made a feature-length film before.

'What Dal contributed', Pat Jackson wrote to me half a century later, 'was enabling us to get the work done uncluttered by bureaucratic interference. He kept the enemy at bay. He was modest in the extreme and very rarely tried to contribute during the creative process. He did not want to take credit as producer of

Western Approaches. He said that he didn't deserve one. He realized that he had joined a unit whose tradition of film-making was new to him. He felt that we were the originators of a new style of film-making and he was there to fight for our freedom to get on with it. This he did, brilliantly. I knew nothing of the fights that he must have had with the Admiralty and heaven knows who while I was struggling to get *Western Approaches* on the screen. He kept that well away from me. I had enough troubles without being burdened with his and he must have had plenty.'[11]

He did. As his original estimated budget of approximately £16,000 was revised continually upwards, so he was harried by yet more memos from the finance officers of the Ministry. These he would deal with attentively but at times with ill-concealed exasperation. 'We should wish to be in a position to know that the course we propose to follow in the production of the film does not involve undue risks or avoidable expense,' reads one memo from the finance department.[12] To which Dal replied: 'All our films involve undue risks.'[13]

Expenditure on *Western Approaches* was so great that in the late summer of 1942 Dal had to apply for a substantial increase in the budget for the Crown Film Unit as a whole. After consultation with the Treasury authority was granted, but Dal was warned: 'The Treasury emphasized that we were risking a good deal by putting all our eggs in one basket and that if this film did not come up to expectations, the whole programme of the Unit would have to be reconsidered.'[14] In the end *Western Approaches* exceeded everyone's expectations, but its successful completion owed much to Dal's readiness to withstand enormous pressure from a phalanx of bureaucrats. This resistance was all the more admirable because he was not combative by nature.

There was perhaps no task so thankless as being producer of the Crown Film Unit. When a new director general arrived, scrutiny of the unit's activities was increased, and Dal was required to report monthly to a new 'Board of Management'. It was the last straw. His report to the first meeting on 25 March 1943 ended with a 'Personal Note': 'I took up the Post of Producer of the Crown Film Unit on 12th August, 1940,' he wrote. 'I inherited a small Unit of technicians of outstanding ability, imbued with a fine spirit, a lien on 3 or 4 Newman-Sinclair cameras and a Sound Truck. Beyond that, all had to be won, and won within the complexities of Government procedure.'[15]

He listed the unit's achievements, which – on a budget that had not exceeded £100,000 a year – amounted to four feature-length films, fifteen featurettes and two-reelers and thirteen one-reel shorts. In the less than three-year period in which he had been in control there had been a return to the Treasury of £120,000, a figure that did not include the substantial income that would accrue from the release of *Fires Were Started, Close Quarters* and *Western Approaches*. He then pointed out that the unit was now well settled, and concluded: 'I sincerely suggest that one of the first considerations before the Board of Management should be the appointment of a successor to myself. The time has come for a new impetus and new ideas: and for somebody less battle-scarred than myself to act as Producer and Administrator.'

Dal's failing was to expect other people to share his enthusiasm and devotion. He was hurt to have received so little recognition for what he had achieved with the Crown Film Unit; perhaps if he had been more worldly, he would have realized that it was a foolish thing to expect – particularly from civil servants who had no interest in the film unit beyond the immediate purpose it served.

But Dal would still call those years the 'best time of my life'.[16] With his features background, documentary had been a revelation, and he had found a cause which would inspire him long after he had left Crown. The radio talks he wrote to publicize the unit's work convey all the passion of a convert. 'The characteristics of these films,' he observed, was that they relied on 'real life for their drama; that the players were the people themselves; and that the camera was not confined to extremes of artificial weather phenomena, as in studios when all days and nights are perfect. Instead of these excesses, the young specially trained documentary cameramen . . . by experiment in exposure and the use of filters sought to capture the prevailing light tone, to record truly the passing mood of Nature or to express in their pictures the dramatic atmosphere of the scene portrayed.'[17]

When he set up his own production company after the war, Dal tried to bring some of these qualities into feature films. It was called 'Wessex' because Dal planned to film Thomas Hardy's novels. *Far from the Madding Crowd* was going to be the first production. In the event he would make none of the novels. Wessex's second feature was based on the bleak George Moore novel, *Esther Waters*. It was a box-office flop and scuppered Dal's hopes of filming the even bleaker Hardy.

Reminiscences of the film suggest a kind of tragic fatefulness that Hardy himself would have savoured. The cameraman C. Pennington-Richards, who had worked with Dal at Crown, begged him not to make it. He warned that it was too downbeat for audiences to accept. Dal himself was directing with the art director Peter Proud. Neither had directed before, and it is a plausible assumption that it was a second-best arrangement for want of finding someone more suitable. 'I wonder if he felt inadequate when he was doing it,' mused Pennington-Richards. 'I made a couple of suggestions on the first day, and he said, "Why aren't you directing this?" Not nastily: nicely!'[18]

Dirk Bogarde, who was acting before a movie camera for the first time, was overwhelmed by the scale of the production. 'The whole set looked like Cape Canaveral.' But Dal, who was full of sympathy but little guidance, seemed just as lost. 'He simply loved everything you did. He was so astonished to see it happening before his very eyes,' remembered Bogarde.[19] 'There was a sense of enormous innate gentleness and of being out of his depth.' Endlessly responsive to other people's views, he could give no clear sense of his own. He was also painfully shy. When talking he would always nervously be pushing his glasses up. When there was a romantic but mild sand dune scene, the set had to be cleared because of Dal. After Pennington-Richards's qualms about the film sadly turned out to be well founded, Dal wrote him a letter. 'I must have given him a cigarette box or something. He said, "Dear Penny, why should you give me a box, apart from a box on the ears?" '

Whatever people may have thought at the time, and however uncertain Dal appeared on the set, seen today, *Esther Waters* is a beautiful film. It stands out for eschewing the usual studio-bound look of the period. It was a brave attempt to apply the documentary approach Dal so cherished to features, an approach that suited the naturalism of the original novel. For intelligence, sincerity and depth of genuine feeling, it outshone most other British films of the period. There are flaws – the story rambles, and Bogarde, as he himself agreed, was wrong for the part he played; but these shortcomings contributed less to the film's failure than the fact that it was so out of keeping with the mood of audiences of the time.

'He was so quixotic,' commented Nora Lee. The idealism that lay behind Wessex was patent. He admired the quality of truth that the young documentary directors had achieved at Crown, and thought he could import it into features. It was a characteristic act of faith and loyalty to give the Crown director Jack Lee his first chance to direct features. If *The Woman in the Hall* (1947) is an unsatisfactory film, *Once a Jolly Swagman* (1948), set in the world of speedway riding, was remarkable for the 1940s, even if unlikely box office. With its working-class hero, its grittiness and realism, it was a decade ahead of its time, anticipating Free Cinema. But looking at Dalrymple's career in films, perhaps that was his fate – to be out of step. Pennington-Richards described him as belonging to a 'gentlemanly age': he seemed uncomfortable both in the time he found himself and in his chosen profession. 'You know, in many ways he shouldn't have been in the film business.'

Wessex enjoyed one success, the prisoner-of-war drama *The Wooden Horse* in 1950. It was not enough to prevent Dal from losing money badly as, typically failing to distinguish between the professional and the private, he poured his own resources into his films. A man who had been of some means, he died extremely poor.

Dal's importance as the driving force behind the wartime achievements of the Crown Film Unit is beyond dispute. As the *Times* obituarist wrote, 'under Dalrymple it transcended its immediate purpose to produce work of lasting quality which has triumphantly stood the test of time'.[20] *London Can Take It, Listen to Britain, Western Approaches* – Dal deserves his share in the glory of films which are acknowledged classics of British cinema. But he also deserves to be remembered for his valiant attempts to build on the achievement of the documentarists and to bring a realist approach into features.

Pat Jackson

I knew I was going to write about Ian Dalrymple and the Crown Film Unit, so I was pleased when I discovered that the single most important documentary made during the war was going to be given a rare outing. And perhaps because it is never shown on television, when I saw *Western Approaches* for the first time at the 1994 London Film Festival I expected little more than a historical curiosity. Instead it was an unforgettable experience. It made *In Which We Serve*, with its studio-tank ocean, seem ridiculous. Yet because it belongs to that hybrid, the story-documentary, only a very few people today will have seen it – dismissed by the TV schedulers as of too limited appeal to warrant transmission. This is a pity, for it is a masterpiece – and I would usually hesitate to use such a word – which has not dated, but has, in the way of masterpieces, kept past experience alive for our own time. If you want to know what it was like to serve in a convoy during the war, watch *Western Approaches*. If you want know how ordinary people faced up to wartime danger, watch *Western Approaches*.

A few weeks after seeing the film at the festival I met Pat Jackson, who wrote and directed it. He treated me to lunch at the Savile Club. Afterwards we played billiards. He gave me a fifty-point handicap, allowed me to retake my miscued shots, but won the game anyway. We started another game, and *Western Approaches*, the Crown Film Unit, Ian Dalrymple – all those things that I had come to talk to him about – were for the time being forgotten. But just being with him, and witnessing his enthusiasm and relish for life, was the best way to understand how such an extraordinary film came to be made.

There can be few eighty-year-olds in such robust good health, and it is an irony that he had only joined the GPO Film Unit

171

because protracted illness had cut short his schooling. Starting as a messenger boy in 1933, he would have found the Oxbridge intellectuals that John Grierson had gathered around him intimidating, but he had the good fortune to meet Harry Watt, who with his healthy disrespect for intellectuals showed that an 'untrained mind' could be a positive advantage. Both were sporty, gregarious and outgoing, and they became natural allies.

Over sixty years ago Jackson had seen what W. H. Auden had so memorably described: 'This is the Night Mail crossing the border/Bringing the cheque and the postal order.' He was on the summit of Beatock Hill with Harry Watt and the cameraman Jonah Jones, waiting for the train to appear. 'It was cold, I remember, and we played rugger with my battered old trilby to keep warm.'[1] His strength as a film-maker was that he partook fully of life; he was at home in the pubs, on the playing fields. He engaged with ordinary people, and understood ordinary pastimes in a way that the brilliant Humphrey Jennings, for example, did not. In Jackson's memories of *Night Mail* the experience of playing tennis with Benjamin Britten (who had a lethal shot) was just as treasured a recollection as any of the making of the film itself.

The revolution which Jackson's mentor Harry Watt had begun – the story-documentary – was about putting people on the screen, putting their characters across. But Watt lacked the dramatic skills to exploit its full potential. It was Jackson who built on this lead and gave us the finest example of the genre, *Western Approaches* (1944). The characters he put on the screen weren't idealized figures as they tended to be in a Humphrey Jennings film, but people he had got to know well and with whom he had laughed and joked on equal terms. There is usually a distance between the artist and what he portrays. *Western Approaches* was remarkable for the absence of such a barrier. No sense of tremendous artifice; just a man showing what his fellow human beings were like at a momentous period in their history. *Western Approaches* is less a translation of reality into drama than a fusion of the two. The story that Pat Jackson tells is the story that the seamen he portrays in the film might have told themselves, a story flowing directly from their experience of war, a story compelling for its simplicity.

A lifeboat is adrift in the Atlantic. A merchant ship picks up its distress signal and goes to the rescue. A U-boat which has sighted the lifeboat realizes that if it waits it will have the chance of sink-ing the ship that answers the distress signal. Just as the ship, the *Leander*, appears on the horizon, the men in the lifeboat spot the U-boat's periscope. They try to warn the *Leander*, but the message gets through only in time for it to avoid one of the two torpedoes that the U-boat fires. The crew abandon ship and the U-boat surfaces to finish off the stricken vessel with gunfire. But two crew members who have stayed behind manage to get the ship's gun working and sink the U-boat when it surfaces. Despite its damage the *Leander* stays afloat and its crew and the survivors in the lifeboat are picked up by another ship in the convoy.

All through the long ordeal of making *Western Approaches* the reality of war and its dramatic representation were closely entwined. Many of the 'actors' were recruited in a seamen's pub in Liverpool. The captain of the lifeboat was played by a real merchant ship captain – Captain Pyecraft – who had just returned from a convoy to Malta which had lost a third of its ships to enemy action.

With the exception of one scene, the film was shot not in a studio but at sea. Sharing the lifeboat with Captain Pyecraft's men was another crew: Pat Jackson's film-makers. Every day for six months a trawler would haul the lifeboat out into the Irish Sea, with its double complement of crew, made even more top heavy with lights and a Technicolor camera the size of a fridge. One day, towards the end of this period, some of the seamen refused to get back in the boat unless they were paid more money. The Crown cameraman C. Pennington-Richards remembers that Jackson walked into a hut on the harbour where the seamen were drinking and threw them out on to the jetty. 'I could kill you for that,' threatened the ringleader, 'but I'm going to save it till I'm sober.'[2] By the time he was sober the threat had been forgotten. Jackson had won their respect.

To film the scenes of the convoy, Jackson went on one with a small crew. On the return voyage from New York, they were playing bridge one evening, when their cards were scattered by the impact of an explosion. They rushed on deck to see the red glow of the unlucky vessel that had been hit.

Jackson made an appearance in the film, playing one of the officers on board the *Leander*. This was not a Hitchcock-like conceit, but expedience: there was no one else available. The film director in the uniform of an officer in the merchant navy – it symbolized how closely the film-makers had come to share the experience of the filmed.

Western Approaches is unlike any other film its audience could have seen. It defied the conventions. The Technicolor that usually signposted garish make-believe – the palette for Disney and MGM musicals – was here used to capture reality. One is so used to wartime films being shot in black and white, with the artifice of the studio, that it is a shock to see the wartime world as it really was. Supplies being loaded in New York Harbour; ships of the convoy at sea; moonlight dancing on the calm waters of the Atlantic; the hues of a mid-ocean sunset. Some of the shots are vertiginous, as the camera pitches with whatever vessel it happens to be on, plunging precipitously into one massive wave, then rising with another. In no other film of the period was the sensation of *being there* so strong.

Part of the truth of *Western Approaches* lies in the way that, as the simple drama unfolds, no incident seems to receive artificial heightening but occurs at a natural pace. When a sailor goes delirious and has to be knocked unconscious, the moment is accorded none of the prominence it would be in a Hollywood feature – the swell of music, the cut to a close shot of the man taking the blow, an amplification of knuckle hitting flesh. On the contrary it happens almost casually, over before we've remarked on it.

And the German U-boat crew. They are depicted not as villains but as tired mariners, caught up in a conflict which they did not choose, and wanting to fire off their last two torpedoes so that they can go home. The shifts of human behaviour are faithfully recorded from the moods of desperation to those of lyrical tenderness – the radio operator tapping a distress signal long after he knows the battery is dead, to reassure the youngest member of the crew. 'The film is devoid of heroics although it is impregnated with heroism,' wrote Richard Winnington in the *News Chronicle*.[3]

Western Approaches depends on that oldest staple of the cinema – suspense – as our gaze is switched between U-boat, lifeboat and ship, but it is not the manipulative suspense of a Griffith or a Hitchcock, winding up our anticipation like a child's toy, but just inherent in the situation.

'A man who has spent his life at sea looks different from other men and he carries the indelible stamp of his working environment upon him,' wrote Pat Jackson. 'No actor can give you that indefinable quality of being the "real thing".' Whether Cockney or Liverpudlian, the seamen in *Western Approaches* speak in their own accents. With the cadences of everyday speech their performances possess an extraordinary freshness: the passage of fifty years vanishes with the discovery, which is surprising although it should not be, that people then spoke as people speak today. Even the slight awkwardness of the sailors – the selfconsciousness of the non-actor – serves as a mark of their authenticity. As they play out their roles, similar to the ones they had in real life, their performances seem like a tribute to their colleagues.

When *Western Approaches* was first shown at the end of the war, it was a triumph. Suddenly Pat Jackson was one of the hottest directors in British films. But the war was nearly over and it was clear that the future of the Crown Film Unit would be far from certain in peacetime. In an article called 'Crisis in Documentary' Jackson argued that as government sponsorship ended the film industry itself should support the story-documentary tradition: 'We have not needed your costly Casting Directors to find our talent,' he wrote. 'We have found it for ourselves by listening and observing at the workplace or the pubs . . . [The non-actor] has a place in the film which attempts to capture the character and problems of the people in any given environment and the effect of that environment on the people, their looks, their ways of thinking and speaking. A story using these raw materials can be told with greater conviction, faith and realism than the artificiality of a studio and the familiar stock face, however big their fan mail.'[4]

It was an argument for what the Italians would later call neo-realism. *Western Approaches* and *Fires Were Started* were of course neo-realist films – even if no one at the time had thought of such a name, and this kind of film-making could have flowered in Britain had the film companies been prepared to back it. But it was so at odds with a system to which the 'familiar stock face' was a central notion that not even Pat Jackson could have been surprised that they chose not to. So instead he followed the familiar path to Hollywood, taking up an option for a contract with MGM that Korda had negotiated for him.

In the years that followed he learnt the painful lesson that the Crown Film Unit, with its scope for experimentation, had shielded him from – that film-makers are rarely free to make films as they would choose. After weeks of highly paid idleness in

Hollywood, he demanded to be given an assignment or to be released from his contract. MGM duly obliged and offered him a *Lassie* picture. He turned it down. 'All I knew was that I wasn't going to make tripe: Lassie tripe or any other tripe. It wasn't pride, it was respect for the Cinema.'[5] It was an understandable reaction. But MGM were probably just as surprised that Jackson should have taken exception. In return for their generous salary, like executives in any other business their directors were expected to implement the policy of the company. Jackson called MGM the 'civil service'. The great German director Fritz Lang explained the system to him: 'Darlink boy, in this place out of the ten films that you may have to make only one perhaps you half wanted to make. If you can't accept this, then you must get out of here, if you can afford to, and have another country to go to.'[6]

Jackson took Lang's advice. He made one film for MGM, *Shadow on the Wall*, before taking advantage of the studio's wish to renegotiate his contract to return home. Back in England, in 1951, he made the hospital film *White Corridors*. It applied the story-documentary approach to commercial cinema, without the one being compromised by the other. Among the cast were three non-actors, including H. F. Hills who had been one of the seamen in *Western Approaches*. It was a commercial and critical success, but made very much against the odds in an industry that had now firmly turned its back on such realism. 'Pat Jackson's direction is a miracle of understanding,' wrote Dilys Powell in the *Sunday Times*.[7] 'Had *White Corridors* been made in France, we should never hear the end of its virtues.' If in the coming years Pat Jackson worked only infrequently in features, it was because the instinct for truth which had produced a masterpiece at one point in the British cinema's history was an obstacle to a successful career at another.

My friend Pat Jackson, director of *Western Approaches,* the best story documentary ever made. Then ...

... and now.

Jack Beddington, the director of the Films Division of the Ministry of Information, here talking to Roger Livesey on the set of *A Matter of Life and Death*. Michael Powell rightly described him as 'one of the most unjustly forgotten men of the war'.

Ian Dalrymple, producer of the Crown Film Unit and later one of Rank's Independent Producers. Here his threadbare and moth-eaten jersey undermines the efforts of the portrait photographer to make him look glamorous. Shy and erudite, many people thought him too much a gentleman to be in films.

Dal's folly. *Esther Waters* was an expensive flop that few people remember today. But it was one of the most beautifully made films of the forties. Ian Dalrymple is at the extreme right-hand side of the picture, a typically marginal figure, looking on from the sidelines at an enterprise that he had made possible. Deeply impressed by his experience of documentary at Crown, he sought to bring a realism into features. In abandoning the back projection of the studio and taking the cameras out into the countryside, he was something of a pioneer.

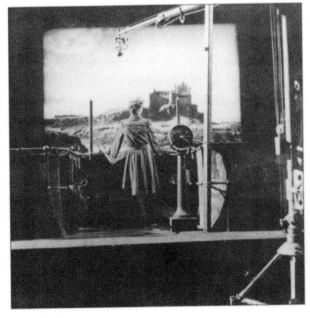

This is how it was more usually done. The outdoors indoors (on the set of *I Know Where I'm Going*).

Sidney Box, 'The Man Who Did Too Much', looking resilient but tired. His sister, Betty, gave me this picture, which was taken at a premiere: 'I find the studio portraits so very formal, and this one shows his lovely smile.'

Starlet Susan Shaw pops out of a plaster cake to offer Sidney an Austerity slice. The occasion was a lavish jubilee party to mark Box's twenty-fifth feature film as a producer, *The Bad Lord Byron*, a mere five years after his first, *Flemish Farm*.

Herbert Wilcox with his wife Anna Neagle, the biggest star in British pictures and here looking like the Madame Tussauds waxwork she could often seem to be in her films.

During most of the year-long production of *Caesar and Cleopatra*, Gabby Pascal and Claude Rains were not on speaking terms. It was something of a feat to capture them in the same picture.

A British studio during wartime. The words scrubbed out in defiance of the Luftwaffe are 'Merton Park'.

Pro Patria 1942: The actresses Peggy Ashcroft, Joyce Carey, Ann Todd and Celia Johnson (seated) appear in a government information film, *We Serve*.

The director was Carol Reed, here snapped 'taking five'. During the war stills film was hard to come by. The editor of *We Serve*, Peter Tanner, who gave me these pictures, took them on motion picture stock.

The monocle was merely decorative. The actor Esmond Knight could not see when in 1942 this production still of him as a Nazi officer was taken for the film *Silver Fleet*. Only a few months before, he had been serving as an officer on board HMS *Prince of Wales* and was blinded during its action against the *Bismarck*. If in the 1940s the British cinema was more committed, serious, realistic and personal than it had ever been before or since, there were obvious reasons why this was so.

In the mid-1940s Britain possessed the most innovative and exciting film industry in the world. Hollywood producers and technicians flocked across the Atlantic to find out what was going on. Here the lighting cameraman Erwin Hillier shows his legendary American colleague Gregg Toland (of *Citizen Kane* fame) around Denham Studios.

The British cinema has often received derision for its portrait of the British as having a 'stiff upper lip' and drinking endless cups of tea. But in the 1940s people really did drink endless cups of tea! Here, on the set of *I Know Where I'm Going*, is Wendy Hiller, with Michael Powell and Roger Livesey looking on.

Jack Beddington

The early days of the Ministry of Information were ones of inauspicious confusion and muddle. When the war began the director of the Films Division was Sir Joseph Ball, recently arrived from Conservative Central Office where he had been in charge of publicity. According to his successor, Sir Kenneth Clark, Ball owed his advance through the ranks of the Tory Party to the excellent fishing to be had on his reach of the River Test. Neville Chamberlain, who was a keen angler, visited often and rewarded him with his patronage. Ball was as hopeless at running the Films Division as his angling companion had been at standing up to Hitler. A couple of days after war was declared, the film directors Thorold Dickinson and Anthony Asquith visited him to discuss how the film industry might contribute to the war effort. 'It's no use coming here,' he said, 'you're all going to be drafted, you'll all be in the forces, we're going to close all the cinemas, there won't be any more film production.' Dismayed, his two visitors argued that film as propaganda was a vital weapon of war. 'Oh, no, no,' he replied, 'it's been decided.'[1]

Asquith and Dickinson used their considerable political influence to get Ball booted out. Together with George Elvin, the general secretary of the film trade union the ACT, and the producer Dallas Bower, they enlisted the support of Lord Beaverbrook, who had been Minister of Information during the First World War and was a close ally of Churchill.[2] Three weeks later Ball was replaced by Sir Kenneth Clark, director of the National Gallery. 'It was an inexplicable choice,' wrote Clark, who had originally applied to join the MoI's censorship department, 'and was commonly attributed to the fact that in those days films were spoken of as "pictures", and I was believed to be an authority on pictures.'[3]

But the new director was eager to learn and over-optimistically thought that a visit to his predecessor might be useful. 'I paid him a routine call and found a small, fat man sitting behind an empty desk, with lines of cigarette ash stretched across the folds of his waistcoat. He cannot have moved for a long time. He did not bother to be polite to me, and when I asked him about his staff said that he had never met them.'[4] The staff turned out to be just as dismissive of the film industry as their erstwhile boss, believing that the division should have as little as possible to do with such a tawdry business. Clark himself would soon move on to another post, but not before nominating Jack Beddington as his successor.

It was an inspired suggestion. Beddington was just as keen on pictures as Clark. As publicity director of Shell in the 1930s he had built up a reputation for discovering promising new artists. Those he had supported included Graham Sutherland, Paul Nash, Barnett Freedman, Rex Whistler and Edward Ardizzone. And he was just as discerning in those he chose to pen his advertising slogans; there was the poet John Betjeman, the travel writer Robert Byron and the scholar Peter Quennell, who in his memoirs would call Beddington what all the artists and writers and eventually film-makers knew him indisputably to be – the 'modern Maecenas'.

This little elite was all the more unusual because it existed in the midst of a strait-laced company whose executives were thought of as 'gentlemen who sold petrol to gentlemen'. It must have been a considerable feat for Beddington to persuade his colleagues that these painters and writers could have any useful role in an oil company. Probably it helped that he had already spent eight years as an executive of Shell in China. Although he would champion the cause of artists with a missionary zeal, he never allowed his enthusiasm to blunt an instinctive pragmatism.

Descriptions of Beddington suggest a man who would have felt as comfortable in the clubs of the Establishment as in the galleries and artists' studios. Nicolas Bentley was impressed by his 'savoir-faire' and remembered him as 'military-looking'.[5] Peter Quennell thought his face 'suggested the portrait of an Austro-Hungarian hussar on a large egg'.[6] There was a mournful quality to his mien which led Michael Powell to describe his expression as 'normally that of a pessimistic basset hound',[7] while for Bill MacQuitty his melancholy face reminded him of Adolphe Menjou.[8] These features were at odds with the positive personality of someone who was 'gregarious' and 'unquenchable in his bonhomie'. He was of medium height, but, remembered Moira Beaty, who worked for him towards the end of the war, 'so filled a room with his personality that he seemed much bigger than he actually was'.[9] He was swift and light on his feet. No sound of footsteps would give his staff time to prepare themselves for his bracing presence.

Ultimately the wholehearted support he was able to pledge to artists stemmed from his conviction, as John Betjeman pointed out, that there was no such thing as commercial art. 'He said either people were artists or they were not.'[10] This attitude allowed those who did work for him an enormous freedom. Bill Mitchell, one of his copywriters at Shell, described the sort of brief he might give: 'Here's a list of follies. Would you choose which one you think you'd like to paint. You'll bring in a rough in three weeks' time. I promise you I'll not mess about and say, "Oh, that tree ought to be blue instead of green . . . I shall either reject it or accept it." '[11] Here in one person was a very rare mixture of authority, decisiveness and an understanding of the creative process.

Beddington regarded companies as patrons of art in the way Renaissance princes had once been. The return, however intangible, was an enhanced reputation. His attachment to this principle meant that in certain circumstances he could even go to lengths *not* to mention Shell, as Paul Rotha found out when he was commissioned in the early 1930s to make a film about Imperial Airways. Only one thing Beddington insisted on: 'There must be in the film no direct reference to Shell, although they were footing the bill. If an air-stocking at some God-forsaken air-strip had on it the name SHELL, then I couldn't help but film it. But he emphasized that in no way at all was it to be considered a piece of advertisement.'[12] What, one wonders, would Beddington, who so detested crude association, have made of today's commonplaces of football divisions named after building societies and brewery logos on Test cricketers' shirts?

Beddington was about as far removed from the conventional image of a civil servant as it was possible to be. He was flamboyant, energetic and volatile. He could be bullying and was often impatient; on the other hand those who enjoyed his approval were offered endless support and encouragement. If he was intolerant, it was usually of the petty and the prosaic. He did not dodge arguments but plunged into them with relish, and his natural dynamism could manifest itself in a lethal bluntness of speech. Michael Powell remembered him as 'a shrewd, jerky conversationalist who liked to throw a bomb into a discussion and then wait for it to explode'.[13]

He was brought up in a devoted Jewish family. The Beddingtons had come over to England as refugees from Portugal during the reign of Queen Anne. They had been merchants and their original name was Moses. Jack's grandfather changed the name to Beddington in the 1860s after the Surrey town where he owned land. It is easy to imagine how such a background would have instilled the 'understanding of the worries and troubles of humanity' that Jack Beddington's daughter Carol observed in her father. She also remembers her mother, who was a High Anglican, referring to him 'as the most Christian man she had ever met'.

He was emotional and, as his daughter put it, 'cried at the drop of a hat'.[14] There was one occasion when he was showing a film to Churchill in the MoI cinema. They both sat there watching with tears pouring down their cheeks. At the end Churchill turned to Beddington and said, 'Not much good, is it?' and Beddington, mopping his eyes, agreed. Like Churchill, whom he admired and resembled in temperament, Beddington loved the movies. His favourite star was Rita Hayworth and he used to run *Cover Girl* about once a week on the pretext of raising staff morale. It was an example of the enthusiasm that would have endeared him to film-makers, if not to civil servants.

This picture of a man that people either hated or adored is borne out by the dramatic manner of Beddington's arrival at the MoI in the spring of 1940. He refused to work with his deputy director, a G. E. G. Forbes, and stopped going into the office.[15] The business of the Films Division, which had in any case been thrown into disarray by the Fall of France, became severely disrupted, and a deputation of senior members of the MoI – Alberto Cavalcanti, Thorold Dickinson, Basil Wright and Dallas Bower – was organized to visit Beddington at Lily Farm, his house in the country. Like Achilles in his tent – a comparison which seems the more apt for the embattled state of the country at the time – Beddington announced that he would not return until Forbes was removed. It was an example of the brinkmanship he was prepared to resort to if necessary, and he duly got his way.

The Ministry of Information's office circular no. 17 was a fine example of Civil Service finesse: 'Mr G. E. G. Forbes is being transferred on the 11th June from the Ministry to the Petroleum Department at the urgent request of that Department. He will be succeeded as Deputy Director, Films Division, by Mr A. G. Highet.'[16] As Beddington had himself just arrived from the petroleum world, for those in the know there was an irony to savour.

A lesser man might have allowed himself to be lulled along while he tried to find his feet in the strange new world of government service, and the British cinema owes a huge debt to Beddington for his early vigilance and determination to do things his own way. Mr Highet, his new deputy director, was the officer in charge of the GPO Film Unit, for which the MoI had recently become responsible. A select committee was due to report on the Ministry's activities and there was considerable pressure to cut costs. Highet's response was to emasculate the GPO Film Unit by ordering the dismissal of its most experienced staff. 'In view of the present policy in the Films Division under which the main work of production is a programme of theatrical shorts, I cannot justify the retention of highly-paid film directors,'* he declared in a memo dated 11 July 1940 (in fact, they were paid a pittance by film-industry standards and had been waiting for a pay rise for years).[17]

Beddington, cross not to have been consulted, asked his superior Eric Bamford – the Deputy Director General – that the instructions be rescinded. From the tone of his memo addressing the matter,[18] the DDG (as he was known) was clearly irritated that Beddington should so disrupt the smooth running of the department, but complied with his request. Beddington then commissioned a report on the unit's future and fashioned a policy which enabled it, as the reborn Crown Film Unit, to make some of the most memorable and – in terms of propaganda – effective films of the war. As for Highet, his services were soon found to be vitally needed in another division.

* The names on Highet's hitlist were: Alberto Cavalcanti, Harry Watt, Humphrey Jennings, Charles Hassé, Ralph Elton, Stewart McAllister, Fred Gamage, Julian Spiro, Gordon Hales and Joe Mendoza.

At the the MoI Films Division Beddington promoted Britain's cause with the same subtlety as he had petrol for Shell. If documentary film-makers were able to find a large popular audience with such feature-length films as *Target for Tonight*, *Desert Victory*, *Fires Were Started* and *Western Approaches*, it was because they were 'profusely financed and fanatically supported by Jack Beddington'.[19] But he also expertly harnessed the efforts of the commercial features industry.

The Films Division wielded huge influence over production. It controlled the allocation of film stock, it could secure the release of film technicians from the Services, and sanction the supply of scarce materials. So there was every incentive for production companies to make films that the Ministry approved of. It was a relationship of dependence that under someone less imaginative could easily have been stifling, but Beddington exploited it to encourage producers to make far more ambitious films than they would have done if left to their own devices.

He set up an 'ideas committee' which consisted of film-makers from both documentary and features. They would meet every two weeks, chat 'over beer and rather lousy sandwiches',[20] then go and watch some films. It took an individual of rare sensibility to appreciate the importance of mulling time in the middle of a war. Paul Rotha thought this informal discussion group was one of the chief reasons 'why the British feature film was beyond question at its best during the war years'.[21]

Beddington's skill at cutting through bureaucracy, and the pleasant change it made from the treatment film-makers more usually received from official quarters, is suggested by this note to him in the MoI's files from the actor David Niven (then an army officer), who had been trying to set up the production of *The Way Ahead*:

Just a note to thank you so much for all you have done to get this army picture made. Things certainly began to move when you arrived on the scene and I am very grateful to you. The pathetic thing is that the success of this particular picture depends almost entirely on our love and enthusiasm for the Service – well, the double crossing, the apathy and the general fiddling about that we encountered at the War Office during the two months immediately before you took a hand very nearly killed any wish to make the picture at all.[22]

One's impression is that Jack Beddington had a far greater affinity with the film-makers than he did with civil servants. In this respect his Jewish background was important. Having some knowledge of what it was like to be an outsider (which being a wartime amateur civil servant could only have accentuated), he could identify with the feeling that artists – whether painters, writers or film-makers – often have of struggling to do something that society at large neither understands nor cares about.

He found it natural to be their advocate. To some extent he even regarded it as a mission. Shortly before he died he compiled a catalogue devoted to 'Young Artists of Promise'. In his introduction, begging the reader's leave to get on one of his 'hobby horses', he wrote: 'I have never found that artists are either unpractical or difficult to get on with, or particularly dirty. Some are, but they are rarely the best ones. If they wear beards, why shouldn't they? If they like to have strange hats, why shouldn't they? If you will ignore this and remember that they are probably just as intelligent and just as hard-working and just as anxious to have a happy life as you are, you will probably find them very much easier to get on with. My experience has always been that they are infinitely more adjustable than businessmen.'[23]

But as director of the MoI Films Division it was not enough for him just to defend the character of film-makers, he also had to demonstrate that their contribution to the national cause justified public expenditure. That he was successful is shown by the fact that the Films Division produced over 800 films during the war. After victory in Europe, however, getting money out of the Treasury, which had always been difficult, became impossible.

When Beddington left the Films Division in early 1946, he wrote an article setting out his hopes for the future. The Civil Service 'must learn something of the ambitions and temperament of artists and craftsmen, must try to enter into their daily lives and treat with sympathy their imaginative ideas even if it takes time to make them practical'.[24] He suggested that short courses could be arranged during which civil servants and film-makers could 'get to know, to understand, and possibly even to like each other'.

The piece was typical of his efforts to bridge the gap between the artist and the rest of society. But with the professional bureaucrats firmly back in charge, the MOI made way for the ineffectual Central Office of Information and Beddington cannot have been surprised to see his recommendations ignored. Probably they were deemed Utopian by the very civil servants they were aimed at, but in any case only someone of his imagination and vitality could have implemented them.

He died in 1959. It was notable that tributes came from businessmen as well as film-makers, writers and artists. When the managing director of Shell wrote a tribute in *The Times*, he recalled that Beddington 'sometimes described himself as a frustrated artist'.[25] Perhaps there was an element of vicarious satisfaction that led him to encourage so many artists, but to do so was in any case an implicit part of his philosophy – his way of showing faith in humanity. Shortly before he died, he wrote of his admiration for artists: 'Their lives are to a certain extent dedicated to that frightening word Beauty. They do not go about the world inciting people to oppress others; they do not foment wars nor covet other people's goods. They delight in the play of light and shade and the skill of hands. They study their fellow men, usually with sympathy and insight. True, that what they see sometimes causes them great misery, but this they usually take out on themselves and not on others. I believe, in fact, that the aesthetic emotion can inspire a life as pure and spiritual and blessed as the religious.'[26] Applying this attitude to film-makers, Beddington had as much responsibility as anyone for the vitality of British cinema in the 1940s, and Michael Powell rightly called him 'one of the most unjustly forgotten men of the war'.[27]

'Puffin' Asquith

Anthony Asquith, or 'Puffin' as he had been known since child-hood, was one of the most loved men in British films. That is why it has been so hard to write about him. In describing the selfless integrity that he displayed, there is the inevitable danger of seeming dull, even though behind such conduct lay a man of considerable complexity.

A difficulty also lies in the fact that his background was so exceptional as to provide few reference points of common experience with which to explain him. His mother Margot was one of the great Society figures of the early twentieth century, famed for her wit and forthrightness. His father Herbert Asquith was Prime Minister of Great Britain from 1908 to 1916. During his most formative years – from the age of six to fourteen – he lived in 10 Downing Street. The last two of those years were overshadowed by the catastrophe of the First World War, in which one brother was killed and another badly shell-shocked. His father was forced to resign as Prime Minister over the conduct of the war, and imme-diately became embroiled in a political feud with his successor Lloyd George that would lead to the virtual collapse of the Liberal Party. These 'Great Events' left their mark on the young Asquith.

It was an upbringing of unique privilege but not one you would wish on anybody. The burden that the Great War placed on his family of all families meant that Puffin's childhood years were far from carefree. Instead, they instilled in him a sense of duty: his privilege was not something to enjoy, but to pay for, to live down. His dilemma was that of the high-born – how to find a sense of real achievement when one's material advantages have put the conventional trappings of success and status within easy grasp.

Puffin's answer lay in a single-minded altruism. But if his excellence of character was finally a more worthwhile achievement, it prejudiced his considerable gifts as a film director, making him hesitate to devote himself too completely to this calling. He loved films but was convinced that, in the greater scheme of things, they were unimportant. David Lean once said that Puffin was a fine director but too gentle to be a great director. But it was much more, I think, that he didn't *presume* to be a great director, that in his long career integrity and friendship and loyalty seemed more important. This attitude has a sad aspect, because – as his friend David Cecil would write in an obituary for *The Times* – 'his most precious and significant experiences were aesthetic'.[1]

To know the sublime, yet to live without it – Puffin had learnt this lesson from an early age. His first love was music, but he renounced his wish to be a composer because he did not think he had the talent. At home he played for friends songs he had written himself on a small upright piano. When he was directing, it was a part of his contract that a piano should be available for him to play in the intervals during set-ups. However much comfort it might have provided, its presence would have been a reminder that he had not quite made the grade. 'The thing that struck me most,' recalled Diana Menuhin, 'was his tremendous frustration. Here was somebody born to be a musician and hadn't the equipment and this perhaps was what gave him that truly deprecating quality.'[2]

Puffin's tendency was to lead a cerebral, ivory-tower life. He possessed a wistful manner that made him seem to his friends to be in a dream. 'When Puffin was in the room or Puffin was speaking, he brought some other time dimension into the room and into the conversation,' remembered Yehudi Menuhin. 'He did not belong to the ordinary world; he felt out of his element in it.'[3] This unease revealed itself in his manner. In company he was rarely still, but paced up and down as he discoursed distractedly on a range of subjects.

Puffin won scholarships to Winchester and Balliol, where he read Classics, only then to be one of the college's first scholars in living memory to fail to get a first. A new undergraduate enthusiasm that would no doubt have hampered his studies was film. During his four years at Oxford he haunted the cinemas, sometimes seeing three films a day. When a motion was put at the Oxford

Union 'that cinema degrades the mind', Puffin spoke against it. A trip after graduation to Hollywood with his sister Elizabeth fuelled his passion. There he was a guest of Douglas Fairbanks and Mary Pickford, and watched some of the great directors of the American silent cinema at work. He came back to England determined to get into the film business.

At the time it was an extraordinary aspiration for someone of his class to have, the cinema generally being frowned upon as a rather tawdry diversion for the masses, but this in itself may well have been part of its appeal. Puffin's background was so unusually rarefied that the movies offered for him not the escape from 'real life' that they represented for most of their audience but some contact with it, however tenuous. He was aware of his own withdrawn nature and sought to temper it. Throughout his life there was a continual tension between his aesthetic pursuits and his efforts to engage with the real world.

In November 1926 Bruce Woolfe, the production manager of the Stoll Film Company at Cricklewood, gave Puffin a job as a general assistant. Early duties included acting as stand-in for Lilian Hall Davies in the studio's production of *Boadicea*, driving her chariot dressed in a blond wig and a pale blue robe. But with the encouragement of Woolfe he was soon writing and directing his own scripts, and by the last days of the silent cinema he would be mentioned with Hitchcock as one of Britain's two leading film directors.

These early films revealed a keen visual sense, an enthusiasm for German expressionist cinema and a willingness to experiment. But Puffin struggled to find satisfying stories. The films he made for Woolfe, at Stoll and then, with the coming of sound, at British Instructional, were conventional in subject matter, and the admiration of many reviewers was tempered by their awareness of this.

'The acting is excellent throughout and the photography is admirable,' the *New York Times* wrote of his last silent film, *Cottage on Dartmoor* (1929). 'His admirers are convinced that Anthony Asquith will in course of time make a great film. Everybody hopes he will; but at present he gives the impression of not exactly knowing what he wants to do.'[4] His first sound film, *Tell England* (1931), was based – in the words of one commentator – on a 'painfully class-conscious novel'[5] by Ernest Raymond about the

Gallipoli landings. 'No war film yet produced has been more convincing than these scenes of the landings,' wrote Paul Rotha. 'It is all the more unfortunate that such brilliantly produced scenes should have to be intermixed with a story of such poorness, in fact with a story of any kind. Yet again we who care for the cinema have to submit to the sight of splendid material being pulled down to the depths of bathos by the introduction of story-interest.'[6]

'If that boy ever gets a story you will see the film of your life,' Robert Flaherty commented after seeing *Dance Pretty Lady* (1931), Puffin's last film for British Instructional.[7] Maybe Puffin would eventually have found his story had he been able to stay on at the company that had nurtured him – he had been quietly developing his skills as a writer-director and was planning a film called *Covent Garden* set in the Royal Opera House, a subject which was obviously close to his heart. But in 1931 the studio was merged with British International Pictures and Puffin's friend and mentor Bruce Woolfe left the company.

Puffin joined Gaumont-British in 1932, but was offered few suitable opportunities. 'We already employed several well-known directors,' commented Michael Balcon, who was then in charge of production, 'and I suppose they had the first choice of subjects.'[8] Much of Puffin's time was spent idle, and when he did work the circumstances were not those he would have chosen. While still at British Instructional he had declared in a newspaper article, 'I have always written my own screenplays, and it seems to me to be an absolute necessity for a director to do so,'[9] but the two films he directed at Gaumont-British were assignments from other people's scripts, and when he was given the job of directing the location unit on *Forever England* (1935) it must have felt like a demotion.

Why was he overlooked? Puffin's reputation was so considerable when he joined Gaumont-British that it is difficult to take Balcon's explanation at face value. A possible answer is that the enthusiastic support of his famous mother – who regularly turned up to watch her son direct – was more a hindrance than a help. Clearly unhappy at Gaumont-British, Puffin applied for a job at the BBC soon after the television service was set up in 1936. According to Dallas Bower, one of the BBC's first TV producers, the then director of television Gerald Cock turned him down because he did not want to have to put up with the disruptive influence of Lady Oxford. Perhaps Balcon had felt the same.

The setbacks of the 1930s would have schooled Puffin in the harsh realities of commercial film-making and tempered his idealism. So far from being an 'absolute necessity' he came to find that writing one's own screenplays was a rare luxury for a film director – that even to feel halfway comfortable with the assignments that producers might offer him was fortunate indeed.

In 1938 Puffin's fortunes took a dramatic change for the better when he was engaged to direct *Pygmalion*. The film's huge international success restored his reputation as one of Britain's leading directors. It also set the pattern of his future career. Henceforth he did not push forward his own vision, but became an interpreter of other people's material. The most important partnership, which would last the remainder of his career, was with the writer-producer Anatole de Grunwald and the playwright Terence Rattigan. The three, who were associated for the first time on *French Without Tears* in 1939, would work together on and off for the next thirty years.

The inevitable tendency of many critics was to regard Rattigan as the prime creative force. Puffin's own identity became subsumed, and over time he suffered a kind of typecasting in critics' minds that did his reputation no good at all. So David Thomson, writing in the 1970s, could describe him in his *Biographical Dictionary of the Cinema* as 'a dull, journeyman supervisor of the transfer to the screen of proven theatrical qualities'. It was an obvious but grotesquely unfair criticism that said more about the prejudices of a later generation in love with the idea of the *auteur* than it did about Puffin's abilities as a director.

While such adaptations hardly stretched Puffin, some sensitive critics appreciated the qualities he contributed. Writing in the *Spectator*, Graham Greene described *French Without Tears* as 'a triumph for Mr Anthony Asquith', whose 'witty direction and firm handling of the cast . . . conquer the too British sexuality of Mr Rattigan's farce'.[10] The piece's 'English levity', he went on, 'would be unbearable if it were not for Mr Asquith's civilized direction (unlike most adaptations from stage plays it is the padding that is memorable).' What Puffin Asquith could bring to often indifferent material was a poise and a restraint, a gentle humour and a quiet sense of realism that could make stock situations and characters believable.

189

Just as Hitchcock's career can be conveniently divided into his British and American periods, Puffin's falls into pre-Rattigan and post-Rattigan phases. In the first he wrote his own scripts, often cut his own films, was what the French would have called an *auteur*. In the second he brought to the screen the works of other people; he was a *metteur en scène*. In the change one can trace a coming to terms with the realities of the British film industry, which his years of unemployment would certainly have impressed upon him. But I think there was also a degree of willing self-effacement, and a sense of community that made him want to fit in with the prevailing system.

Puffin's approach was founded on a fundamental respect for his source material. 'The aim,' he wrote, was 'to preserve the essence of the play while recreating in a different medium.'[11] It may have seemed a lesser skill to some critics, but it allowed him to develop as a film-maker in a direction that had been neglected before. Previously noted for his technical virtuosity, now he concentrated on truth of performance.

Puffin thought deeply about his craft. Among his papers in the British Film Institute Library can be found several rough notebooks dating from the early 1940s. In these he used to scrawl, in a soft and scarcely legible pencil, ideas for the films he was working on, bits of diary, drafts of letters or articles. A perusal gives some insight into his state of mind at the time. When he wrote the following, perhaps to some extent he was thinking of his younger self.

> It is a great temptation, even for the experienced director – to the young it is irresistible – to devise something about which he can say with misplaced pride: '*That* has never been done before.' If he is referring to a new technical trick which has not arisen out of the necessity of the scene, then to be the first has no more merit than to be the first man to walk backwards down Piccadilly, singing 'Land of Hope and Glory' in a minor key. A director is only the first to do something when he produces a richly imagined scene, even if the technique has been used a thousand times before, because the only thing in art that is really new is something new-born and living.

*

In a profession where by and large we expect directors to be self-seeking and even a little ruthless, Puffin was extraordinary for habitually going out of his way to help other people. Muriel Box, then a continuity girl at British Instructional, was laid off with the arrival of the talkies. On hearing this Puffin at once offered both his commiserations and money to tide her over until she found another job. She refused, but accepted his offer to write her a personal recommendation. She remembered his letter as 'a glowing overstatement' of her experience and abilities, but it gave her the courage to write to other studios.[12] When the editor and producer Sidney Cole was trying to get into the film industry in the early 1930s Puffin was one of the people he wrote to. Puffin met him and offered what advice he could.

In the early 1930s he was the first director to join the film technicians' trade union, the ACT, and – in the words of the union's then general secretary George Elvin – did so 'not for what he could get out of it, but for what he could put into it, in fact to help other members'.[13] At that early point in the union's history, before it had been properly established, it was a brave act of solidarity. 'Some members were victimized in those days for being active Trade Unionists,' remembered Elvin, 'but that didn't deter Asquith although, whilst he never spoke about it, he was more than once on the receiving end of the pressures.'[14]

Why did Puffin become so involved? Sidney Cole, who was a leading figure in the union, conjectured that he was aware of his privileged upbringing and wanted to give something back.[15] I think this is true. But I think also that the difficulties Puffin had experienced in achieving his own ambitions – whether to be a musician or to realize his full potential as a film director – bred a strong fellow feeling. He knew how painful it was to have one's aspirations thwarted.

A noble resignation characterized his life. It was perhaps underpinned by the fact that he was homosexual at a time when society was intolerant of homosexuals. If, as seems to have been the case, he sought to suppress this tendency, it was yet one more sacrifice that he had to come to terms with.

In May 1937 Puffin became president of the union, a position he held – with one brief interlude – until his death thirty-one years later. It was not a position that he had sought; he undertook it at the union's request. It was a key time for the film industry, which was in the midst of a severe slump, and facing the expiry of the 1927 Quota Act. Having revealed itself to be anything but viable, in spite of the help of the quota, many felt that the film industry did not deserve any further protection.

Puffin, who had the huge advantage of knowing most of the government ministers socially, spearheaded the lobbying for the renewal of an improved Act, enlisting the powerful support of his mother. 'If the ministers weren't prepared to accept our arguments,' remembered Puffin's fellow campaigner, the film director Thorold Dickinson, 'she went for them, denounced them for not having the sense to see how important films were to the country, for they did not just entertain, they educated the public and showed the world what Britain was able to do. She was a stalwart fighter – a crusader in fact.'[16] On the surface so unalike, mother and son had in common a tenaciousness.

Puffin's first assignment of the war was a propaganda film called *Freedom Radio* (1940). It told the story of a Viennese doctor who sets up an underground radio station to fight against Nazism, while his wife accepts a post in the Party. The film was remarkable for its honesty. At a time when Nazis portrayed on the screen were invariably gross caricatures of evil, it provided an intelligent insight into how decent people could become seduced by fascism.

Puffin's next film, *Quiet Wedding* (1941), was an inconsequential return to the light comedy of *French Without Tears*. He then embarked on a four-film contract for Gainsborough. They were conventional subjects with uneven scripts, but his sincerity of approach brought moments of real distinction. In *We Dive at Dawn* (1943), the story of a British submarine attack on a German battleship, the early domestic scenes of the men on leave were marred by cliché and stock types, but the scenes on board the submarine itself are gripping and brilliantly cinematic.

Notes Puffin made on the source novel of another of his Gainsborough assignments give some insight into the sort of constraints he would routinely have had to deal with. 'The main danger of *Fanny by Gaslight* (1944) is not of impoverishing the characters by simplification. They are already simple, and not particularly subtly analysed. Indeed to give them reasonably accurate incarnation would I think add to their life. The difficulty is first of all compressing a diffuse and rambling narrative into reasonable length and giving that narrative a strong story which it lacks.'[17]

Away from Gainsborough he would find the conditions to work more freely. *The Demi-Paradise*, made in 1943, was written and produced by de Grunwald for Two Cities. It is the story of

Ivan Kouznetsoff, a Soviet engineer who invents a new propeller and comes to England to oversee its manufacture. The visitor is at first infuriated and puzzled by the ways of his hosts, but then gradually comes to appreciate them. It is a curious film, which hovers between gentle satire and occasionally awkward caricature, leaving the viewer sometimes confused as to which is intended. But finally – much in the way of the Russian visitor – one is won over by its tolerance, affection and *Englishness*. This is what we English are like, it seems to say. We have our virtues and mean well, however peculiar we may seem. In the context of the time the visit of the Russian was an opportunity to show goodwill to a new ally, and the fact that Anatole de Grunwald was himself Russian would have lent a candour to the exercise, but it was really a pretext in a quiet way to celebrate being English.

Explaining the English became something of an Asquith speciality. *Welcome to Britain*, made in the same year, was very much a documentary companion piece to *The Demi-Paradise*. Made for the Ministry of Information, the film's purpose was to provide American troops with an introduction to the country. Asquith devised and directed the film in collaboration with Burgess Meredith – this Anglo-American partnership a counterpart to the Anglo-Russian one he had had with Anatole de Grunwald. Meredith acts as a guide to the British, visiting homes, schools and pubs and explaining the native customs. 'A brilliant little elucidation of character,' commented the *New Statesman and Nation*.[18] 'Anthony Asquith ... has drawn his types with great restraint and truth,' wrote Richard Winnington in the *News Chronicle*.[19]

Without actively looking for it, Asquith was finding a subject and an approach that suited him. He had discovered the English, and the detachment of his own ivory-tower life lent his observations an engaging quality of disinterested affection. As in so many other cases the catalyst of war had served to release his talents. He was, as many critics described him, a kind of 'English René Clair', but a gentler and more dreamy one.

The English at war provided Asquith with a continuity of theme that ran through *The Demi-Paradise* and *Welcome to Britain* to *The Way to the Stars*. This last was a near masterpiece, if flawed by the artificial yoking together of two themes.

In 1942 Asquith had directed on the stage Terence Rattigan's play *Flare Path*, which focused on the drama of the home front – as the wives of RAF pilots wait for them to return from a night raid over Germany. Rattigan had written the play while serving as a gunnery officer in the RAF. Then in 1943 he was commissioned, under the aegis of the MoI, to work with the American screenwriter Richard Sherman on a script about a British airbase which is handed over to the American airforce. *Rendezvous*, as the project was called, was part of the MoI's effort to promote Anglo-American relations. In the event this film was never made.

The Way to the Stars (1945) drew on Rattigan's play and the shelved *Rendezvous* script. The join is visible. The first half of the film – the *Flare Path* part – is set in the early years of the war and deals with the lives of the RAF officers and their loved ones. The second – the *Rendezvous* part – begins with the arrival of American airmen, and traces the bonds of friendship they come to share with their hosts after initial misunderstanding and antagonism. It is skilfully grafted, but its propaganda purpose is too obvious for it to fit naturally into an organic whole. The Hollywood-style heroism of the ending in particular strikes a false note, all the more apparent for the realism and poetic restraint of the English part of the film. Returning from a mission, the American pilot Johnny Hollis disregards instructions to bail out and steers his crippled, bomb-laden plane away from a nearby village, sacrificing his life.

But the handling of the English material is flawless and I can think of nothing that surpasses it for pathos. The central story is simple. When the squadron leader is killed, leaving behind a widow and young child, his friend and fellow pilot vows never to marry, breaking off a relationship with the girl he loves. The emotional force lies in showing people who usually lived comfortable, untroubled lives under threat. However much of a cliché the romantic theme might have seemed, it captured the tragic essence of wartime. When death was so near, courtship and marriage took on renewed significance as precious symbols of life.

The RAF pilots skirt routine tragedy with a forced calm, using banter and euphemism to shut away their pain. So much meaning lay in the unsaid, and Puffin managed to find the perfect visual expression of these wordless emotions. 'Toddy', played by Rosamund John, tries out her wedding dress and looks at herself in a mirror with a bride's last-minute worry over her appearance.

Her expression chills as she hears the sound of an aircraft's engines and then, with an effort of will, she regains her composure. Fifty years on, this sequence is still ineffably moving.

'The best of cinema,' wrote Thorold Dickinson, 'like music, is usually indescribable in words.'[20] The English part of *The Way to the Stars* is certainly the best of cinema and Asquith's feel for music is plain in the flair with which he marries images with words – uses music itself to underline and counterpoint the narrative.

Indeed his whole approach to the cinema was conceived in musical terms. 'I score my effects just as one orchestrates a symphony,' he once explained in an interview. 'There are all the emotions of a sonata in a film; one has the *scherzo* passages, the *andantes*, the *allegro* and *appassionata* and *rallentando* effects not merely in the action but in the actual photography of the scenes, in the treatment of lighting and shade and right emphasis. It is this rhythm which makes the beauty and balance of a film.'[21]

'The nearest he could come to music', Yehudi Menuhin observed of Puffin, 'was in the creative art of the film.'[22] It was a vicarious way of being the composer he had always wanted to be. 'I remember "Puffin" Asquith calling at my room at the end of the second day's shooting,' wrote Michael Redgrave in recollection of *The Way to the Stars*, 'and lending me Donald Tovey's book on the Concerto, which has the following: "One of the first essentials of creative art is the habit of imagining the most familiar things as vividly as the most surprising." I cannot now recall whether it was he or I who underlined those words, but they sum up rather well what he did and what made the film memorable.'[23]

The Way to the Stars was shot not in a film studio, but in an RAF base near Catterick in Yorkshire that had just been decommissioned (which perhaps inspired the haunting opening shots as the camera wanders through the empty buildings). The actors and technicians lived on the airbase. With 'its corridors spotlessly painted in regulation cream, its narrow beds hard and yet unbelievably comfortable', the camp reminded Michael Redgrave of his time in the Royal Navy earlier in the war. 'To tumble into such a bed at night after an evening spent in the Sergeants' Mess, or with the WAAFs in the village pub, was to be transported back two and a half years to the first few weeks of my naval training at Plymouth. The same indescribable friendliness, the same wartime atmosphere of living for the moment.'[24]

One marvels at the depth of feeling with which Puffin conveyed the domestic tragedy of war, its effect on those left back home, but it was something that he would have had personal experience of. Doubtless, in *his* memories he was transported back considerably further, to the First World War and the news of his half-brother's death, here described by his mother Margot in her diary:[25]

> The moment I took up the telephone I said to myself, 'Raymond is killed.'
>
> With the receiver in my hand, I asked what it was and if the news was bad.
>
> Our secretary, Davies, answered. 'Terrible, terrible news. Raymond was shot dead on the 15th . . . he was shot leading his men the moment he had gone over the parapet.'
>
> I put back the receiver and sat down. I heard Elizabeth's delicious laugh, and a hum of talk and smell of cigars came down the passage from the dining-room.
>
> I went back into the sitting-room.
>
> 'Raymond is dead,' I said, 'he was shot leading his men over the top on Friday.'
>
> Puffin got up from his game and hanging his head took my hand.

When in *The Way to the Stars* Toddy is told of the death of her husband on a raid over Germany, it was an echo of this reality.

It was the familiar things that made *The Way to the Stars* a great film. The film faltered only where it strayed away from the personal key. Puffin may well have realized these failings, but with the sense of co-operation that was second nature to him he would have accepted them as the necessary compromise of working within the system.

He offered a perceptive insight into that system in an article for the *Penguin Film Review*:

> A man who makes a film must spend, literally, thousands. Therefore films, unless they are made by the State or quixotic millionaires, must be made by companies. Companies aim at profits for their shareholders, so they cannot be blamed for playing safe – underrating the taste and intelligence of their

public. Economically this may be excusable: aesthetically it must be deplorable; and yet is not this the reason why the film is the only example of popular art – art where the unbridgeable chasm between art with a capital A and mere popular entertainment has not been irrevocably dug – where some artists create for the intelligent few while a mass of artisans cater for the unintelligent, undiscriminating many? And this, surely, gives the film immense strength, because whatever it may lose in intellectual quality and even in subtleties which properly belong to it, its gains in vitality are out of all proportion. Its material is the stuff of the imagination of the people, and the director must take advantage of that fact and, if strong enough, master and mould that stuff into a work of art.[26]

Reading Puffin's words, one is struck by his democratic spirit. For all its compromises, he loved the cinema because it was an art that belonged to the people. He was a complex man who wanted to be simple. His life was a paradox. He continued to live with his mother in a large house in Bedford Square, where guests included the King and Queen, but felt happiest in the company of the technicians on the film set. Maybe it was the knowledge that he could never completely resolve these two worlds that inspired in him a humility. Reminiscences suggest an almost monastic quality. When he was directing films he would wear a blue boiler-suit – all the more striking because the members of a film unit in those days dressed formally in jackets and ties.*

In April 1945 Puffin's sister Elizabeth died at the age of only forty-eight. Married to the Romanian Prince Bibesco, she lived during the war in Bucharest and the Asquiths had been looking forward to the reunion that peace would bring. Three months later Puffin's mother died. The double bereavement shook him badly, and in the years that followed he drank heavily. But a surprising new friendship would eventually provide a new stability. When he was directing *The Way to the Stars* at Catterick, he would often go to a café for lorry drivers, and there he became

* One of the more objectionable travesties of character that occurs in David Thomson's mostly admirable *Biographical Dictionary of Film* is to write that Asquith 'affected a boilersuit'. He was the last person on earth to 'affect' anything.

197

friends with the proprietor, Joe Jones, who was a former regimental sergeant-major and had a wife and two young children. Puffin would eventually become an extra member of the family, spending weekends and holidays there.

It was a great story for the newspapers. 'To the lorry drivers on the Great North Road,' wrote a *Daily Mirror* reporter in 1950, 'the dishwasher in Joe's transport café at Old Catterick is just Tony. At Catterick airfield he is the newsboy in baggy corduroys and sloppy pullover who comes round with the morning newspapers at 6.30. But you may know him better as the Hon. Anthony Asquith, film director son of Lord Asquith. He is all three. For when Mr Asquith gets bored with the beauty of films stars and cocktails at film premieres, he turns into dishwasher, newsboy Tony.'[27] The relationship, which lasted until the end of Puffin's life, was far more profound than the tone of the piece suggested, and offered a contact with reality that he could not otherwise find.

In his career Puffin seemed content to continue adapting Rattigan's plays for the screen, none of which had the sense of purpose and cogency of *The Way to the Stars*. It was an under-use of his talents, but in some way, one senses, served a wider purpose. Perhaps he came to regard his aesthetic aspirations as a sort of vanity. Of *While the Sun Shines* (1947), a minor Rattigan farce, Richard Winnington wrote in the *News Chronicle*, 'There are brief delightful moments when one recognizes the hand of Anthony Asquith, but they are all too few and too brief.'

Puffin's own comments on the film suggest that he would have been quite happy if his presence had been completely invisible. 'A good director – or at least a director who knows his job – can adapt his technique and ideas to the differing subjects of each new film. Perfection requires that his style always be apparent, but directors reach perfection only rarely. The film version of *While the Sun Shines* sets out to make audiences laugh, and it succeeded, I am told, admirably in this purpose.'[28] The notion of 'making audiences laugh' being enough in itself would, I think, have appealed to Puffin – it was another example of the simplicity he yearned for as a counterbalance to his own sophistication. His career in films became a renunciation of elitism. Entertaining a mass audience was more important to him than being an artist treasured by just a select few.

'You might say he gave himself to the cinema,' wrote Dilys Powell in an appreciation of Puffin after his death, 'not only as an artist but as a servant.'[29]

Sydney Box

If at all, Sydney Box is perhaps best remembered for making *The Seventh Veil* and for running Gainsborough Studios in the late 1940s. I knew he had also at one time been a journalist and thought I would try to find out if he had had any books published. I sat down at a computer terminal in the British Library and called up the 'General Retrospective Catalogue of Printed Books'. When I typed in Sydney Box's name, a message flashed up: 'LARGE NUMBER OF ENTRIES: Your search has found over 30 entries.' I declined the invitation to 'refine' my search, and brought up the long list of his works that either in partnership with his wife Muriel, or by himself, he was responsible for. There were countless plays that he had written with Muriel, and as many more that he had written alone – *The Woman and the Walnut Tree: A Modern Play in Six Scenes* or *Blossom Time: A Musical Play in Two Acts*, and so on. Then there was Sydney Box the writer of film companions and technical guides – for example, in 1937, *Film Publicity: A Handbook on the Production and Distribution of Propaganda Films*; and then – but nowhere nearly finally – Sydney Box the writer of crime novels – *Alibi in the Rough, Second Only to Murder*.

All this activity. But Jack of all trades as he certainly was, one feels that if he had wished he could certainly have been a master of one, two, or possibly even three. *The Seventh Veil* (1945), with Ann Todd as a concert pianist and James Mason as her overbearing guardian, was a brilliant example of popular film-making. Box produced, wrote the Oscar-winning script with his wife Muriel, and helped Bob Compton-Bennett – a newcomer to features – to direct.

The film was a big success in America, and looked so lavish

that Hollywood producers visiting England were amazed that such a film could have been made in the small Riverside Studios in Hammersmith. They would have been even more amazed had they been around to witness the conditions of its production. In the winter of 1944–5 V1s and V2s were raining down on the capital. As London struggled to cope with the arrival of these deadly visitors, shrapnel riddled the studio roof with holes, rain dripped on to the sets, and sound recording was disrupted by explosions or the wail of sirens. The chaos caused by the destruction of nearby buildings and bomb craters in the road meant that just getting to the studio became a major effort. Yet the film – which featured Britain's biggest box-office star – cost only £92,000. It was an example of Box's ability to overcome obstacles and make the most of meagre resources.

The Box family lived in Beckenham, Kent. Frank Sydney was born with a congenital dislocation of the hip. He shared the same name as his father, who was a keen sportsman. Although these circumstances may have made the young Sydney more than usually aware of his handicap, his response was characteristically positive. If he was unable to compete with his father physically, his disability seemed to spur an extraordinary mental energy.

At fourteen he became a sportswriter for the local papers. Sydney's sister Betty Box – who would become a notable producer in her own right – remembers that the letter offering the job had originally been sent to their father. He 'just threw the letter back on the table to my mother and said, "Oh, tell them I can't do it, I haven't got time for that." Sydney waited until he was gone and said, "I can do that." '[1] In the years ahead always the hardest admission for Sydney would be that he did not have the time or something was beyond him. It was one that he would very rarely have to make.

The young Box was also an enthusiastic member of the local amateur dramatic society, writing and producing plays and revues. When he was eighteen, he put on the six-hour-long *Peer Gynt* in its entirety. Betty Box remembers that he approached a man called David Greig, who was the owner of a local chain of grocery shops: would Mr Greig like to offer some financial assistance in view of his family connection with the author of the play? Whether this was cheek or teenage ignorance, the application was successful. The story is revealing not just as an example of

Sydney's enterprise, but because of his assumption that a man would want to help his relations in this way. He would later run his film company like a family business, involving both his wife and sister.

An important motivation for Sydney was the awareness that his family were not well off, and he did what he could to contribute to the household finances. One such venture was opening a string of station confectionery kiosks in Beckenham and Bromley, which Betty Box remembered was moderately successful. Bill MacQuitty, who worked with Sydney in the 1940s and became his business partner, told me perhaps the most poignant story of Sydney's early days. At the age of fourteen or fifteen, he helped to run a travelling aeroplane show. When the condition of the grass field that served as a runway made taking off difficult, in spite of his lameness he would do all he could to get the plane aloft, running along and pushing from behind.

In the course of his life Sydney Box passed so swiftly through a succession of varied challenges that it seems particularly appropriate that he should also have been a prolific writer of one-act plays. He not only wrote them but judged them, travelling to amateur theatre competitions all over the country. At one such festival at the Welwyn Theatre in 1932 he met a young script editor, Muriel Baker, who would become his collaborator and his wife.

His greatest success in the theatre came when his one-act play *Not This Man* won the British Drama League's National Festival at the Old Vic in 1935. When the actor Michael Hordern wrote in a newspaper that it was blasphemous, the ever resourceful Sydney sued him. He conducted the case himself as he couldn't afford a lawyer. He lost, but didn't mind as he thought it worth the publicity.

Sydney had shown no particular interest in films when he was growing up, but the extraordinary scope of his activities meant that he was bound to come across them sooner rather than later. Soon after his success with *Not This Man* the writer-director Ralph Smart, who was making a documentary for a company called Publicity Films, asked him if he would write the commentary. Sydney accepted and the assignment led to regular work. Within a matter of months, when most people would probably have felt that they had scarcely begun their apprenticeship, he was writing a book on his new profession. *Film Publicity*, published in 1937, was a handbook on the production and distribution of propaganda films – the word 'propaganda' was commonly used to refer to sponsored films whether documentaries or commercials. In a foreword Sydney was described as a 'Master in the Art of Film Publicity' who spoke 'with authority and wisdom'.[2] This description was certainly overstating the case, but a perusal reveals the manual to be full of refreshing common sense. Maybe it was precisely because he *wasn't* a 'Master' that he could write with an attractive broadmindedness. In summing up the tangle of personalities who fell under that misleading term 'documentary', Sydney cut through to the nub of the matter with a clarity that eluded most of the so-called experts:

> The quickest way to set half a dozen people connected with films quarrelling is to collect them together in one room and ask them to define 'documentary' . . . Today the documentary-realist group is producing story-films, ballets, cartoons, utilising hosts of unreal and undocumented effects. Its members (and the film industry has every reason to be thankful for it) are unblushingly experimental . . . All this pother over labels must not be allowed to obscure the fact that the members of this group are the most progressive force in the cinema today.[3]

With the publication of his book, Sydney's genius for moonlighting had reached its zenith: at roughly the same time he was working for Publicity Films, he was sub-editing for London's *Evening Standard* and *Evening News*, he was doing his sports column, he was writing another column for children under the name 'Uncle Sydney', he was writing his plays with Muriel, and he was also editing the *Christian Herald*. This last was 'just another job', recalled his sister. 'He saw it advertised, and he said he felt he could do that in what he called his spare time.'[4]

In the atmosphere of increasing uncertainty just before the war, the documentary work dried up. But Sydney with his usual entrepreneurial flair thought up a way of taking advantage of the moment. *The Black-out Book* would be a collection of games, puzzles, jokes, *pensées* and literary quotations to while away the hours during the pitch-dark wartime nights. The Boxes approached a publisher, who agreed to publish it if they could finish the manuscript in time for the Christmas demand. It came out in November 1939 and quickly sold out.

Muriel Box described Sydney as possessing 'a sanguine, buoyant temperament which helped him take everything in his stride with the minimum of fuss'.[5] Although it's impossible to be entirely certain which of the contributions in *The Black-out Book* he was responsible for, his presence can be detected in the general tone of unquenchable optimism. Perhaps he had a hand in this rhyming reflection on rationing: 'At first, I must admit the prospect seemed a little glum, / and then I reconsidered it, and found the time had come / to count the many things I knew would never be "cut down" / the kind of things we may forget through living in a town. / You may not have the petrol to run a motor-car, / but courage is a spirit that will get you just as far . . .' Then there were the maps of the constellations which appeared under the title 'You can't black-out the stars!'[6]

Making the most of the moment again, he set up a documentary company in the autumn of 1940. After the indecision of the first months of the war the Films Division of the Ministry of Information had at last found a sense of purpose. There was a large and consistent demand for propaganda and information films. Two years later Verity Films was the largest producer of documentary films in the country, with more than ten units working simultaneously.

Thinking up ideas for films, negotiating deals, writing scripts, supervising other people's, organizing the schedules of so many productions, and coping with all the difficulties of wartime when materials and experienced staff were hard to find – it was the sort of workload to cause nervous breakdowns in other people, but still it seemed not to be enough for Sydney. The offer to produce a film version of Frederick Lonsdale's comedy *On Approval* for the actor Clive Brook was a particularly enticing one. It was an opportunity to cross over into features: he and Muriel had written many one-act plays together, and it had been a long-held ambition of theirs to film their own scripts.

The production did not get off to a good start. The director Brian Desmond Hurst and the cameraman Günther Krampf, who had worked on such German Expressionist films as *Nosferatu*, *The Hands of Orlac* and *Pandora's Box*, were better suited to dramatic subjects, as indeed was the great German screenwriter Carl Mayer who was helping Hurst with the script.

The first scene in the schedule took place in the kitchen of a gloomy Scottish castle. Clive Brook was required to enter through a door on the left with a candle in his hand, to sit on the kitchen table, then cross over to the sink to talk to his co-star Googie Withers. Krampf took an age to light this simple scene in a heavy Germanic style at odds with the demands of a light and sophisticated comedy. Then, during the first take, Brian Desmond Hurst, impatient with yet more fussing, this time from Clive Brook, insulted him so badly that he walked off the set. Over the next few days many more rows between star and director followed.* Sydney resigned himself to the inevitable, sacking Krampf and Hurst. Claude Friese-Greene was taken on as a replacement cameraman, and since there was no money for a new director, Sydney and Clive Brook decided to direct the film themselves.

Bill MacQuitty, who worked closely with Sydney Box for twenty-five years, felt that such desperate circumstances were the kind of situation in which he thrived. 'To him the problem would be the ideal thing because he would fix it.'[7] But it can't have helped that Sydney had agreed to produce another feature film, *The Flemish Farm*, for Two Cities at the same time as *On Approval*, and there were signs of strain. In the last week of shooting Sydney and Clive Brook fell out. Sydney told Brook that he could take the production and direction credits, and finish the picture as he saw fit.

Against all odds, as there had been nothing to laugh about during its production, *On Approval* was hailed as a first-class screen comedy. Even Lindsay Anderson, witheringly dismissive of most of the British cinema's offerings, called it 'the funniest British comedy ever made' in an article he wrote for *Sequence* in 1948,[8] and forty years later he was urging me to try to see it. In his article he cited it as a welcome example of the kind of independent, small-scale productions that were so rare in the British cinema of the period. 'They date less, or less damagingly, than more elaborate productions, because they have not compromised with the fashions and prejudices of their time: execution has followed from conception, not from the demands of box office. They remain fresh, spontaneous, individual.'

Sydney Box deserves enormous credit for being one of the very few producers courageous enough to attempt to make films with such a spirit of independence. After producing two more films for

* 'I can't stand his clacking teeth in the love scenes,' Brian Desmond Hurst explained to Bill MacQuitty, who was Sydney Box's assistant on the production.

Two Cities, *English Without Tears* and *Don't Take it to Heart*, he took out a lease on the Riverside Studios in Hammersmith in 1943 in order to produce his own features. He raised £45,000 to make *29 Acacia Avenue*, a light comedy about a young woman who arranges a liaison with her fiancé in her parents' home when they go away on holiday, only to be thwarted by their early return. Box had proceeded on the understanding that the Rank Organisation would be the distributor, but when Arthur Rank saw the film, he declared it to be immoral as it set a bad example to young people. Rank's offer to pay the costs of the film if it was left on the shelf was refused as it would have let down all the people who had been involved.

In spite of turning down Rank's money, Sydney went ahead with the next film planned for Riverside Studios. Somehow he had to scrape together the finance for *The Seventh Veil* while at the same time finding another distributor for *29 Acacia Avenue*. It was a situation few people would have had the courage to face.

Production began on *The Seventh Veil* before all the necessary money was in place. The creditors were kept at bay 'by a process of financial jugglery at which Sydney excelled'.[9] But there was another hurdle. No leading man could be found to play the role of Ann Todd's cruel guardian. 'We started filming without a leading man,' Todd recalled, 'and worked for three weeks while Sydney tried desperately to find one. I was practically unknown in films, especially in America, and no one wished to play with me . . . Sydney gathered us together and said that we couldn't go on unless the money was forthcoming and we had a star.'[10]

Todd prayed for a miracle and within a week it arrived in the form of James Mason, who had become one of Britain's biggest stars after *The Man in Grey* in 1943. It was an extraordinary coup to persuade him to become involved in such a small film, with an as yet incomplete budget. Perhaps the difference was made by the fact that Mason would have had some fellow feeling for Box. He had once been a small independent producer himself.

Before the war, he had made a film called *I Met a Murderer* with Roy and Pamela Kellino (who would later become Mason's wife). The British film industry had been suffering one of its more severe slumps, and, pooling together £4,500, the three decided that the only escape from their unemployment was to make a film of their own. Although Pamela Kellino was the daughter of one of the Ostrer brothers who owned Gaumont-British, they refused to distribute the film and their lack of interest scared off other potential distributors. Eventually the film played to excellent reviews in New York. The experience left Mason deeply disenchanted with the commercial industry.

'I will always support and encourage the practice of film-making on a strictly amateur level,' wrote Mason, reflecting on the experience. 'The technical side of film-making gets easier every year, and in the commercial world the content of film-making becomes more and more restricted by the fancied requirements of merchandizing. The intelligent and cultural future of films is in the hands of amateur film societies. At least that is one of my pet theories. The work that we put into this small project is a memory that I cherish.'[11]

Sydney Box's efforts were of course far from being 'strictly amateur', but they were in the spirit of what Mason had tried to do himself. Mason would have been drawn to Box as an individual risking his own money, rather than an executive implementing the production programme of a faceless corporation, and he would have known all too well the difficulties that Sydney, as a comparative minnow in Wardour Street, would have had to face.

As a contract star at Gainsborough Mason felt a deep contempt both for the studio's output of escapist melodramas and for the executives he deemed responsible for such mediocrity. 'To me producers were men who polluted the artistic aspirations of writers, directors and actors, who responded only to the promptings of vulgar men in Wardour Street.'[12] Working for Sydney, Mason was pleasantly surprised to discover that one could make friends with a producer. 'When he paid his daily visit to the set where we were working his beaming presence gave the impression that for him each new day was a new adventure.' At last Mason had the satisfaction of having his opinions respected and being made to feel part of a rewarding creative process.

Ann Todd felt the same. She remembered the original script the Boxes sent her as 'avant-garde and experimental'. Her character, the concert pianist, was the only person to appear on the screen; the others were to be filmed 'in shadow "voices-off" and reflections in the piano and mirrors'.[13] When she told the Boxes that she lacked the confidence to carry the role by herself, they rewrote the script to show the other characters in a more conventional way, and adapted it to her own life.

Ann Todd's father had wanted her to be a good pianist, and one of her most painful childhood memories was of humiliation when she was to play the piano at a school concert. 'My hands were clammy. I felt sick. When my name was called I prayed to be allowed to faint. I sat down at the piano that seemed to envelop me and started to play. Seven seconds after the beginning my fingers became numb and my mind seemed to float away. I stopped and murmured, "I'm sorry." ' She tried twice more, but each time the same thing happened. 'I left the hated piano and ran back through the audience to my seat, my hand covering my face and crying with shame.'[14]

This real experience became a scene in the film, in which her character breaks down during the same Chopin piece as she herself had struggled vainly to play all those years ago as a child. With her own experience of the burden of parental expectation, Ann Todd could bring a psychological truth to a character who wished both to resist and yield to the Svengali-like influence of her guardian. And Sydney's own experience of lameness, one feels, must have lent an edge to the portrayal of Nicholas, the crippled guardian. The film was remarkable for its intensity of mood and feeling of truth, while at the same time observing the requirements of mainstream entertainment.

Concert pianists were a familar sight in 1940s cinema. There was James Mason himself as a misanthropic virtuoso in *The Night Has Eyes* (1942). Anton Walbrook played the 'Warsaw Concerto' in the hugely popular *Dangerous Moonlight* (1941). In the Gainsborough film *Love Story* (1944) Margaret Lockwood played a pianist with a terminal disease. In the climactic scene she performs a composition inspired by the man she loves, whom she has now nobly turned her back on because she knows she has only a few months to live. These films were by and large novelettish, offering a packaged make-believe.

Sydney Box's great achievement was to marry the romance to a realism. After all the stereotypical villains he had been forced to play at Gainsborough, James Mason was at last given the opportunity to play a three-dimensional character, and encouraged to explore its depths. It was a turning-point in his career. As the cruel, crippled guardian of *The Seventh Veil* he revealed a quality of underlying tenderness which perhaps drew Carol Reed to him when he was looking for someone to play Johnny, the mortally wounded gunman in *Odd Man Out*.

Ann Todd and James Mason were both grateful to Sydney Box

for accommodating their own thoughts about their roles. It was characteristic of a more general responsiveness, which was not limited just to people engaged in his own projects. 'He had enormous sympathy with anybody who had an idea for a film,' remembered Bill MacQuitty. 'He would give them money to develop it and he would also try very hard to get it off the ground.' The writer Jill Craigie wanted to make a film about the war artists. MacQuitty liked the idea and mentioned it to Sydney, who then persuaded Filippo Del Giudice at Two Cities to back the film.

Out of Chaos would have announced the arrival of a gifted and sensitive film-maker had any company been willing to distribute it. 'Some of our most famous artists have been set to work to paint the war, and this is a film showing how it was done,' wrote the film critic Ernest Betts in the *Sunday Express*. 'It tries something new and advances the cause of the cinema as an intelligent medium. It is so good. In fact it isn't being shown anywhere!'[15] Jill Craigie and her producer Bill MacQuitty would have the same trouble with their next two films, *The Way We Live* (1946) and *Blue Scar* (1949). The distributors were reluctant to show films they did not consider to be 'popular entertainment'. Their lack of support is a major reason why Craigie, who was a fine film-maker, is so little known as such today.*

The Seventh Veil was a huge critical and commercial success, both in England and America. It was the crowning achievement of an extraordinary career. There was no one in wartime cinema as energetic, progressive or versatile as Box. Not only had he built Verity into the largest producer of documentaries, he had established himself as a significant producer of features both for Two Cities and on his own account. But this dynamism was also a weakness. He never stayed still for long enough to consolidate his gains. His relationship with Two Cities was enviable. It was the most prestigious production company in Britain, and Sydney

* The careers of many other fine film-makers must inevitably have foundered on the narrow attitude of the distributors. A talent like Humphrey Jennings – who had had his own difficulties with distributors (see p. 9) – could easily have been stifled had it not been for a wartime arrangement between the government and the distributors that documentary films would be shown. But the distributors thought they were granting a special favour.

could propose feature film ideas to its production meetings. If he had possessed a more leisurely temperament, he might have made under Del Giudice's famously generous sponsorship some films of real consequence. Instead, he preferred to face the risks of independent production. There was nothing considered about this. The challenge was an end in itself. He was inclined to accept any task, even if it did not really suit his nature. Beneath the joviality and enterprise he was still the lame child determined to prove that nothing was beyond him.

When Rank, impressed by *The Seventh Veil*, offered Sydney the job of running Gainsborough Studios, inevitably he accepted. He had proved that he could be a journalist, that he could write plays, that he could run a business, that he could produce, write and if need be direct documentaries and features. Now a new challenge. He would run a film factory. The contract also offered security. No more worries about finding finance or securing distribution. Each picture was to have a budget of approximately £200,000 – twice what had been scraped together for *The Seventh Veil*. But there was a catch. Rank was under pressure to increase the production of British films to meet the requirements of the Quota Act, and Sydney undertook to increase production from the three films that Gainsborough had hitherto been making a year to twelve.

Muriel Box was put in charge of the script department, and Betty Box looked after Gainsborough's studio in Islington, but the enterprise was far too large to be run as a family concern. 'In his desire for safety and stability,' wrote Muriel in her memoirs, 'Sydney, always sanguine and optimistic to a degree, forgot to take into account that by agreeing to produce so many pictures yearly, we were tackling a programme even more arduous than our freelance ventures. We were also relinquishing something of much greater value: our independence as film-makers. The running of a large studio and the responsibilities it entailed, were going to leave us no spare time in which to write original screenplays.'[16]

Sydney found himself administering a huge machine. And the films which got made were just the tip of the iceberg. Joe Mendoza, who was a writer at the studio, remembers that Sydney used to publish a weekly report of films in production, films finishing and films planned. 'Every week there were these marvellous titles of films you'd never heard of or seen on the book stalls, and every week we used to have a sweepstake as to which film would not be in next week. The films plan was always changing.'[17] For Sydney, who had always taken a hands-on approach to film-making, contending with the production line must have presented considerable frustrations. There wasn't the leisure to be inventive. It was a struggle just to get the films made at all.

He had also to contend with studio politics. His arrival at Gainsborough had been preceded by some corporate bloodletting, as Rank got rid of the previous studio boss, Maurice Ostrer. Many Gainsborough staff retained a considerable loyalty for the old regime, and felt ill disposed towards Sydney, some to the point of obstruction.

In 1947 Sydney offered Joe Mendoza and his writing partner Tony Skene a chance to direct their own script for a film called *Street Paved with Water*. According to Mendoza, the Gainsborough camera department were furious when Sydney asked a young cameraman he had worked with in documentaries to photograph the film, instead of promoting a camera operator from their department, and they set about sabotaging the production. 'For the first two weeks of our shooting our cameras were out of focus, underexposed, wobbly ... and in the end Sydney said to us, "Look, boys, I'm terribly sorry, but we'll have to stop making this picture." '[18] As an independent Sydney had been able to act decisively and with imagination. Now he was mired in the jealousies and rivalries of an initially unsympathetic organization. Even his renowned readiness to give opportunities to newcomers required a battle to put into practice.

Under the circumstances it was scarcely surprising that no great films emerged from Gainsborough under Box's stewardship – although there was much that was interesting. He did not just settle for the safer and less time-consuming option of adapting novels, but in films like *Holiday Camp* (1947) or *Easy Money* or *Good Time Girl* (both 1948) also showed a willingness to tackle contemporary issues with original scripts. It was an inheritance of his documentary background.

'What Box is looking for', the trade magazine *Kinematograph Weekly* reported, 'are subjects dealing with live people and things – which will lend themselves to production on the actual spot.'[19] There was an element of pragmatism in his thinking as he was seeking to increase production at a time when there was a severe shortage of studio space. But the programme as a whole was marked by a realism and a readiness to treat its audience as intelligent that had never been a concern of the previous regime – responsible for such far-fetched confections as *The Wicked Lady* and *Madonna of the Seven Moons*. Quite a few of the films could have achieved real distinction if they had been executed with less haste. In Richard Griffith's supplement to Paul Rotha's *The Film Till Now*, he wrote: '[Sydney Box] lacks, possibly, good directors; but his pictures are perhaps preferable to the pseudo-art prestige films.'[20] What Box really lacked – had always lacked because of the huge commitments he took on – was time.

In his first year at Gainsborough he produced not the twelve pictures that he had promised with what had seemed to the trade press like crazy optimism, but fourteen. The following year he celebrated his Silver Jubilee. It was perhaps typical that he didn't feel he had to wait twenty-five years. At Shepherd's Bush Studios on 8 December 1947 – only five years after he had made his first feature – he watched his twenty-fifth, *The Bad Lord Byron* , take the floor and celebrated with a party of producers, directors, film critics and stars.

Box didn't really require an excuse for such intense activity, but there was an important underlying reason for the publicity that the occasion attracted. The boycott of British cinemas that Hollywood had imposed a few months before meant that British films were badly needed to make up for the shortfall.

At Gainsborough Box bore the brunt of meeting this crisis. After only three years at the studios he fell seriously ill, and Gainsborough was wound up as the Rank Organisation switched its production to Pinewood. One need only watch *The Seventh Veil* to appreciate that Sydney Box was one of the most gifted people working in British films. The pity was that he never applied himself at anything for long enough to make a permanent mark. He was the Man Who Did Too Much.

Herbert Wilcox

'Serious' film writers and critics have tended to disregard Herbert Wilcox. Even in 1947, when he was by far the most successful producer around, Dilys Powell managed to write a little book on contemporary British cinema without mentioning him once.[1] And the new edition of *The Macmillan International Film Encyclopaedia*, published in 1994, was only stating today's consensus when it called him 'mediocre'. In fact, in their own way, his films were brilliant: expertly photographed and staged, well written and as lavish as anything the British cinema had seen.

The 'London series' of films he produced and directed in the late 1940s were a phenomenon. Anna Neagle, his wife and leading lady, was Britain's top box-office star for six years running. *Spring in Park Lane* achieved the highest attendance figures of any film shown in Britain. And although the highbrow critics spurned him, the tabloids – who after all represented the vast majority of the audience – lauded him. He won National Film Awards (the equivalent of today's BAFTAs) for the best British Film of the Year with *Piccadilly Incident, The Courtneys of Curzon Street, Spring in Park Lane* and *Odette*.

If Herbert Wilcox was the Master of Escapism, then one of his most important qualifications was experience of what audiences wanted to escape from – indeed his whole career, which was based on unmitigated optimism and a refusal to accept drab reality, was a form of personal escapism. He was born in London in 1890, one of five children. His father, an impoverished sculptor, was unable to find steady employment and financial straits forced the family to move to Brighton. Here Herbert was selling newspapers on the street at the age of ten. 'We all knew real hunger,'[2] he would later write of those years. His mother died of tuberculosis at the age of forty-two, but the *coup de grâce*, he believed, was her embarrassment at having to return a piano after falling behind on the instalments. His father died soon afterwards, and the young Wilcox came to London, where he managed to scratch a living as a billiards player.

After serving in the Royal Flying Corps during the First World War, he was briefly a films salesman and then took his first steps as a producer. His first production, *The Wonderful Story*, was 'a realistic short story with a humble cottage setting, and with ordinary country people'.[3] It got excellent reviews,* but no one went to see it. The next, *Flames of Passion*, made in 1922, was 'a florid melodrama'[4] with a finale in which the black-and-white film burst into colour. It was a huge hit and for Wilcox the lesson was simple: 'No more stark realism.'[5]

He was a showman and he was prepared to take enormous risks in the pursuit of box-office success. He was making films at a time – before the first Quota Act in 1928 – when the rest of the industry was supine. A young Michael Powell was among those impressed by *Flames of Passion*.[6] It had a sense of spectacle that seemed extraordinary for a British film. But more extraordinary was that Wilcox managed to get it made at a time when Hollywood seemed to have a virtually total grip on British screens and the enfeebling refrain in the British film industry was: Making Films Does Not Pay.

The setting up in 1925 of the Film Society, where a small coterie of intellectuals gathered to watch foreign films, may have been an important step in getting people to take the new medium seriously, but Wilcox, through his feats of showmanship, was winning it a much wider respectability. A year before the Society's first show he had startled the film world by opening his film *Southern Love* at the Albert Hall. 'It was incredible,' wrote George Pearson, then one of the country's top directors, 'a film-show in that sacred temple of Victorian sobriety! From a platform of flowers an enormous screen faced a vast audience, the great floor and the tiers of circles were packed, evening dress predominant. As I sat amongst that gathering of two thousand or more in the very heart of London's West End, my mind flew back to my pennyworth of cinema in a derelict greengrocer's shop in the Lambeth Walk! Well, Wilcox had dared, and had

---

* The *Times* reviewer (5 June 1922) thought this 'remarkable production' was 'an excellent piece of drama' and 'grimly realistic'.

won. The once despised Cinema had challenged the prestige of the Stage.'[7]

Wilcox himself remembered *Southern Love* as an indifferent film which he had written in twenty-four hours on a train to Vienna, where it was made. But 'the ballyhoo took everyone by surprise – so much so that the shortcomings of my film were scarcely discussed'.[8] Here was the essence of his genius: to take an ordinary film and make it seem extraordinary. 'I say unhesitatingly that he is the greatest showman and publicist I have ever known in England,' commented Richard Norton,[9] who would work with him at British and Dominions (B & D), a company that Wilcox set up in 1928 with the actor Nelson Keys. This flair for 'ballyhoo' may have won him little admiration from the highbrow critics, but it was vital for breathing confidence into an industry and inspiring it with a sense of the possible.

Herbert Wilcox possessed the ability of great entrepreneurs to take big decisions instantaneously. When sound came in, he rushed to Hollywood to exploit the new technology, making a crime film called *Black Waters*. Having acquired a licence to use the Western Electric sound system, he then returned to England and built one of the country's first sound studios at Elstree.

The West End stage was an obvious resource to exploit in this new medium, and in the early 1930s Jack Buchanan musicals and adaptations of Aldwych farces provided a staple diet for the studio. Wilcox spotted Anna Neagle in a Buchanan show called *Stand Up and Sing*, and in 1931 cast her opposite Buchanan in *Goodnight Vienna*. The film made a star of her, but it is important to appreciate that at this stage she was just a part of the much larger enterprise that Wilcox was running.

I spoke to Freddie Young, who joined Wilcox as Chief Cameraman of B & D in 1928 and stayed with him until the beginning of the war. He thought that Wilcox had been 'very underrated', and was impressed by his ability to juggle directing with all the other responsibilities of running a studio. At his peak Wilcox was responsible for over thirty films a year. 'He was the quickest man to start making pictures you ever saw,' remembered Richard Norton. 'If you took your eye off him for a moment two or three more would be on the way.'[10] There were severe cash-flow problems, but Wilcox took them in his stride with his usual buoyant energy. Friday, Freddie Young remembered, was Wilcox's day for going up to London to raise money. He would discuss a set-up in the morning, and in the afternoon 'he would come back and I would have a set-up arranged, and we would shoot that and he would have got the money to pay the wages for that week. He was wonderful in that way.'[11]

B & D's films were unashamed crowd-pleasers, but extremely well made. Wilcox made a point of hiring the best people. At B & D he gathered a formidable team which he kept together for ten years, this rare continuity making it an important training ground for the British film industry as a whole. There was the legendary American editor Merrill White, known as 'The Doctor' for his ability to patch up apparently irredeemable films. There was the art director L. P. Williams, who would later design *Brief Encounter*. And of course there was Freddie Young, 'the undisputed doyen of British cameramen'[12] in the words of Jack Cardiff, who was briefly one of his assistants. Young reckoned that 'the quality of films photographically and in every other way were equal to Hollywood'.[13] At the time he prided himself on working for the best film company in Britain.

When the B & D studios burnt down in 1936, Wilcox went into partnership with C. M. Woolf and Rank, who owned General Film Distributors and the newly built Pinewood Studios. Wilcox took a half-share in the studios and shot the first film ever to be made there, *London Melody* (1937). But his stay was brief. He fell out with Woolf over his plans to star Anna Neagle in *Victoria the Great*, and made the film at Denham. It was with the enormous worldwide success of this film that Wilcox discarded his studio interests and concentrated on his principal asset, Anna Neagle.

Sixty Glorious Years (1938) offered more episodes out of the life of Queen Victoria, and secured Wilcox a contract to make four films starring Neagle in Hollywood. *Nurse Edith Cavell* (1939) was yet another remake – of his 1927 silent film, *Dawn* – and three light musicals followed, *No, No, Nanette* (1939), *Irene* (1940) and *Sunny* (1941). These films met with only modest success. Although Wilcox understood the populist soul of Hollywood better than perhaps any other British producer, it was the English setting that lent conviction to his brand of escapism. Returning to Britain to make *They Flew Alone* in 1942, he embarked on a series of films which would flawlessly mix English themes with Hollywood story values to make him the country's undisputed king of make-believe.

During the 1940s, his heyday, it was often difficult to distinguish between the fairy-tale existence of the characters in his films and the life Wilcox seemed to lead himself. He treated film-making as a society occasion, to be conducted with endless rounds of champagne and caviar. A biopic of Wilcox's own life would have been like a Fred Astaire musical, and Jack Buchanan – B & D's biggest star – would have played him. Margaret Lockwood's welcome to his court was extravagant but standard treatment: 'I had never worked in such an atmosphere before. With Gainsborough, and then with Rank, filming was very much a routine job. You were expected at the studios very early in the morning; you went about your acting in a methodical way, and while they looked after you well enough they certainly did not spoil you. Not so with Herbert Wilcox. Only an hour after signing the contract a magnificent bouquet was delivered at my flat. It was from Herbert and Anna, expressing their delight that I had joined them. This was followed by several greetings telegrams and a dinner to celebrate the contract. From that day I was never allowed to forget that I was a really bright and dazzling star on their horizon. They were going to look after me as no one else had done before.'[14]

It was not only his stars that Wilcox looked after. Few journalists failed to respond favourably to his lavish hospitality. Bob Dunbar, who became Wilcox's general manager in 1949, remembered that they 'had lots and lots of separate shows for the journalists and plied them with drinks and sat them down. It worked.'[15] For Wilcox public relations was just another more subtle kind of fiction, a natural part of the film-making process. 'We would sometimes have no film in the camera at all,' Dunbar recalled, 'and he'd be shooting shot after shot with journalists on the set.'

Some of the best performances were given well away from the studios. Wilcox kept a suite at Claridge's, where he entertained regularly: 'He would ask a daily magazine and an evening, say, journalist – never two from the same category – and he'd give them tea and drinks, and then just at the right moment out from the bedroom Anna would sail in.' And Wilcox's genius for convincing people that all was for the best in the best of all possible worlds applied perhaps most of all to his own wife. 'He kept her absolutely wrapped in cotton-wool all the time. If there was a bad review he'd send everyone around buying all the *Evening Standards* so she wouldn't read it.'

Wilcox's formula took three basic forms: the biopic, the melodrama, the romantic musical comedy. By the 1940s he had honed these variants to perfection: in the biopics (or more accurately the hagiographies) unwavering, spotless heroism and dedication to duty; in the melodramas, a girl who will sacrifice her heart to do the right thing; and in the romantic comedies, glamour, opulence, music and dance.

What impresses is the rigorous calculation with which he focused on the elements of popular success. He understood the importance of continuity in a successful product, and was, as we have seen, not embarrassed to repeat himself wherever he could. Anna Neagle was always the star, and it didn't much matter whether she appeared as Queen Victoria, Amy Johnson or Florence Nightingale, for of course it was the same film. The titles of the romantic comedies he made in the late 1940s – *Spring in Park Lane*, *Maytime in Mayfair*, *The Courtneys of Curzon Street* – were models of movie branding, unmistakably announcing variations on a popular theme.

His flair for escapism was perfectly suited to the times. There was a vast audience who wanted to forget for a few moments the hardship and muddle of an austerity Britain. Wilcox presented them with a world in which the reassuring certainties of convention would always prevail. Indeed, part of the satisfaction of a Wilcox film was to see endings of perfect propriety – although not necessarily happy ones – being engineered out of the most awkward and unpromising of situations.

In *I Live in Grosvenor Square* Anna Neagle is a WRAF going steady with a British army officer (Rex Harrison), but falls in love with a gunner in the American airforce. Many English girls must have been in a similar position back in 1945 when the film came out, but few can have emerged from the situation quite so tidily. In the film the forces of confusion are swiftly dispelled by everyone behaving impeccably: Anna Neagle tries to forget her passion, the British officer retires from the scene so that the true lovers will be free, and the gunner returns to active service rather than break up the original couple. The possibility of any embarrassment at a future date is removed by the death of the gunner on combat duty. The status quo is beautifully restored.

Wilcox's next film, *Piccadilly Incident* (1946), evoked the previous success with its title and stuck close to the proven formula, with a few diverting modifications. This time Anna is a Wren who meets an army officer during an air-raid in Piccadilly. They fall in love and get married, but are soon parted when Anna is posted overseas. Her husband learns that her ship has been torpedoed and is convinced that she is dead. In due course he marries again and has a child.

In fact Anna managed to scramble into a lifeboat, and is now marooned on a desert island, where she spends much of her time, inspired by the memory of her husband, defending her virtue from an amorous sailor. Anna is eventually rescued and returns to England. How will she cope with the very trying circumstances that her presumed death has led to? Selflessly, of course. When she learns what has happened, she resolves to keep her identity secret and not to break up the new family, realizing that the child will be declared illegitimate should it be known that she is still alive.

But in the last reel fate brings her face to face with her husband, when for old time's sake she returns to Piccadilly where they first met. Anna pretends that when she was on the desert island she fell in love with someone else. The husband, overwhelmed to find her still alive, reveals that he loves her as much as ever. In this grand finale of fine feelings Anna can now no longer hide the truth, but at this point enemy action, as in *I Live in Grosvenor Square*, makes a timely intervention. Another air-raid leaves Anna mortally wounded and saves her husband from the disgrace of bigamy. Wilcox, who treated such conventions of society with enormous respect, was the Establishment film-maker, the defender of the status quo.

As Anna lay on her deathbed, many in the audience must have reached for their handkerchiefs, but in a way it was the ultimate happy ending – to meet one's maker in a perfect state of grace and sanctity. Wilcox had used it more than once before. Amy Johnson in *They Flew Alone* (1942), Nurse Edith Cavell in the film of the same name – both perish but achieve a kind of immortality through the perfection of their lives.

So what was Anna doing playing a Nazi sympathizer in *The Yellow Canary* (1943)? Reviled in England, she sets off to live in

Canada, where she is soon spying for the Germans. It's a wonderful idea – to pitch the natural sympathy the audience would feel for the star against their repugnance for her behaviour – a chance, some would think, to explore the muddle of human nature, where from time to time apparently decent people do end up batting for the wrong side. A few years later Hitchcock would attempt something similar in *Notorious*. Ingrid Bergman was the disillusioned daughter of a captured Nazi agent, dragged along by a suspicious Cary Grant to spy on her father's Nazi friends in Rio. Being a star, Bergman of course had to be working for the right side in the end, but within this framework she played a role of genuine disenchantment and moral ambivalence. Anna Neagle, by contrast, is permitted no doubts. Her virtue is unwavering from the outset. Some time after the film had come out Neagle saw *The Yellow Canary* at a matinee in Newcastle. Sitting in front of her were two ladies. One was rather deaf, and her companion had to keep on explaining what the film was about. 'Oh no,' the deaf lady muttered. 'Oh dear me *no*, Anna Neagle would never do that.'

'When I finally appeared in my WRNS uniform and all was made clear' – that Anna was really a double agent gathering information for the British – 'she gave a very relieved sigh. "There," she said, turning in triumph to her patient neighbour. "I *told* you Anna Neagle wouldn't do things like that." '[16]

Wilcox's films carried the unstated guarantee that, however disturbing the situation, goodness would be shown to be unalloyed and heroes to be trusted without reserve. They reaffirmed the certainties of the nursery.

Wilcox once urged British producers to make 'happy, unclouded pictures. We do not want sadism, abnormality and psychoanalysis. That sort of thing is no good for the average audience – they do not understand it and in most cases do not want to understand it.'[17] No one was more qualified than Wilcox, with his record of box-office success, to put forward such an opinion. When he passed on the opportunity to create a more complex character for Anna Neagle in *The Yellow Canary*, this was not a director's lack of insight into character, but a producer's astute appreciation of what the audience *wanted*.

He certainly was not a great artist if art is to provide some profound insight into life, but he was brilliant at what he chose to do. His talent lay in his nose for a good story, and, as Freddie

Young commented, the ability to tell that story with absolute conviction.

Herbert Wilcox's greatest discovery of course was Anna Neagle. Her personality suited his brand of safe entertainment perfectly, but he built her into Britain's biggest box-office star with considerable skill. Early in their partnership Neagle had played the title role in *Nell Gwyn* (1934),* but in the many films that followed rarely would such demands be made on her acting ability. Conscientious and hard-working, she saw the key to most of her roles was simply to be herself. This woman who played Edith Cavell and Florence Nightingale would confide in her memoirs that she had 'always had a great admiration for nurses', and that while at school she had toyed with the idea of becoming a missionary. She was a Head Girl type, and her outlook was geared to playing the saintly.

In her memoirs Anna Neagle reminisced fondly about her time in Hollywood, where the stars were treated with formality. 'I was never "Anna" in Hollywood except to my intimates. I was always "Miss Neagle".'[18] Bob Dunbar recalled that 'she was really rather like the royal family'. He was struck by her graciousness, the courtesy she showed to even the most humble of her colleagues. 'She remembered everybody, just like the Queen.'

Wilcox made sure she was treated like a queen, yet perhaps the secret of her appeal lay in her very ordinariness. She was not beautiful or naturally graceful. There was something stiff, slightly awkward about her, a prosaic edge to her voice. She was just a little bit dull, like the sensible elder sister. But her very plainness provided comfort. She was the perfect surrogate for the dreams of a largely female audience. If *she* could wear such wonderful dresses, dance with such charming men, find romance, then there was hope for them too. She offered an obtainable kind of glamour – the only qualifications one needed were virtue, dedication and hard work.

'Why don't you get swollen-headed?' a journalist asked her on a triumphant tour of North America. 'Why should I?' she replied.

---

* Such was the propriety of Anna Neagle's later roles that it seems strange that the word 'cleavage' should have been coined in wrangles with the American censor over Nell Gwyn's low-cut dress.

'I'm lucky, that's all. I call myself Lucky Neagle. There are plenty of girls who deserve my success just as much as I do, but they have not been lucky.'[19]

With Anna Neagle as his vehicle, Wilcox presented a world of Truth, Honour and Virtue, a world where right and wrong are easily distinguished, where order can be imposed on chaos. Almost exactly two years after he died, there was a spectacular revival of these values. Margaret Thatcher celebrated a famous election victory with these words of St Francis:

> Where there is hatred let me sow love;
> Where there is injury, pardon;
> Where there is despair, hope;
> Where there is darkness, light;
> Where there is sadness, joy.

They could easily have served as Wilcox's manifesto as a film-maker.

At times in her march through history Margaret Thatcher, with her regal bearing and carefully arranged golden locks, seemed to be playing Anna Neagle, and it is perhaps one of the great mis-timings of fate that Anna Neagle never played her. Britain's first woman prime minister – it would have been an ideal role for the biopic queen who had already portrayed Queen Victoria twice, but could also play (and indeed *was*) the ordinary girl who achieves greatness through hard work.

'Born to be one of millions, she became one in a million. This career – rather like a rocket out of a match-box – was her own. She dreamed it; lived it, until all that happened to her shouted from headlines!' The words preface *They Flew Alone*, in which Anna Neagle portrayed Amy Johnson. But they could as easily be applied to Margaret Thatcher. Two ordinary girls who even began life with similar names: Marjorie Robertson became a film star,* while Margaret Roberts went into politics . . .

Writing in the late 1950s, Richard Norton observed: 'Wilcox had to find the money himself for almost every film he made. The

---

* It was the producer-director J. B. Williams who suggested that she should swap her name for one of more star appeal when she appeared in his film *The Chinese Bungalow.*

highest praise that can be given him is the mere fact that he has stayed in the business for so long; he could not have got money unless his films showed a profit in the long run, and that is a claim very few British producers can make.'[20]

In 1964, not too long after these words were written, Wilcox did go bankrupt. His downfall came when two films flopped, *King's Rhapsody* and *Lilacs in Spring* – typically frothy entertainments. As Wilcox acknowledged himself, he had finally failed to keep up with the mood of the times. 'I was making films about pleasant themes and pleasant people. Now they make films about unpleasant people. I do not think I would fit in with that.'[21] Wilcox and Neagle swapped their Park Lane penthouse for a flat in Brighton. It was fate coming full circle for Wilcox, whose father's impecuniousness had occasioned a similar journey a lifetime ago. Anna, true to form, emerged as the staunch heroine. Her jewels were sold and she supported her husband with a £40 a week allowance. A year later she took to the boards again. *Charlie Girl* was a smash hit and made her as big a star as ever. This pattern of pluckiness turning misadventure to triumph was of course the perfect Herbert Wilcox story.

His bankruptcy certainly was not pleasant, but one has the feeling that his showman's heart enjoyed its sensational aspect. If the arrival of the bailiffs had caused his mother fatal embarrassment, Wilcox – who had far more to lose than just a piano – seemed only too happy to advertise the fact. His friends the journalists were as welcome as ever, and he made the most of the pathos of the situation. He showed the man from the *Mirror* around the penthouse that had to be sold in much the same way as he once had taken journalists on a tour of his set or entertained them in his Claridge's suite. The resulting article showed that he retained all his old instinct for the publicity stunt. At one point he pulled out of his pocket a £100,000 cheque that he had made out to Terence Rattigan for the screen rights of his play *Ross*. He explained that the film was never made. ' "Every penny of that went down the drain," said Wilcox grimly.' But he did not explain – nor would *Mirror* readers have cared – how he still managed to have the cheque. 'As we talked together, Anna Neagle – still beautiful at 54 – came into the room . . .'[22]

When he began to write a column for the *News of the World* under the heading 'I Made the Stars', it was less a reluctant necessity than an embrace of a true *métier*. Once again he was selling newspapers, only this time by writing for them. As he named the six sexiest women he had met in fifty years of film-making,* or described how he once had to boot a drunken Errol Flynn on to the set, he wrote with the sure populist touch that he had demonstrated in his long career as a film producer.

In the aftermath of losing his fortune the qualities that had made it became only more evident – a robust opportunism, a happy-go-lucky spirit, and, above all, an incorrigible optimism. As soon as he had received his discharge for bankruptcy, he announced plans for an epic film set in the Congo – with Anna Neagle, now fifty-five, as the star. 'The film will put us back where we belong.'[23] No one could have been surprised if this time the dream failed to materialize, but it was, after all, such reckless belief that had made his fortune in the first place.

* Lucille Ball, Elizabeth Taylor, Zsa Zsa Gabor, Diana Dors, Marlene Dietrich and Greta Garbo.

Gabriel Pascal

Gabriel Pascal's story was that of a typical British movie mogul at large in an industry of continual false dawns and phoenix-like rises from the ashes: not only was he not British, but his career moved from penury to fabulous success, to boundless ambition and extravagance back to penury again.

Pascal's film version of Shaw's *Pygmalion* in 1938 was an enormous worldwide box-office hit, and on the strength of it – difficult to credit now when, film historians apart, few have heard of him – he joined Hitler and the Pope on *Time* magazine's list of the world's ten most famous men. Faithful to the original and with the active participation of Shaw himself – who would win an Oscar for the screenplay – the film was as significant a shot in the arm for the British film industry as Korda's *Private Life of Henry VIII* had been five years earlier. It established Pascal but was also Rank's first big-budget production: its success set the pattern for the next decade as Rank committed his resources to making prestige films which would find a world market.

Pascal deserves acknowledgement for his part in bringing about the boldness that characterized British films in the 1940s, but he duly succumbed to *folie de grandeur* when in 1944 (and a good deal of 1945) he produced and directed Shaw's *Caesar and Cleopatra*. It cost a staggering £1¼ million (the equivalent today would be over £20 million); never had so much money been spent to so little effect.

It was difficult to stay awake when I watched the film recently. It was the opposite of everything I had imagined cinema to be: static, verbose scenes instead of movement, rhythm and montage; a claustrophobic world of enormous sets that the camera chose never to explore, everything reminding you of the sound stage – the still seas of a water tank, the shininess of the studio floor and strange blue skies where no wind ever seemed to blow. Its only possible merit was in being faithful to Shaw, which Pascal always was, to a fault.

According to Pascal's own account, which his widow would record in a book about him, he first met Shaw in the mid-1920s when he was producing films in Germany and Italy. He was on holiday at Cap d'Antibes on the French Riviera and there mistook the Irish playwright for a red buoy floating off the coast. Swimming out, he quickly recognized the Shavian beard and the following conversation ensued:[1]

'What is your nationality, young man?'

'I am Hungarian.'

'I could perhaps be wrong, but you struck me more as a gypsy.'

'. . . and an ex-Hussar who is still fighting under the banner of Beauty and Truth with the Hussar sword of artistic integrity . . . It is a rather hopeless fight, though, as I am in the stinking *métier* of producing films.'

The quixotic nobility of this response struck a chord with Shaw, who was both fascinated and appalled by the film business, and as the Hungarian swam back to shore he called out that he should look him up when he was in England.

They next met over ten years later. Pascal arrived in England broke and made his way to Shaw's house. When he said he wanted to film Shaw's plays, the playwright asked him how much money he had. 'I have all the money one needs to make a start – provided one has talent as well – which I have limitless.' He threw a half-crown on the table. 'This is all I have on earth, and even this was a loan.'[2]

It was the sort of encounter that agents exist to prevent, but once Pascal had gained access it is easy to see how he would have beguiled the playwright.* As Pascal's widow wrote of the meeting, 'Shaw must have had an eerie feeling that the man facing him couldn't be real. He was an incarnate figment of his own brain, a type of character only he could invent.'[3] His name alone would have charmed, with its suggestion of an angel and a philosopher. It was apt too. Pascal had just come back from India, where he had toured the holy places in the company of an Indian mystic called Shri Meher Baba. 'For the first time in my life I was really free,' he said of the trip. 'I was poor and my poverty was pure, as I desired nothing.'[4]

---

* Shaw gave the same account of their meeting. See Kenneth Clark, *The Other Half: A Self-portrait* (John Murray, 1977), p. 37.

Presumably he must also have been able to show a genuine enthusiasm and appreciation of Shaw's plays. The film producer Richard Norton, who would set up the finance deal for *Pygmalion*, remembered him as 'an intellectual with a love of good literature' who 'had a genuine admiration and understanding of Shaw'.[5] After all the businessmen who had tried to get hold of the rights, Shaw would have found Pascal a refreshing change.

Only Pascal's own account exists for his early life. He was an orphan brought up by gypsies. A mysterious patron, a Jesuit priest, put him into a military school. But Pascal wanted to become an actor and joined the Imperial Hofburg Theatre in Vienna. It was here that he first became a Shaw enthusiast. During the First World War he was an officer in a Hussar cavalry regiment and fought on the Italian front. His entry into the film business was glamorous by modern standards, but unexceptional for those pioneering days. When the war was over he got a job looking after horses. One morning, after taking a swim in the nude, he galloped past a film crew who were shooting a scene close to the field where he had left his horses to graze. Stirred by the swashbuckling dash of the bare bare-backed rider, the director hired him on the spot.[6]

This early curriculum vitae was about as ideal as anyone hoping to be a close collaborator of the unconventional Shaw could hope to have. At any rate a relationship of immense affection and loyalty developed between the two men, who as far as films were concerned in practice became a team. The key was Pascal's readiness to respect the integrity of Shaw's plays. After a preview of *Pygmalion*, the playwright wrote jubilantly to Pascal: 'An all-British film, made by British methods without interference by American scriptwriters, no spurious dialogue, but every word by the author, a revolution in the presentation of film. In short, English *über alles.*'[7]

Contrary to the widely held view that Pascal had somehow 'captured' Shaw, it was really the other way round. Shaw had found a tame producer who would go to any length to fulfil his least whim. With the triumph of *Pygmalion* they now planned to produce definitive screen versions of Shaw's other plays on a film-by-film basis. Pascal had made *Pygmalion* with the able assistance of Anthony Asquith and Leslie Howard, who were credited as co-directors. But egged on by the Old Man himself, he became more and more convinced that he was the only person who could interpret Shaw correctly. On the next Shaw production, *Major Barbara* (1941), David Lean and Harold French fulfilled the functions that Asquith and Howard had on *Pygmalion*, but Pascal kept the directorial credit for himself. This was not just a sign of vanity; it was an indication of the degree to which Shaw had come to regard Pascal as the only man he could trust to observe his wishes. According to Valerie Pascal, after *Pygmalion* Shaw stipulated that a condition of any future production of his work was that Pascal should be sole director.[8]

Major Barbara was shot during the Blitz. Bombs were constantly exploding around Denham and production was seriously disrupted. But Pascal, who clearly viewed himself as the oracle of a god, contributed just as much to the film's spiralling costs with his fussing after perfection. After the original shooting schedule had been completed, he insisted on additional scenes and retakes. Even Shaw had sent an anxious letter to try to knock some common sense into him. 'You must finish, finish, finish at all sacrifice until a Barbara film is ready for release no matter how far it may fall short of the film of which you dream . . .'[9]

The American release of *Major Barbara* was prefaced by a prologue in which Shaw addressed the American people: 'Citizens of the United States of America, the whole 130 millions of you, I am sending you my old plays, just as you are sending us your old destroyers.' Only partly tongue in cheek, it was an index of how he viewed the enterprise. A diet of GBS would, through the mass medium of the cinema, help to bring about the moral salvation of the free world.

Major Barbara was successful enough for the Shaw–Pascal partnership still to seem attractive to backers. Pascal would have liked to make further productions away from wartime England, and when plans for making films in the Bahamas or Canada came to nothing he turned to the Hollywood studios. He spent two years in America trying to set up a deal. But his negotiations always foundered on Shaw's refusal to surrender rights to more than one play at a time. This obstacle miraculously disappeared once Pascal returned to England. The Old Man wanted his acolyte to stay where he could keep an eye on him.

Pascal signed a deal with Rank to make *Saint Joan*, *Caesar and Cleopatra* and *The Doctor's Dilemma*. Plans to make *Saint Joan* first were abandoned when the Ministry of Information questioned the wisdom during the war of making a film about the English burning a French saint. So *Caesar and Cleopatra* was undertaken instead. Two years' inactivity and a budget of £500,000 from Rank had whetted Pascal's appetite. His quest for perfection reached new levels of craziness. Months before the production was due to begin he was conducting countless tests for even the smallest roles. There was a joke running around London about any actor who was more than five minutes late for a drink in a pub: 'He's being held up. He's just being tested for *Caesar and Cleo.*' [10]

Stanley Holloway had a small part as a Greek soldier called Balzinar. For a year he made 'practically a career' of it as he returned for retake after retake: 'What *are* these Romans? Peasants – sons of smiths, millers, and tanners,' he had to say. 'Bring out the "millers" very loud, ' Pascal advised him, 'and Arthur Rank will be very pleased and give you fifty pounds a week more salary.'[11] The flippancy was perhaps a sign of how little concern he had for the ever-increasing cost. But in his self-delusion he believed he was attaining immortal performances. In fact, as he shouted and cajoled in a heavy Hungarian accent, most of the actors found him more of a nuisance. 'If only you'd go away and let me get on with my job,' Claude Rains said.[12]

Over the year and a bit that the film was in production there was plenty to keep the newspapers both outraged and amused. Top of the list perhaps was an excursion to Egypt in the midst of wartime restrictions to film some battle scenes. In coals to Newcastle fashion the unit took its own sphinx.

Pascal was at first denied permission to travel as he was classified as an enemy alien. The cinematographer Freddie Young was entrusted with the task of directing, which in Pascal's absence was a relatively straightforward one.[13] The biggest difficulty was the coldness of the desert nights: the Egyptian extras, who were encamped in the desert, made bonfires of their wooden spears and papier-mâché armour to keep warm, and replacement props had to be continually reordered from Cairo.*

After a few weeks Young received a telegram that Pascal had

* A less plausible version of this story is that the Egyptian extras ate their papier-mâché shields when they discovered that the glue holding them together was nourishing.

been granted permission to visit the location for forty-eight hours. Next day he had to stop filming when a strange car crossed the desert towards the unit. At last a huge Rolls-Royce drew to a halt, and out stepped Pascal wearing white jacket, jodhpurs, riding boots and a red fez, and carrying a gold-mounted cane. (When Freddie Young told me this story, I couldn't help thinking of how nearly twenty years later he would eclipse even Pascal's desert entry, in a sublime moment of cinema filming the mysterious figure of Omar Sharif on his camel gradually issuing forth from the desert mirages in *Lawrence of Arabia*.)

Pascal soon demonstrated the sort of behaviour that had sent the budget soaring over a million pounds. The next day some senior Egyptian army officers turned up to see how their soldiers were faring as film extras. The unit shot a scene in which Ptolemy's soldiers galloped round the bottom of a hill on horseback. When several of the extras fell off, Pascal grabbed a megaphone and yelled: 'I am an officer of the Hungarian Hussars and you are a lot of Jewish bastards!' After a stunned silence the Egyptian officers ordered their men to march away. Freddie Young had to plead with them to come back, which they did only on condition that Pascal left the location.

As Pascal seemed to be a magnet for disaster, perhaps no one should have been surprised when Hitler's V1s paid a visit to Denham. One doodlebug exploded on the backlot where *Caesar and Cleopatra* was being shot, narrowly missing Pascal. Many people in British films might well have wished that it had hit. Pascal had monopolized Denham for a whole year at a time when there was a severe shortage of studio space (half the studio had been requisitioned during the war), and other productions had to be rescheduled, with the added expense that this entailed.* For *Caesar and Cleopatra*'s final cost of £1,250,000 Hollywood could have made one and a half *Gone with the Wind*s, or Michael Balcon ten Ealing comedies. Maybe Pascal could have been forgiven if he had produced a fine film, but he hadn't.

In spite of a barrage of hostile comments from the press and the industry itself about the disruption he had caused, Pascal was unrepentant. In a book published as part of the film's publicity

---

* Roy Boulting told me that the delays caused by *Caesar and Cleopatra* led to £68,000 being added to the budget of the Boulting brothers' *Fame is the Spur*. The actors, who had been contracted, had to be paid while they waited for studio space.

Pascal had intended to write a foreword which would have included these words: 'I tell you, my friends, who says this is a man who never had a real sweetheart and never made a woman happy, but calculates only how much he will spend on his girl before he invites her for a weekend holiday? Such people are not worthy that the sun shines on them. In love and art there is no economic consideration. The more generous you are, the more you can get back.' It was as well that his assistant Marjorie Deans persuaded him to think again.[14]

'I was surrounded by saboteurs and I made the picture without joy and inspiration,' Pascal would later say of *Caesar and Cleopatra*.[15] Perhaps it was these difficulties that led him to ponder some Utopian alternatives. The director Pat Jackson, soon after he had made *Western Approaches*, remembers being invited to tea by Pascal to discuss an idea for a floating film studio, which would be built in an ocean liner and cruise to the necessary locations.[16]

But Shaw also deserved to take some responsibility both for the film's extravagance and for its critical failure. It was inherent in the nature of the partnership, according to which he closely followed the course of the production and made his views known on every aspect. If Pascal was centre-stage, then the Old Man was certainly pulling the strings. Shaw looked to the cinema to provide a definitive interpretation of his plays for a mass audience, not a departure from them. This attitude allowed little scope for an imaginative filmic treatment. The script conferences for *Caesar and Cleopatra*, which lasted eight months, were particularly comic affairs: expensive consultants were hired only to have their suggestions turned down by Pascal exclaiming loudly: 'I have promise Shaw, that sweet man, we don't change one little word.'[17]

Caesar and Cleopatra played to large audiences, but not nearly large enough to justify the huge outlay and disruption Pascal had caused. In 1946 Rank pulled out of its contract to make *Saint Joan* and *The Doctor's Dilemma*, and the film technicians' union, the ACT, passed an unprecedented resolution that Pascal should not be allowed to make any more films in England 'unless subject to special control'.[18] The only solace Pascal had was Shaw's continued loyalty. 'In our next venture,' he advised Pascal – thinking big as usual – 'we must try to secure an up-to-date studio reserved (perhaps built) for our use exclusively, and lettable only during your holidays . . .'[19] But the next venture would not materialize in

Shaw's lifetime. Pascal, who had once called himself 'a scholarly vagabond',[20] toured the world in a fruitless search for finance to produce more Shaw films.

The film producer R. J. Minney saw Shaw in 1950 just a few days before he died. The conversation turned to Pascal, and Minney noticed a sadness in the Old Man's eyes. He was sorry that Pascal hadn't been to see him. 'I hear he's in Rome,' said Minney.

'Rome,' replied Shaw. 'I read in the newspapers that he had gone to India to try to raise money from the Maharajahs for my next film. Then I read that he had gone to Hollywood to arrange the filming of one of my plays there. Now you say he's in Rome. That's the trouble with the man. Rome, Roam, Roam. All over the place.'[21] Not vintage Shavian wit perhaps, but appropriate and impressive for a ninety-four-year-old on his deathbed.

Shaw had fared from the partnership far better than he could possibly have hoped. He received substantial financial reward and, with all the publicity and the kudos, was saved from the sad dotage that normally awaited a man of his age.

Most people regarded Pascal as a charlatan and a buffoon. He was looked down on as a funny foreigner even by the more enlightened members of the Establishment. The only reason why he had been taken seriously at all was because of Shaw's support of him, which itself was greeted with incredulity. 'Why did Mr Shaw allow himself to be conned by this impostor?' mused Sir Kenneth Clark who, when he was briefly in charge of the Films Division of the MOI, had had dealings with Pascal.[22] But who would have been more of an impostor? Pascal, who in spite of his recklessness with other people's money, made every effort to respect the artistic integrity of the film versions of Shaw's plays? Or the businessmen who might otherwise have got hold of the rights, and who would have pretended an appreciation they didn't happen to have? Pascal's chief failing was, if anything, to have been too loyal.

One is reminded of another 'funny foreigner', Filippo Del Giudice. Both men showed the sort of real respect for artists – if occasionally misguided – that most others in their profession mouthed as platitudes. It comes as no surprise that they knew each other and got on, or that they should both have ended up as outcasts. Pascal's wife describes a meeting with Del Giudice in

Rome shortly after Del had fled England. 'He invited us to his elegant suite at the Excelsior and explained that we were to have dinner there, as he hadn't one lira to take us out but still had credit in the hotel. He talked feverishly, and with more gesticulations than ever, about a film he was to make, and his cheeks burned with two red circles. I thought of Gabriel's unsuccessful attempts and wondered, shivering, if we were headed toward the same end.'[23]

In 1950, shortly before he died, Shaw wrote this letter to Pascal: 'I have been uneasy about you lately. You are laying out your life as if I were sure to live another fifty years and putting all your eggs in that quite illusory basket, accordingly. It is extremely unlikely that I shall live another three years and not certain that I shall live another three days; and when I die, your connexion with me will have been a mere episode in your career. You will have half your life before you which you must fill up with new friendships and new interests . . . never forget that dealing with very old people can be only transient . . . look for a young Shaw; for though Shaws do not grow on gooseberry bushes, there are as many good fish in the sea as ever came out of it. Anyhow, you must live in your own generation, not in mine.' A postscript read: 'Devotion to an old crock like me is sentimental folly.'[24]

Pascal did not heed Shaw's advice, but he must have felt that his fortunes were taking a positive turn when RKO, owned by the fabulously rich Howard Hughes, agreed to back his production of *Androcles and the Lion*. Pascal told Stewart Granger, who was working in Hollywood, how this new film 'would make *Caesar and Cleopatra* seem like a quickie'.[25] But he was soon to find that Hughes lacked Rank's forbearance. When Pascal inevitably sought to alter various production arrangements, he was thrown off the picture. 'He wasn't even allowed to collect his personal papers from his office; they had just been dumped in a box and left outside the gates.'[26]

It was the final confirmation that he was a has-been. No one wanted to be associated with him. He floundered around trying in vain to set up deals but getting poorer and poorer. Things were so bad that he even had the crazy idea of turning *Pygmalion* into a musical. In 1951 he contracted a couple of songwriters called Lerner and Loewe to write it but they backed out, no doubt having been warned of Pascal's talent for trouble.

Three years later he died a bankrupt, and the songwriters

resurrected the idea of the musical. They called it *My Fair Lady*, and as Pascal was adjudged to be the co-author of the 1938 film version of *Pygmalion*, on which it was based, his estate shared in the huge royalties – which almost did make *Caesar and Cleopatra* seem like a quickie.

Olwen Vaughan

The best place to go to find the spirit that shaped the British cinema of the 1940s would not have been the sound stages of Denham or Pinewood or Ealing but a town house not far from Piccadilly. A small signboard, decorated with a fleur de lys, hung outside no. 4 St James's Place and announced 'Le Petit Club Français'.

Inside it was cramped and threadbare, but animated. Even the first-time visitor would have recognized a few faces, for included in the membership of the club were famous artists, writers, musicians and, especially, film-makers. The stalwarts included several people who have been written about in these pages – Cavalcanti, Robert Hamer, Harry Watt, Angus Macphail. But the individual who would have left the most lasting impression on a newcomer was the woman who had founded the establishment. She would be as likely as not sitting at her special table in the restaurant upstairs, or on a stool at the bar on the ground floor, a large portrait of herself nestling among the array of bottles behind. Even if Olwen Vaughan was in a good mood, her basilisk stare could cause the confident to falter and the fainthearted to leave instantly.

A gold Alice band held her shoulder-length hair firmly in place, bright red lipstick was extravagantly applied to her lugubrious face, and from behind her thick, heavy glasses her brown eyes sized up everyone and missed nothing.

She presided over her domain as an autocrat, and few members dared to question her will. But her mien masked the warmest of hearts. The French Club was a place that had been built out of love, and through its decades of existence it continued to be run with the idealism that was plain in its founding. Olwen Vaughan was a Francophile and had opened up the basement in the summer of 1940 as a place where the Free French in London might find a little of the spirit of the country they had been forced to leave behind. As her passion for France was matched by an equal one for the cinema, the Frenchmen were soon joined by a large contingent of film-makers, who – delighted to find a place where they could share their enthusiasms –remained long after the war had ended and the French had returned home.

Olwen Vaughan was born on 27 May 1905, the daughter of a Unitarian minister from Liverpool, the Reverend Hemming Vaughan.[1] Oddly for a time when the clergy tended to regard the cinema as a den of iniquity, the Reverend Vaughan was a devotee who founded some early film societies. For the young Olwen the picture house became a second home, and she would recall her passion for films as having begun in earnest with the First World War, when her nurse would routinely leave her in the stalls while she went out with a soldier.[2]

In 1933 Olwen became the secretary of the newly formed British Film Institute. Here she showed the independence of spirit that institutions find so difficult to accommodate. Required on one occasion to produce the Institute's ledgers in court, and asked by the judge why they had been kept in pencil, she replied, 'They're always changing their minds and it's so much easier to rub out.'[3] She was finally dismissed after ten years for sneaking a film out of the National Film Archive to show to film societies. The zealous Ernest Lindgren was then the Archive's curator, and regarded many of the films in his care as far too precious to be seen. Perhaps the only surprise was that the unconventional Olwen had remained at the Institute for as long as she had.

Her decision to start a club in the middle of London just as the Blitz was about to begin was a wonderful example of her unorthodoxy. But although she had no experience of running restaurants and had to contend with the increasingly tight restrictions of rationing, she made the club work with her enthusiasm. In its early days the restaurant was squeezed into the basement, offering members a token protection from bombs. Olwen would do much of the cooking herself, operating out of a kitchen that had once been a lavatory: the bowl had been removed and the plumbing detoured to a single tap. There was no space for anything else besides a cooker, and the ingredients had to wait on a table outside. But Olwen thrived on overcoming obstacles, and did not find such conditions dispiriting.[4] The 'Documentary Boys' of the GPO Film Unit, whose offices were close by in Soho Square, were regulars of the club from the outset, and when their erstwhile producer Cavalcanti, a close friend of Olwen, moved to Ealing there was a new influx of members. The club's fame spread until it was really the unofficial headquarters for people who loved the cinema. Its reputation was such that, as Basil Wright put it, 'if during the war you heard that Orson Welles, say, or Rita Hayworth was in town, the practical thing would be to try the French Club first and the Savoy second.'[5]

Occasionally the club's hospitality was abused, most notoriously when Irwin Shaw, using a thin disguise, wove it unflatteringly into fiction in his bestseller *The Young Lions*: 'The Canteen of the Allies, for all its imposing name, was merely three small basement rooms decked with dusty bunting, with a long plank nailed on a couple of barrels that did service for a bar. In it, from time to time, you could get venison chops and Scotch salmon and cold beer from a tin washtub that the proprietress kept full of ice in deference to American tastes. The Frenchmen who came there could usually find a bottle of Algerian wine at legal prices. It was the sort of place where all ranks could fraternize on a mildly alcoholic basis with the certain knowledge that the cold light of day would erase the military indiscretions of the previous night.'[6]

It was extraordinary to suggest that Olwen would defer to anybody, let alone American servicemen, but the even greater crime was to characterize this bastion of civilized values – if a dilapidated one – as a low dive. Olwen was furious and Shaw anxiously sought to placate her, offering a full apology and a new red carpet for the stairs. Members joked that it was dyed with his blood.[7]

Once the air-raids had abated, the club took on the appearance it would keep for the next thirty years – kitchen in the basement, bar and clubroom on the ground floor, restaurant on the first, and Olwen's flat above that. But Olwen was always short of cash and the upkeep of the property posed a constant challenge to her ingenuity. The wartime bombs and doodlebugs never came close to competing with the destruction that the building managed to achieve under its own momentum. Bits were always falling off, and members grew used to being asked to contribute to the latest renovation fund or to provide their services about the club as unpaid labour. On one occasion in the 1950s when Olwen was – not for the first time – behind with the rent money and threatened with eviction, she enlisted the help of the Free French Association, who valiantly came to her aid with radio appeals in France that raised a thousand pounds. She flew triumphantly over to Paris to pick up the cheque.[8]

As the club always seemed to be skirting along the edge of insolvency, some members suggested that she should put up the charges, but she always refused on the grounds that young people would no longer be able to afford to come. She was recklessly generous. If people couldn't pay for a meal, she wouldn't insist on it, and there were beds on hand to put up people who had had too much to drink or had nowhere to go. 'There was usually some sort of stray from the Czechoslovakian film industry up in the attic,' remembered Sir Denis Forman.[9]

The French Club was always much more a cause than a business, and the commodity Olwen dispensed most profusely was encouragement. Early on in the war, when she was still secretary of the British Film Institute, she lent the BFI's only complete set of *Close-Up** to the future film-maker Peter Hopkinson. He was an unknown private soldier on a week's leave in London, and she couldn't have been sure that she would ever get it back.[10]

There were many events in the club's social calendar, but two stand out in people's memories. On Bastille Day flags were stretched across St James's Place, and revellers spilled out of the bar on to the street, dancing to the tune of an accordion. At Christmas Olwen organized a party for the members' children, to which the parents were strictly forbidden to come. She addressed the invitations to the young guests themselves and with great care chose a present for each child.

Olwen needed love in as large a measure as she doled it out, actively sought it but never found the ideal arrangement. When Helen Blackburne first came to the club in the late 1940s, it was generally known among the members that Olwen had been deeply in love with the homosexual Cavalcanti.[11] One day in the early 1950s to everyone's astonishment she got married to a homosexual member of the club called Duncan Melvin, who photographed ballet dancers. He moved into her flat upstairs, but

---

* Published between 1927 and 1930 by a group of expatriate cinéastes in Switzerland, the magazine was the film bible of its time.

apart from that there was no visible change in the routine of the club. Not long afterwards they were divorced.

She was prone to black moods, which in turn would lead to severe drinking bouts. She would hole up in her flat for days until she had recovered. 'She used to get very depressed sometimes,' Brenda Danischewsky recalled. 'She was very emotional. She Loved. She Hated. She would. She wouldn't . . . Life was stormy sometimes in the French Club, very stormy.'

The wealth of dramatic material that Olwen and the club presented was too much for one regular member to resist. In Rodney Ackland's play *Absolute Hell* Olwen becomes the character Christine, a proprietress of 'a drinking club in the West End of London' called La Vie en Rose. If Olwen was angry this time, it would have been because the play was too close to the bone. Christine is generous, impulsive and often drunk. She develops mad infatuations for people, and seeks love wherever she may find it. One moment she is singing with joy, the next she is miserable. Towards the end of the play she marries a gay writer. Her devotion to the club and her imperfect love affairs are both impelled by a sense of emptiness and a fear of loneliness.

Although Ackland's portrait of Christine was unmistakably Olwen, and probably touched the truth in its suggestion of an essential unhappiness, Olwen herself was altogether more resolute. While Christine succumbs to the safety regulations and closes her crumbling club soon after the 1945 General Election, Olwen battled on to her death nearly thirty years later. Ackland's play ends on a note of despair with Christine a wretched, pitiful figure, but the reminiscences of people who knew Olwen leave a far more positive impression – of someone triumphing over adversity with considerable relish.

The French Club, with all its dramas, was a heavy burden but Olwen still found time for other activities. After the war she was films officer for the United Nations Relief and Rehabilitation Fund, and in the late 1950s she was a research 'assistant' to John Grierson on his television series *This Wonderful World*. She travelled all over the world and attended countless festivals in search of suitable material. All Grierson had to do was turn up at the studio.

But she made perhaps her most memorable contribution in the film society movement. Basil Wright spoke of her 'genius in creating a social and artistic ambience',[12] and her film society work was really part of the same exercise as running the French Club in enabling people to savour art and life. She had been involved with the original Film Society until its close at the beginning of the war, and had also organized the screenings for the Forum Cinema at Charing Cross. During the war she ran the London Film Institute Society. Serious film enthusiasts came to depend on it. Dilys Powell wrote in the *Sunday Times* towards the end of 1945: 'Even in the dreariest winters we could refresh ourselves, thanks to the energy and enterprise of its secretary, Miss Olwen Vaughan, with programmes of French and other Continental films, varied now and again by American and English works.'[13]

After the war Olwen, together with Rodney Ackland, decided to form a successor with increased resources: the New London Film Society. Ackland described the occasion of its inception. 'Olwen and I were deploring the debased state of contemporary cinema and expressing the opinion that unless something was done to educate the movie-going public which had never seen silent films it would have no standard by which to condemn the current trash; we wept for those like ourselves who had recognized the cinema as an art form, we wept for those who had had no opportunity to do so, we wept for the cinema which was being strangled to death by the vulgar film industry. Then we dried our eyes and *thought*.'[14]

I can see them having the conversation at Olwen's special table at the French Club, drinking far too much and very possibly weeping. And there would have been little trouble finding at the other tables the people required to make the thought a deed. Basil Wright, Dilys Powell, Leonard Russell, Jack Beddington, Cavalcanti, Anthony Asquith and Edgar Anstey were all signatories on the programme for the first season. Most of them also became members of the Society's Committee. Olwen, who really ran the show, enjoyed the teasingly self-effacing title of Honorary Secretary.

The New London Film Society's performances took place at the Scala Theatre in Charlotte Street, which, as the programme for the first season pointed out (written, one assumes, by Olwen), was imbued with cinema history and a particularly suitable temple for such an occasion. 'In 1915 it was at the Scala Theatre that Griffith's *The Birth of a Nation* had its record-breaking run. Emil Jannings, Pola Negri and many of the great German film stars made their first English appearances on the Scala screen. When the ban on the great Russian masterpieces was finally lifted it was the Scala Theatre which gave them their first public showing.' The first season celebrated fifty years of cinema with a 'Festival of Great Films'. It opened on 3 December 1945 with the return to the Scala of *The Birth of a Nation*. There was a live orchestra so huge that not all its members could fit into the orchestra pit, and the overflow of musicians was squeezed, wretchedly cramped, into boxes.

The showings were so popular that repeat performances in the evening were put on. In the first season eleven programmes of mostly silent films were shown at fortnightly intervals, including *Intolerance, The Cabinet of Dr Caligari, Greed*; and there were other less well-known treasures, such as Mauritz Stiller's *The Atonement of Gösta Berling*, with a young Greta Garbo, and G. W. Pabst's *The Loves of Jeanne Ney*.

That hugely popular first season had the kind of success that forty years later greeted the presentation of the restored version of Abel Gance's *Napoleon* with a live orchestra. A new generation marvelled at the artistry of the past.

Today, when old films are shown again and again on TV or can be bought on videocassette, it's difficult to appreciate how indispensable film societies and repertory cinemas were. Dilys Powell, with her customary wisdom, explained why the New London Film Society was to be welcomed. 'While the literary critic can refer to his library or somebody else's, while the art critic has at worst the reminder of the photographic record, in the cinema there is no guide but memory, perhaps a few still photographs and the occasional, unreliable evidence of the written word. The cinema public, too, suffers; constantly badgered for its tolerance of the current folderols, constantly referred to the yardstick of former achievements, it is still debarred from seeing anything except a stray reissue or two and, now and then, some piece from the past disinterred by the few indefatigable and invaluable repertory cinemas.'[15]

The New London Film Society ran for ten seasons. There was a heavy emphasis in its programming on the silent cinema, and there probably hasn't been such an in-depth and representative sampling of this lost art since. But Olwen also organized a number of premieres, which directors could be relied upon to go to great lengths to attend. When Jean Grémillon's 1943 film

Lumière d'Eté was shown, despite the grounding of all regular airlines by fog, he chartered a private plane from Paris to get to the Scala in time.

Olwen did everything she could to encourage members of the Society to participate. A note in one programme read: 'Arrangements are being made for members to meet at the Society's offices, no. 4, St James's Place, SW1, to discuss the previous day's programme, and to meet members of the Committee and people connected with film-making.' The 'Society's Offices' of course was just a grand way of saying the French Club. 'In this way,' the note continued, 'the Committee hope that members will get to know each other and have free discussions which will help to create a more "active" interest in the Society than just a "film-going" membership.' It requires only a visit to the National Film Theatre today – where asking a few questions at a *Guardian* lecture is about the extent of audience participation – to realize what a wonderful invitation this was. Nothing was more likely to facilitate free discussion and to melt people's shyness than a few drinks in the French Club.

Naturally Olwen got her friends to pitch in: Cavalcanti contributed programme notes and introduced programmes; Dilys Powell promoted the Society in her *Sunday Times* column; and Richard Winnington did likewise in the *News Chronicle*.

The New London Film Society filled a gap between the old Film Society which had closed with the war and the rejuvenation of a hitherto moribund British Film Institute under the directorship of Denis Forman. Olwen had been in a state of virtual war with the previous director, Oliver Bell, a figure in the Magistrates' Association who, in the fashion of bureaucracies, had somehow been given the reins of an organization about which he knew little and which he ran with scant commitment. Rather than have to rely on the Institute, Olwen formed an alliance with Henri Langlois of the Cinémathèque Française and Iris Barry at the Museum of Modern Art in New York.[16] The Festival of Great Films that opened the first season depended mostly on the Museum's film library: the photograph of Iris Barry that appeared in a published retrospective was probably Olwen's personal touch of gratitude.

Her 'heroes and villains' approach can be detected between the lines of the Society's programmes. Both Iris Barry and Henri Langlois would often be thanked by name; Ernest Lindgren of the

National Film Archive, from which on a very few occasions she had to borrow prints, not at all. 'She took a slightly malicious pleasure in getting a print of, say, an early Stroheim film, from the Museum of Modern Art when it had been refused to the Institute,' remembered Sir Denis Forman.

Forman's appointment as Director of the British Film Institute in 1949 marked a sea-change in attitude. Clearly a hero in Olwen's mind, he was someone whose assistance she was glad to acknowledge in the Society's programmes. The British Film Institute, which Olwen had frostily ignored for so many years, now developed a close partnership with the Society. In 1953 the Society began to show films at the Institute's new National Film Theatre under Waterloo Bridge, and in retrospect this move from the Scala looks like a passing-on of the baton: seven of the fourteen programmes in that ninth season were arranged by the British Film Institute. When the New London Film Society ceased after its tenth season, it was simply an acknowledgement that an invigorated British Film Institute had inherited its role.

Olwen Vaughan died on 18 August 1973. She died as she had lived much of her life – cross. She was on holiday in Greece with a friend and had a heart attack after a row. Because she had been such an active presence in their lives, people who knew her found it more than usually difficult to come to terms with her death. 'A shattering sense of loss was combined with the extreme difficulty of believing that she was gone,' said Basil Wright in his tribute to Olwen at a memorial service held in St James's Church, Piccadilly.

When the staff of the French Club heard the news that she had died they carried on as usual. 'It is what Miss Vaughan would have wished,' said one of them. Attempts were made to keep the club going, but no one could match Olwen's talent for defying economic reality. The club was making losses and the building looked as if it might finally fall down, Westminster Council threatening to serve a dangerous structure notice on it. The French Club was finally wound up in 1977.

If you go along to 4 St James's Place today – which surprisingly is still standing – you will find no sign that Olwen Vaughan or the

French Club ever existed – just a blue plaque put up by the GLC: 'From this house in 1848 Frederic CHOPIN, 1810–1849, went to Guildhall to give his last public performance.'

Postscript

After Olwen Vaughan's death some of her friends got together to think of a fitting way in which she might be remembered. The portrait of her that had hung in the French Club was given to the British Film Institute, who for many years displayed it prominently in their premises in Dean Street. When the BFI moved to its present headquarters in Stephen Street, the picture moved to the bar of the National Film Theatre. This of course could not have been more appropriate, marrying as it did Olwen's two chief pleasures in life – the cinema and conviviality.

But some years later the picture disappeared. Peter Hopkinson, an old friend of Olwen, wrote to ask what had happened to it and was assured that it would be displayed in the Museum of the Moving Image. More years went by but the picture failed to materialize in the Museum.

Thinking that there could be no more appropriate image of Olwen for my book, I made enquiries about the picture. Well-meaning people said that they would try to find it, a few telephone calls followed, but after a while they gave up looking and the whereabouts of the portrait remain a mystery. 'Poor Olwen,' I thought. I imagined her picture lost in a sea of crates like Charles Foster Kane's sledge with no one to appreciate its significance.

The idea of commemoration has a powerful appeal. Recently I received a letter – a form letter – from the Curator of the National Film and Television Archive, offering me an opportunity 'to help preserve our cinematic heritage for years to come'. If I wrote a cheque for £500, they would include my name in a personal credit, which would appear at the beginning of one of the historic British films the Archive was seeking to preserve. 'This credit will remain on the film for ever,' I was assured, 'and will appear whenever the print is screened.' There was even an enticing example, each line neatly framed between sprocket holes:

Presenting Alfred Hitchcock's *The Lodger*
Preserved and restored thanks to the generous support of
MR CHARLES DRAZIN

What would future audiences make of this I wondered. What would they know of 'Mr Charles Drazin' except that he had once signed a cheque? The names of many of the individuals who made these films are almost as meaningless since we know so little about them. Hitchcock has been endlessly written about, but most others hardly at all. 'Few things are more distressing for me than prising open a can of film to find nothing but a congealed, crumbling film, its images lost for ever,' wrote the curator in her letter. I think it's as distressing to see the lives of the people who made those films slip into oblivion.

It's marvellous that the National Film and Television Archive should be preserving old films, but we can't really expect such institutions to do the same for people. They lack the necessary sympathy and imagination. Olwen Vaughan's friends getting together to decide how to remember her, Diana Morgan rescuing the bust of Robert Hamer from a back room in the BFI – just as it took individuals to bring about the British cinema's finest years, it requires individuals to pay them fitting tribute. Ultimately this book is about individuals – often at odds with the prevailing order – making a difference.

Notes

Preface

1. Satyajit Ray, *Our Films, Their Films* (Orient Longman, 1976), p. 145.
2. *The Dilys Powell Film Reader* (Oxford University Press, 1992), p. 20.
3. Interview, 26 September 1994.
4. James Park, *British Cinema: The Lights That Failed* (Batsford, 1990).
5. *Daniel Martin* (Picador, 1989), p. 307.

Introduction

1. *Silver Spoon* (Hutchinson, 1954), p. 161.
2. *The Film Till Now: A Survey of World Cinema* (Vision Press, 2nd edn 1951), p. 550.
3. Quoted in the Political and Economic Planning report on the British Film Industry (1952), p. 73.
4. Alan Wood, *Mr Rank* (Hodder & Stoughton, 1952), p. 67.
5. Peter Noble (ed.), *British Film Yearbook 1947–48* (British Yearbooks), p. 82.
6. Ibid., p. 83.
7. Sydney Box's cuttings book, Kevin Brownlow collection.
8. *Motion Picture Herald*, 11 October 1947.
9. Ibid., 31 January 1948.
10. Ibid., 26 July 1947.
11. Interview, 1 February 1995.
12. *Cinéma, notre métier.* Quoted in Pierre Billard, *L'Age classique du cinéma français* (Flammarion, 1995), p. 387.

13. 'French Films', broadcast on the BBC Third Programme, 26 October 1946.
14. *French Film* (Falcon Press, 1953), p. 111.
15. Figures taken from a table in Georges Sadoul, *Histoire Générale du Cinéma*, vol. 6 (Editions Denoël, 1954).
16. *Daily Film Renter*, 19 May 1943.
17. INF 1/212, Public Record Office (PRO).
18. *The Long View* (Secker & Warburg, 1974), p. 106.
19. Quoted in *The British Board of Film Censors: Film Censorship in Britain 1896–1950* (Croom Helm, 1985), p. 74.
20. *Odd Woman Out* (Leslie Frewin, 1974), pp.192–3.
21. *Observer*, 29 June 1947.
22. *Sunday Pictorial*, 12 October 1947.
23. *Red Roses at Night: An Account of London Cinemas under Fire* (Quality Press, 1948), p. 73.
24. *Penguin Film Review*, vol. 1 (Penguin, 1946), p. 29.
25. *Twenty Years of British Film 1925–45* (Falcon Press, 1947), p. 7.

Filippo Del Giudice

1. Thorold Dickinson, *A Discovery of Cinema* (Oxford University Press, 1971), p. 77.
2. Michael Powell, *A Life in Movies* (Heinemann, 1986), p. 236.
3. Noël Coward, *Future Indefinite* (Heinemann, 1954), p. 206.
4. Ibid., p. 212.
5. Ibid.
6. Anthony Havelock-Allan, interview, 1 February 1995.
7. 24 December 1942.
8. Guido Coen, interview, 17 March 1995.
9. Adrian Brunel, *Nice Work* (Forbes Robertson, 1949), p. 193.
10. Del Giudice Papers, BFI Library Special Collection, item 1.
11. Guido Coen, interview.
12. Quoted in Leslie Ruth Howard, *A Quite Remarkable Father* (Longmans, 1960), p. 257.
13. Ibid., p. 258.
14. Guido Coen, interview.
15. John Barber, *Leader Magazine*, 21 June 1947.
16. Michael Powell, *A Life in Movies*, p. 603.
17. Del Giudice Papers, BFI Library Special Collection, item 3.
18. Ibid.

19. Ibid.
20. Ibid.
21. Basil Wright, *The Long View* (Secker & Warburg, 1974), p. 199.
22. Conversation with the author, autumn 1996.
23. Anthony Havelock-Allan, interview.
24. Richard Norton, quoted in *The Diaries of Sir Robert Bruce Lockhart* (entry for 25 May 1946), vol. 2, ed. Kenneth Young (Macmillan), p. 546.
25. *Daily Film Renter*, 16 April 1946.
26. Sir Robert Bruce Lockhart, *Friends, Foes and Foreigners* (Putnam, 1957), pp. 176–7.
27. Sir Nicholas Henderson, *The Private Office* (Weidenfeld & Nicolson, 1984), p. 32.
28. See Woodrow Wyatt, *Confessions of an Optimist* (Collins, 1985), p. 143.
29. Ibid.
30. *Leader Magazine*, 21 June 1947.
31. Sir Robert Bruce Lockhart, *Friends, Foes and Foreigners*, p. 178.
32. Bill MacQuitty, interview, 27 October 1995.
33. Jill Craigie, interview, 14 November 1994.
34. Guido Coen, interview.
35. The original budget was £350,000, and it finally cost £475,000. See Alan Wood, *Mr Rank* (Hodder & Stoughton, 1952), p. 139.
36. Ibid., p. 143.
37. Memo to Jack Beddington, dated 31 May 1943, INF 1/218, PRO.
38. Anthony Havelock-Allan, interview.
39. *The Diaries of Sir Robert Bruce Lockhart*, vol. 2 (Macmillan, 1973), p. 546.
40. *Leader Magazine*, 21 June 1947.
41. Del Giudice Papers, BFI Library Special Collection, item 13.
42. 21 June 1947.
43. Del Giudice Papers, BFI Library Special Collection, item 2.
44. *Inside Pictures* (Cresset Press, 1960), p. 27.
45. Del Giudice Papers, BFI Library Special Collection, item 16.
46. According to the Political and Economic Planning report on the British Film Industry (p. 88), in 1944 the Rank Organisation owned 619 cinemas, ABPC 442.
47. A copy of this undated letter can be found in the Board of Trade files at the Public Record Office, BT 64/2366.

48. Ibid.
49. 12 April 1948, ibid.
50. As Woodrow Wyatt reported to Harold Wilson in a letter dated 8 July 1948, ibid.
51. Letter dated 10 August 1948, Del Giudice Papers, BFI Library Special Collection, item 10.
52. *Evening Standard*, 27 April 1950.
53. Letter dated 27 November 1949, Del Giudice Papers, BFI Special Collection, item 21.
54. Letter dated 9 March 1950, Del Giudice Papers, BFI Library Special Collection, item 24.
55. Interview with Roy Baker, 25 October 1995.
56. 8 March 1950.
57. Letter dated 13 July 1959, Del Giudice Papers, BFI Library Special Collection, item 27.
58. *Daily Mail*, 30 April 1958.
59. See *Reynolds News*, 4 May 1958.
60. *Daily Mail*, 30 April 1958.
61. See Woodrow Wyatt, *Confessions of an Optimist*, p. 144.
62. *Daily Sketch*, 29 September 1958.
63. Quoted in the Italian monthly review *Derby* (Milan), February 1950.

John Davis

1. Supplement to *Today's Cinema*, 12 November 1971.
2. Bill MacQuitty, *A Life to Remember* (Quartet, 1991), p. 324.
3. Roy Baker, interview, 25 October 1995.
4. Alan Wood, *Mr Rank* (Hodder & Stoughton, 1952), p. 102.
5. Ibid.
6. Ivor Montagu, *The Youngest Son: Autobiographical Chapters* (Lawrence & Wishart, 1970), p. 347.
7. Ibid., p. 354.
8. Alan Wood, *Mr Rank*, p. 84.
9. Supplement to *Today's Cinema*, 12 November 1971.
10. Richard Norton, *Silver Spoon* (Hutchinson, 1954), p. 210.
11. Alan Wood, *Mr Rank*, p. 242.
12. Jill Craigie, interview, 14 November 1995.
13. Bill MacQuitty, *A Life to Remember*, p. 297.
14. Bill MacQuitty, interview, 27 October 1995.

15. Michael Powell, *A Life in Movies* (Heinemann, 1986), p. 597.
16. Bill MacQuitty, interview.
17. Michael Powell, *A Life in Movies*, p. 663.
18. Interview in Brian MacFarlane (ed.), *Sixty Voices* (BFI Publishing, 1992), p. 73.
19. Roy Baker, interview.
20. Dirk Bogarde, interview, 14 June 1996.
21. Michael Powell, *A Life in Movies*, p. 397.
22. Ibid., p. 662.
23. Roy Baker, interview.
24. Guido Coen, interview, 17 March 1995.
25. Michael Powell, *Million Dollar Movie* (Heinemann, 1993), p. 297.
26. Supplement to *Today's Cinema*, 12 November 1971.
27. Michael Powell, *A Life in Movies*, p. 664.
28. Bill MacQuitty, interview.
29. Alan Wood, *Mr Rank*, p. 243.
30. Michael Powell, *Million Dollar Movie*, p. 7.
31. Bill MacQuitty, interview.
32. Alan Wood, *Mr Rank*, p. 242.

David Lean and Carol Reed

1. Quoted in Stephen M. Silverman, *David Lean* (André Deutsch, 1989), p. 90.
2. *Here Lies Eric Ambler* (Weidenfeld & Nicolson, 1985), p. 188.
3. Quoted in Stephen M. Silverman, *David Lean*, p. 49
4. Quoted in Nicholas Wapshott, *The Man Between: A Biography of Carol Reed* (Chatto & Windus, 1990), p. 98.
5. Interview, 1 February 1995.
6. *The Eighth Veil* (William Kimber, 1980), p. 70.
7. Ibid.
8. Michael Redgrave, *In My Mind's Eye* (Weidenfeld & Nicolson, 1983), pp. 43–4.
9. Mrs Robert Henrey, *A Filmstar in Belgrave Square* (Peter Davies, 1948), p. 157.
10. Stanley Holloway, *Wiv a Little Bit o' Luck* (Leslie Frewin, 1969), p. 263.
11. Michael Korda, *Charmed Lives* (Random House, 1979), p. 230.
12. Jack Hawkins, *Anything for a Quiet Life* (Elm Tree Books, 1973), p. 21.

13. Freddie Young, interview, 18 February 1997.
14. John Hawkesworth, interview, 7 April 1997.
15. Quoted in Stephen M. Silverman, *David Lean*, p. 21.
16. Noël Coward, *Future Indefinite* (Heinemann, 1954), p. 211.
17. *Red Roses Every Night: An Account of London Cinemas under Fire* (Quality Press, 1948), p. 72.
18. Quoted in Nicholas Wapshott, *The Man Between*, p. 179.
19. 3 October 1948.
20. 3 October 1948.
21. 3 October 1948.
22. *Sunday Times*, 3 October 1948.
23. Preface to thc Collected Edition of *The Third Man* and *The Fallen Idol* (Penguin, 1976), p. 123.
24. Ibid., p. 124.
25. Quoted in Orson Welles and Peter Bogdanovich, *This is Orson Welles* (HarperCollins, 1992), p. 220.
26. Graham Greene, Preface to the Collected Edition of *The Third Man* and *The Fallen Idol*, p. 119.
27. Joseph Cotten, *Vanity Will Get You Somewhere* (Columbus Books, 1987), p. 97.
28. Ibid., p. 98.
29. Interview in Charles Thomas Samuels, *Encountering Directors* (Putnam & Sons, 1972), p. 166.
30. Quoted in Nicholas Wapshott, *The Man Between*, p. 285.
31. *Independent on Sunday*, 30 September 1990.

Robert Hamer

1. Brenda Danischewsky, telephone conversation with the author, 1993.
2. 'Obituaries', House and School Notes, Rossall School, September 1930.
3. Brenda Danischewsky, interview, 2 August 1995.
4. John McCallum, *Life with Googie* (Heinemann, 1979), p. 11.
5. *The Cinema 1952*, ed. Roger Manvell and R. K. Neilson Baxter (Penguin, 1952), p. 53.
6. Freda Bruce-Lockhart, *Sight and Sound*, October–December, 1951, p. 75.
7. *Monthly Film Bulletin*, 1947, p. 171.
8. Letter to author dated 11 October 1993.

9. This and all subsequent quotations from the minutes of the meetings of Ealing's Associate Producers and Directors come from copies in the Ivor Montagu Papers, BFI Library Special Collection.
10. Interview, 1 September 1994.
11. Ivor Montagu Papers, BFI Library Special Collection, item 243.
12. *Michael Balcon Presents: A Lifetime of Films* (Hutchinson, 1969), p. 163.
13. *Sight and Sound*, spring, 1959.
14. *Almost a Gentleman* (Peter Davies, 1966), p. 190.
15. Ibid., p. 213.
16. Ibid., p. 214.
17. Ibid., p. 212.
18. Ibid.
19. *Between Hell and Charing Cross* (Allen & Unwin, 1977), p. 83.
20. *Almost a Gentleman*, p. 213.

Angus Macphail

1. T. E. B. Clarke, *This is Where I Came In* (Michael Joseph, 1974), p. 149.
2. Undated letter in the Ivor Montagu Papers, BFI Library Special Collection, item 404.
3. T. E. B. Clarke, *This is Where I Came In*, p. 149.
4. Diana Morgan, interview, summer 1993.
5. Brenda Danischewsky, interview, 2 August 1995.
6. Brenda Danischewsky was told this story by a Cambridge contemporary of Angus Macphail.
7. Ivor Montagu, *The Youngest Son: Autobiographical Chapters* (Lawrence & Wishart, 1970), p. 225.
8. Ibid., p. 228.
9. Ibid., p. 225.
10. *Granta*, 29 February 1924.
11. Ibid., 23 January 1925.
12. Ivor Montagu, *The Youngest Son*, p. 266.
13. Quoted in Adrian Brunel, *Nice Work* (Forbes Robertson, 1949), p. 113.
14. Ibid., p. 145.
15. Ibid.

16. *Michael Balcon Presents: A Lifetime of Films* (Hutchinson, 1969), p. 20.
17. Mark Benny, *Almost a Gentleman* (Peter Davies, 1966), pp. 198–9.
18. Michael Relph, interview, 19 January 1995.
19. Harry Watt, *Don't Look at the Camera* (Elek Books, 1974), p. 193.
20. Stella Jonckheere, interview, 30 November 1994.
21. Brenda Danischewsky, interview.
22. Stella Jonckheere, interview.
23. Donald Spoto, *The Dark Side of Genius: The Life of Alfred Hitchcock* (Ballantine Books, 1983), p. 394.
24. Letter dated 2 December 1960 in the Ivor Montagu Papers, BFI Library Special Collection, item 404.
25. 6 July 1961.

Michael Balcon

1. *Michael Balcon Presents: A Lifetime of Films* (Hutchinson, 1969), p. 100.
2. Ibid., p. 107.
3. Ibid., p. 105.
4. Ibid., p. 99.
5. *The Youngest Son: Autobiographical Chapters* (Lawrence & Wishart, 1970), p. 322.
6. Elizabeth Sussex, *The Rise and Fall of British Documentary* (University of California Press, 1975), p. 19.
7. *Michael Balcon Presents: A Lifetime of Films*, p. 66.
8. Ibid., p. 130.
9. Interview, 2 August 1995.
10. *Michael Balcon Presents: A Lifetime of Films*, p. 94.
11. Interview, *Made in Ealing*, Omnibus, BBC, 1986.
12. Interview, ibid.
13. Sidney Cole, interview, 12 March 1997.
14. Interview, *Made in Ealing*.
15. *Michael Balcon Presents: A Lifetime of Films*, p. 138.
16. *Odd Woman Out* (Leslie Frewin, 1974), p. 205.
17. Dated 20 November 1928, Ivor Montagu Papers, BFI Library Special Collection.
18. Ivor Montagu Papers, BFI Library Special Collection, item 47.
19. *Almost a Gentleman* (Peter Davies, 1966), p. 199.

Cavalcanti

1. Interview with Judy and Charles Hassé, 29 September 1996.
2. Judy Hassé.
3. Brenda Danischewsky, interview, 2 August 1995.
4. For an account of Cavalcanti's early career see Hermilo Borba Filho, in Lorenzo Pellizzari and Claudio M. Valentinetti (eds), *Alberto Cavalcanti* (Editions du Festival international du film de Locarno, 1988), pp. 89ff.
5. Elizabeth Sussex, 'Cavalcanti in England', *Sight and Sound*, autumn, 1975, p. 207.
6. Elizabeth Sussex, *The Rise and Fall of British Documentary* (University of California Press, 1975), p. 47.
7. Ibid., p. 98.
8. Elizabeth Sussex, 'Cavalcanti in England', p. 207.
9. Ibid.
10. Elizabeth Sussex, *The Rise and Fall of British Documentary*, p. 51.
11. Ibid., p. 53.
12. Harry Watt, *Don't Look at the Camera* (Elek Books, 1974), p. 68.
13. Interview, 2 August 1995.
14. Elizabeth Sussex, *The Rise and Fall of British Documentary*, p. 51.
15. *Documentary Diary: An Informal History of the Documentary Film 1928–1939* (Secker & Warburg, 1973), p. 130.
16. Ibid., p. 220.
17. Elizabeth Sussex, *The Rise and Fall of British Documentary*, p. 51.
18. Interview, 29 September 1996.
19. INF 1/57, PRO.
20. Ibid.
21. *Screen*, summer, 1972.
22. INF 1/57, PRO.
23. Interview, 21 October 1995.
24. 'Comedies and Cartoons', *Footnotes to the Film*, ed. Charles Davy (Lovat Dickson, 1938) p. 83.
25. Ibid., p. 84.
26. *Michael Balcon Presents: A Lifetime of Films* (Hutchinson, 1969), p. 131.
27. Douglas Slocombe, interview, 1995.
28. Elizabeth Sussex, 'Cavalcanti in England', p. 209.
29. Quoted in Penelope Houston, *Went the Day Well?* (British Film Institute, 1992), p. 51.
30. *News Chronicle*, 26 August 1944.

31. Quoted in an Ealing Studios publicity profile, Cavalcanti microfiche, BFI Library.
32. *Late Joys at the Players' Theatre* (Boardman & Co, 1943), p. 27.
33. 'Comedies and Cartoons', p. 86.
34. Interview with John Harrington and David Paroissien, *Literature/Film Quarterly*, 6, 1 (winter, 1978), p. 49.
35. Interview, 1995.
36. For an account of this trip, see Hermilo Borba Filho, in Lorenzo Pellizzari and Claudio M. Valentinetti (eds), *Alberto Cavalcanti*, pp. 161–4.
37. 29 June 1947.
38. Elizabeth Sussex, 'Cavalcanti in England', p. 211.
39. Bob Huke, interview, 16 March 1997.
40. Elizabeth Sussex, 'Cavalcanti in England', p. 211.

Harry Watt

1. Elizabeth Sussex, *The Rise and Fall of British Documentary* (University of California Press, 1975), p. 29.
2. Harry Watt, *Don't Look at the Camera* (Elek Books, 1974), p. 27.
3. Ibid., p. 29.
4. Ibid., p. 28.
5. Elizabeth Sussex, *The Rise and Fall of British Documentary*, p. 29.
6. Ibid., p. 30.
7. Ibid., p. 76.
8. Ibid., pp. 76–7.
9. Ibid., p. 98.
10. Ibid., p. 131.
11. Harry Watt, *Don't Look at the Camera*, p. 102.
12. Ibid., p. 110.
13. Elizabeth Sussex, *The Rise and Fall of British Documentary*, p. 109.
14. Julian Spiro, interview, 17 April 1996.
15. Harry Watt, *Don't Look at the Camera*, p. 101.
16. Ibid.
17. Joe Mendoza, interview, 21 October 1995.
18. Harry Watt, *Don't Look at the Camera*, p. 161.
19. John Krish, interview, 12 October 1994.
20. Harry Watt, *Don't Look at the Camera*, p. 152.
21. Elizabeth Sussex, *The Rise and Fall of British Documentary*, p. 131.

22. 24 February 1941, INF 1/81, PRO.
23. Elizabeth Sussex, *The Rise and Fall of British Documentary*, p. 29.
24. Ibid., p. 189.

Humphrey Jennings

1. *Heart of Britain: An Affectionate Portrait of Humphrey Jennings*, BBC, transmitted September 1970.
2. *Sight and Sound*, spring, 1954.
3. Gerry Bryant, 'Wartime Rhymes by members of the Crown Film Unit, 1940–1946', unpublished, compiled by Mavis Ilsley.
4. Joe Mendoza, interview, 21 October 1995.
5. John Krish, interview, 12 October 1994.
6. Nora Lee, interview, 21 June 1994.
7. 28 July 1942, reproduced in *The Humphrey Jennings Film Reader*, ed. Kevin Jackson (Carcanet, 1993), p. 60.
8. 16 January 1944, ibid., p. 91.
9. 12 April 1942, ibid., p. 58.
10. BBC Home Service, 26 May 1943, ibid., p. 74.
11. Letter to Allen Hutt, undated, ibid., p. 82.
12. Reproduced in ibid., p. 297.
13. Joe Mendoza, interview.
14. In Robert Vas's *Omnibus* documentary.
15. Betty Jenkins, interviewed by Robert Vas.
16. Anthony Hodgkinson and Rodney Sheratsky, *Humphrey Jennings: More than a Maker of Films* (University of New England, 1982), p. 82.
17. Ibid., p. 57.
18. Quoted in Dai Vaughan, *Portrait of an Invisible Man* (BFI Publishing, 1983), p. 55.
19. 19 October 1941, *The Humphrey Jennings Film Reader*, p. 32.
20. Quoted in Elizabeth Sussex, *The Rise and Fall of British Documentary*, pp. 10–11.
21. 31 August 1949, *The Humphrey Jennings Film Reader*, p. 161.
22. Joe Mendoza, interview.
23. *Hitchcock by Truffaut* (Paladin, 1986), p. 321.
24. Joe Mendoza, interview.
25. 29 January 1943, *The Humphrey Jennings Film Reader*, p. 76.
26. Ibid., p. 78.

27. Sir Denis Forman, interview, 2 November 1994.
28. 13 January 1944, *The Humphrey Jennings Film Reader*, p. 93.
29. Postscript to his *Sight and Sound* article on Jennings, reprinted in *Humphrey Jennings: Film-maker, Painter, Poet*, ed. Mary-Lou Jennings, British Film Institute, 1982, p. 58.
30. Ian Dalrymple, 'Humphrey Jennings, 1907–1950: A Tribute', *British Film Academy Quarterly*, no. 11, January 1951.

Ian Dalrymple

1. *Independent*, 1 May 1989.
2. Official papers relating to the reorganization of the GPO Film Unit are contained in INF 1/81, PRO.
3. Elizabeth Sussex, *The Rise and Fall of British Documentary* (University of California Press, 1975), p. 125.
4. Memo dated 7 November 1940. INF 1/81, PRO.
5. INF 1/81, PRO.
6. 25 September 1940. INF 1/81, PRO.
7. 15 May 1941. INF 1/210, PRO.
8. John Krish, interview, 12 October 1994.
9. Nora Lee, interview, 21 June 1994.
10. Interview, 2 November 1994.
11. Letter to author, 22 December 1994.
12. 18 May 1942. INF 1/213, PRO.
13. 21 May 1942. INF 1/213, PRO.
14. 7 September 1942. INF 1/213, PRO.
15. INF 1/58, PRO.
16. Elizabeth Sussex, *The Rise and Fall of British Documentary*, p. 125.
17. 'British Films in Wartime', African transmission, BBC Radio, 24 September 1941.
18. Interview, 26 September 1996.
19. Interview, 16 June 1996.
20. 2 May 1989.

Pat Jackson

1. Pat Jackson, unpublished manuscript.
2. C. Pennington-Richards, interview, 26 September 1996.

3. 9 December 1944.
4. Quoted in Pat Jackson, unpublished manuscript.
5. Ibid.
6. Ibid.
7. 17 June 1951.

Jack Beddington

1. From a transcript of an interview published in *Film Dope*, 12, Thorold Dickinson Papers, BFI Library Special Collection, item 31.
2. For an account of the campaign see R. J. Minney, *Puffin Asquith* (Leslie Frewin, 1973), pp. 102ff.
3. Kenneth Clark, *The Other Half: A Self Portrait* (John Murray, 1977), p. 10.
4. Ibid., p. 11.
5. Nicolas Bentley, *A Version of the Truth* (André Deutsch, 1960), pp. 132, 139.
6. Peter Quennell, *The Marble Foot: An Autobiography 1905–1938* (Collins, 1976), p. 224.
7. Michael Powell, *A Life in Movies* (Heinemann, 1986), p. 455.
8. Bill MacQuitty, *A Life to Remember* (Quartet, 1991), p. 271.
9. Letter to author, 3 March 1997.
10. Tribute in *The Times*, 27 April 1959.
11. *A Brush with Industry*, Shell video, 1983.
12. Paul Rotha, *Documentary Diary: An Informal History of the Documentary Film 1928–1939* (Secker & Warburg, 1973), p. 72.
13. Michael Powell, *A Life in Movies*, p. 455.
14. Letter to author, 22 October 1996.
15. Dallas Bower, interview, 1996.
16. INF 1/30, PRO.
17. INF 1/460, PRO.
18. 13 July 1940. INF 1/460, PRO.
19. John Grierson, *Grierson on Documentary*, ed. Forsyth Hardy (Faber & Faber, 1979), p. 355.
20. Paul Rotha, quoted in Elizabeth Sussex, *The Rise and Fall of British Documentary* (University of California Press, 1975), p. 140.
21. 'Forgotten Lessons in Realism', *Rotha on the Film: A Selection of Writings about the Cinema* (Faber & Faber, 1958), p. 308.

22. 27 March 1943. INF 1/224, PRO.
23. *Young Artists of Promise* (Studio Publications, 1957), p. 8.
24. *Kinematograph Weekly*, 7 February 1946.
25. *The Times*, 17 April 1959.
26. *Young Artists of Promise*, p. 10.
27. *A Life in Movies*, p. 383.

'Puffin' Asquith

1. *The Times*, 27 February 1968.
2. R. J. Minney, *Puffin Asquith* (Leslie Frewin, 1973), pp. 162–3.
3. Ibid., p. 158.
4. 16 February 1930.
5. Peter Noble, *Anthony Asquith* (BFI, 1952), p. 14.
6. Paul Rotha, *Celluloid: The Film Today* (Longmans, Green & Co., 1935), p. 175.
7. Quoted in Peter Noble, *Anthony Asquith*, p. 7.
8. Ibid., pp. 20–21.
9. *Observer*, 15 February 1931.
10. 27 October 1939.
11. From a notebook in Box 1, Anthony Asquith Papers, BFI Library Special Collection.
12. Muriel Box, *Odd Woman Out* (Leslie Frewin, 1974), p. 107.
13. R. J. Minney, *Puffin Asquith*, p. 90.
14. Address to the ACTT annual meeting, 30 March 1968.
15. Interview, 12 March 1997.
16. R. J. Minney, *Puffin Asquith*, p. 91.
17. From a notebook in Box 1, Anthony Asquith Papers, BFI Library Special Collection.
18. 15 January 1944.
19. 23 December 1943.
20. *A Discovery of Cinema* (Oxford University Press, 1971), p. 21.
21. *The Queen*, 25 June 1930.
22. R. J. Minney, *Puffin Asquith*, p. 159.
23. *In My Mind's Eye* (Weidenfeld & Nicolson), p. 173.
24. Ibid., p. 172.
25. Quoted in *The Autobiography of Margot Asquith*, vol. 2 (Thornton Butterworth, 1922), p. 243.
26. *Penguin Film Review*, vol. 1, August 1946, p. 18.
27. *Daily Mirror*, 30 May 1950.

28. *News Chronicle*, 8 March 1947.
29. *Sunday Times*, 25 February 1968.

Sydney Box

1. Interview, 11 August 1995.
2. *Film Publicity: A Handbook on the Production and Distribution of Propaganda Films* (Lovat Dickson, 1937), p. 3.
3. Ibid., pp. 43–4.
4. Interview, 11 August 1995.
5. *Odd Woman Out* (Leslie Frewin, 1974), p. 138.
6. *The Black-out Book* (Harrap, 1939).
7. Interview, 27 October 1995.
8. 'A Possible Solution', *Sequence*, spring, 1948, p. 8.
9. Muriel Box, *Odd Woman Out*, p. 171.
10. Ann Todd, *The Eighth Veil* (William Kimber, 1980), p. 57.
11. James Mason, *Before I Forget* (Hamish Hamilton, 1981), p. 107.
12. Ibid., p. 111.
13. Ann Todd, *The Eighth Veil*, p. 57.
14. Ibid., p. 25.
15. Quoted in Bill MacQuitty, *A Life to Remember* (Quartet, 1991), p. 293.
16. *Odd Woman Out*, p. 186.
17. Interview, October 1995.
18. Telephone conversation with author, 1997.
19. *Kinematograph Weekly*, 25 September 1947.
20. *The Film Till Now: A Survey of World Cinema* (Vision Press, 2nd edn, 1951), p. 555.

Herbert Wilcox

1. *Films Since 1939* (Longmans, Green & Co., 1947)
2. Herbert Wilcox, *Twenty-five Thousand Sunsets* (Bodley Head, 1967), p. 5.
3. Ibid., p. 53.
4. Ibid.
5. Ibid.
6. See Michael Powell, *A Life in Movies* (Heinemann, 1986), p. 111.

7. George Pearson, *Flashback* (George Allen & Unwin, 1957), p. 122.
8. Herbert Wilcox, *Twenty-five Thousand Sunsets*, p. 58.
9. Richard Norton, *Silver Spoon* (Hutchinson, 1954), p. 169.
10. Ibid., p. 170.
11. Freddie Young, interview, 18 February 1997.
12. Jack Cardiff, *Magic Hour* (Faber & Faber, 1996), p. 27.
13. Interview, 18 February 1997.
14. Margaret Lockwood, *Lucky Star*, p. 160.
15. Bob Dunbar, interview, 14 February 1995.
16. Anna Neagle, *There's Always Tomorrow: An Autobiography* (W. H. Allen, 1974), pp. 143–4.
17. *Kinematograph Weekly*, 18 December 1947.
18. Anna Neagle, *An Autobiography*, p. 122.
19. *Picturegoer*, 1 January 1938.
20. Richard Norton, *Silver Spoon*, p. 169.
21. *Daily Express*, 16 September 1964.
22. *Daily Mirror*, 28 January 1965.
23. *Daily Despatch*, 13 January 1965.

Gabriel Pascal

1. Valerie Pascal, *The Disciple and His Devil* (Michael Joseph, 1971), p. 67.
2. Ibid., p. 77.
3. Ibid.
4. Ibid., p. 74.
5. Richard Norton, *Silver Spoon* (Hutchinson, 1954), p. 180.
6. Valerie Pascal, *The Disciple and His Devil*, p. 66.
7. Ibid., p. 84.
8. Ibid., p. 87.
9. Ibid., p. 98.
10. Stanley Holloway, *Wiv a Little Bit o' Luck* (Leslie Frewin, 1969), p. 266.
11. Ibid., p. 267.
12. *The Leader*, 17 February 1945.
13. Freddie Young, interview, 18 February 1997.
14. Marjorie Deans, 'My Wartime Life with GBS and Gaby', unpublished manuscript, chapter 11, p. 22.
15. Valerie Pascal, *The Disciple and His Devil*, p. 105.

16. Conversation with author.
17. *The Leader*, 17 February 1945.
18. See *Daily Film Renter*, 17 April 1946.
19. Valerie Pascal, *The Disciple and His Devil*, p. 109.
20. Marjorie Deans, *Meeting at the Sphinx*, p. viii.
21. R. J. Minney, *The Bogus Image of Bernard Shaw* (Leslie Frewin, 1969), p. 86.
22. Kenneth Clark, *The Other Half: A Self Portrait* (John Murray, 1977), p. 37.
23. Valerie Pascal, *The Disciple and His Devil*, p. 151.
24. Ibid., p. 197.
25. Stewart Granger, *Sparks Fly Upward* (Granada, 1981), p. 256.
26. Ibid., p. 257.

Olwen Vaughan

1. Rodney Ackland and Elspeth Grant, *The Celluloid Mistress* (Allan Wingate, 1954), p. 168.
2. *Evening News*, 3 December 1945.
3. Penelope Houston, interview, 11 October 1994.
4. Brenda Danischewsky, interview, 2 August 1995.
5. Basil Wright, *Sight and Sound*, autumn, 1973.
6. Irwin Shaw, *The Young Lions* (Jonathan Cape, 1949), p. 380.
7. Patrick Campbell, *Nova*, December 1969, p. 66.
8. *Daily Express*, 24 September 1962.
9. Sir Denis Forman, interview, 2 November 1994.
10. Peter Hopkinson, interview, 11 October 1994.
11. Helen Blackburne, interview, 5 November 1996.
12. Memorial tribute, 10 October 1973.
13. *Sunday Times*, 11 November 1945.
14. Rodney Ackland and Elspeth Grant, *The Celluloid Mistress*, p. 168.
15. *Sunday Times*, 11 November 1945.
16. Sir Denis Forman, interview.

Select Bibliography

Histories and works of criticism and reference

Aldgate, Anthony and Richards, Jeffrey, *Britain Can Take It*, Blackwell, 1986.

Barr, Charles, *Ealing Studios*, Studio Vista, 2nd edn, 1993.

Box, Sydney, *Film Publicity: A Handbook on the Production and Distribution of Propaganda Films*, Lovat Dickson, 1937.

Davy, Charles (ed.), *Footnotes to the Film*, Lovat Dickson, 1938.

Dickinson, Thorold, *A Discovery of Cinema*, Oxford University Press, 1971.

Durgnat, Raymond, *A Mirror for England*, Faber & Faber, 1970.

Forman, Denis, *Films 1945–1950*, Longmans, Green & Co, 1952.

Hopkinson, Peter, *Split Focus: An Involvement in Two Decades*, Rupert Hart-Davis, 1969.

Low, Rachael, *The History of the British Film 1929–1939: Film-making in 1930s Britain*, George Allen & Unwin, 1985.

McFarlane, Brian (ed.), *Sixty Voices: Celebrities Recall the Golden Age of British Cinema*, BFI, 1992.

Macnab, Geoffrey, *J. Arthur Rank and the British Film Industry*, Routledge, 1993.

Morgan, Guy, *Red Roses Every Night: An Account of London Cinemas Under Fire*, Quality Press, 1948.

Murphy, Robert, *Realism and Tinsel: Cinema and Society in Britain 1939–49*, Routledge, 1989.

Noble, Peter (ed.), *British Film Yearbook 1947–8*, British Yearbooks.

PEP (Political and Economic Planning), *The British Film Industry*, 1952.

Perry, George, *The Great British Picture Show*, Paladin, 1975.

Powell, Dilys, *Films Since 1939*, Longmans, Green & Co, 1947.

——, *The Dilys Powell Film Reader*, Oxford University Press, 1992.

Ray, Satyajit, *Our Films, Their Films*, Orient Longman, 1976.
Robertson, James C., *The British Board of Film Censors: Film Censorship in Britain, 1896–1950*, Croom Helm, 1985.
Rotha, Paul, *Documentary Diary: An Informal History of the Documentary Film, 1928–1939*, Secker & Warburg, 1973.
——, *Rotha on the Film: A Selection of Writings about the Cinema*, Faber & Faber, 1958.
Rotha, Paul and Griffith, Richard, *The Film Till Now: A Survey of World Cinema*, Vision Press, 2nd edn, 1951.
Samuels, Charles Thomas, *Encountering Directors*, Putnam & Sons, 1972.
Sussex, Elizabeth, *The Rise and Fall of British Documentary*, University of California Press, 1975.
Thomson, David, *A Biographical Dictionary of the Cinema*, Secker & Warburg, 1975.
——, *A Biographical Dictionary of Film*, André Deutsch, 1994.
Welles, Orson and Bogdanovich, Peter, *This is Orson Welles* (ed. Jonathan Rosenbaum), HarperCollins, 1992.
Winnington, Richard, *Film Criticism and Caricatures 1943–53*, Paul Elek, 1975.
Wright, Basil, *The Long View: A Personal Perspective on World Cinema*, Secker & Warburg, 1974.

Memoirs and biographies

Ackland, Rodney and Grant, Elspeth, *The Celluloid Mistress*, Allan Wingate, 1954.
Ambler, Eric, *Here Lies Eric Ambler: An Autobiography*, Weidenfeld & Nicolson, 1985.
Balcon, Michael, *Michael Balcon Presents: A Lifetime of Films*, Hutchinson, 1969.
Benny, Mark, *Almost a Gentleman*, Peter Davies, 1966.
Bentley, Nicolas, *A Version of the Truth*, André Deutsch, 1960.
Betts, Ernest, *Inside Pictures: With Some Reflections from the Outside*, Cresset Press, 1960.
Box, Muriel, *Odd Woman Out*, Leslie Frewin, 1974.
Brownlow, Kevin, *David Lean*, Richard Cohen, 1996.
Brunel, Adrian, *Nice Work*, Forbes Robertson, 1949.
Cardiff, Jack, *Magic Hour*, Faber & Faber, 1996.
Clark, Kenneth, *The Other Half*, John Murray, 1977.

Select Bibliography

Clarke, T. E. B., *This is Where I Came In*, Michael Joseph, 1974.

Cotten, Joseph, *Vanity Will Get You Somewhere*, Columbus Books, 1987.

Coward, Noël, *Future Indefinite*, Heinemann, 1954.

Danischewsky, Monja, *White Russian, Red Face*, Victor Gollancz, 1966.

Deans, Marjorie, *Meeting at the Sphinx: Gabriel Pascal's Production of Bernard Shaw's Caesar and Cleopatra*, Macdonald & Co., 1946.

Farrar, David, *No Royal Road*, Mortimer Publications, 1948.

Granger, Stewart, *Sparks Fly Upward*, Granada, 1981.

Guinness, Alec, *Blessings in Disguise*, Hamish Hamilton, 1985.

Hardy, Forsyth, *John Grierson: A Documentary Biography*, Faber & Faber, 1979.

Hawkins, Jack, *Anything for a Quiet Life*, Hamish Hamilton, 1973.

Henrey, Robert, *A Film Star in Belgrave Square*, Peter Davies, 1948.

Hodgkinson, Anthony W. and Sheratsky, Rodney E., *Humphrey Jennings: More than a Maker of Films*, University Press of New England, 1982.

Holloway, Stanley, *Wiv A Little Bit o' Luck*, Leslie Frewin, 1969.

Howard, Leslie Ruth, *A Quite Remarkable Father*, Longmans, 1959.

Howard, Ronald, *In Search of My Father*, William Kimber, 1981.

Jackson, Kevin (ed.), *The Humphrey Jennings Film Reader*, Carcanet, 1993.

Korda, Michael, *Charmed Lives*, Allen Lane, 1980.

Kulik, Karol, *Alexander Korda*, W. H. Allen, 1975.

Lejeune, C. A., *Thanks for Having Me*, Hutchinson, 1964.

McCallum, John, *Life with Googie*, Heinemann, 1979.

MacQuitty, Bill, *A Life to Remember*, Quartet, 1991.

Mason, James, *Before I Forget*, Hamish Hamilton, 1981.

Mills, John, *Up in the Clouds, Gentlemen, Please*, Weidenfeld & Nicolson, 1980.

Minney, R. J., *Puffin Asquith*, Leslie Frewin, 1973.

Montagu, Ivor, *The Youngest Son: Autobiographical Sketches*, Lawrence & Wishart, 1970.

Moorehead, Caroline, *Sidney Bernstein: A Biography*, Jonathan Cape, 1984.

Neagle, Anna, *There's Always Tomorow: An Autobiography*, W. H. Allen, 1974.

Norton, Richard (Lord Grantley), *Silver Spoon*, Hutchinson, 1954.

Pascal, Valerie, *The Disciple and His Devil*, Michael Joseph, 1971.

Pellizzari, Lorenzo and Valentinetti, Claudio M. (eds), *Alberto

Cavalcanti, Editions du Festival international du film de Locarno, 1988.

Powell, Michael, *A Life in Movies*, Heinemann, 1986.

——, *Million-Dollar Movie*, Heinemann, 1993.

Redgrave, Michael, *In My Mind's Eye*, Weidenfeld & Nicolson, 1983.

Silverman, Stephen, *David Lean*, André Deutsch, 1989.

Spoto, Donald, *The Dark Side of Genius: The Life of Alfred Hitchcock*, Ballantine Books, 1983.

Todd, Ann, *The Eighth Veil*, William Kimber, 1980.

Trevelyan, John, *What the Censor Saw*, Michael Joseph, 1973.

Ustinov, Peter, *Dear Me*, Heinemann, 1977.

Vaughan, Dai, *Portrait of an Invisible Man*, BFI, 1983.

Wapshott, Nicholas, *Carol Reed*, Chatto & Windus, 1990.

Watt, Harry, *Don't Look at the Camera*, Elek Books, 1974.

Wilcox, Herbert, *Twenty-five Thousand Sunsets*, Bodley Head, 1967.

Wilcox, Pamela, *Between Hell and Charing Cross*, Allen & Unwin, 1977.

Wood, Alan, *Mr Rank: A Study of J. Arthur Rank and British Films*, Hodder & Stoughton, 1952.

Publications since 1997

Aitken, Ian, *Alberto Cavalcanti: Realism, Surrealism and National Cinemas*, Flicks Books, 2000.

Babington, Bruce, *Launder and Gilliat*, Manchester University Press, 2002.

Baker, Roy Ward, *Director's Cut: A Memoir of Sixty Years in Film and Television*, Reynolds & Hearn, 2000.

Box, Betty, *Lifting the Lid: The Autobiography of Film Producer, Betty Box*, Book Guild, 2000.

Box, Sydney, *The Lion That Lost Its Way: And Other Cautionary Tales of the Showbusiness Jungle*, Scarecrow Press, 2005.

Chapman, James, *The British at War: Cinema, State and Propaganda 1939–1945*, I.B.Tauris, 2000.

Christie, Ian and Andrew Moor (eds), International Perspectives on an English Film-maker, BFI Publishing, 2005.

Drazin, Charles, *Alexander Korda: Britain's Only Movie Mogul*, Sidgwick & Jackson, 2002.

Drazin, Charles, *In Search of The Third Man*, Methuen, 1999.

Evans, Peter, *Carol Reed*, Manchester University Press, 2005.

Figgis, Mike and Justin Boyer, *Conversations with Jack Cardiff: Art, Light and Direction in Cinema*, Batsford, 2003.

Glancy, Mark, *When Hollywood Loved Britain: The Hollywood British Film 1939–1945*, Manchester University Press, 1999.

Jackson, Kevin, *Humphrey Jennings*, Picador, 2004.

Jackson Pat, *A Retake Please: Night Mail to Western Approaches*, Liverpool University Press, 1999.

Lean Sandra and Barry Chattington, *David Lean: An Intimate Portrait*, Carlton Books, 2001.

Mayer, Geoff, Roy *Ward Baker*, Manchester University Press, 2004.

McFarlane, Brian, *An Autobiography of British Cinema*, Methuen, 1997.

——, *The Encylopedia of British Film*, Methuen, 2nd edn, 2005.

——, *Lance Comfort*, Manchester University Press, 2000.

Moor, Andrew, *Powell and Pressburger: A Cinema of Magic Spaces*, I.B.Tauris, 2005.

Murphy, Robert, *British Cinema and the Second World War*, Continuum, 2005.

Neame, Ronald, *Straight from the Horse's Mouth*, Scarecrow Press, 2002.

Ryall, Tom, *Anthony Asquith*, Manchester University Press, 2006.

Spicer, Andrew, *Sydney Box*, Manchester University Press, 2006.

Street, Sarah, *Black Narcissus*, I.B.Tauris, 2005.

Sweet, Matthew, *Shepperton Babylon: The Lost Worlds of British Cinema*, Faber & Faber, 2005.

Von Kassel, Elena Siambani, *Poésie et science sociales, sources du documentaire anglais des années 1930–1950. L'exemple de Humphey Jennings*, ANRT, 2003.

Young, Freddie, *Seventy Light Years*, Faber & Faber, 1999.

Index

Krish, John, 149, 157, 160, 161, 164
'Kuleshov effect', 158

La Bern, Arthur, 76
Lamp Still Burns, The, 19
Lang, Fritz, 176
Langlois, Henri, 242
Lassie, 176
Laughton, Charles, 142
Lawrence of Arabia, 63, 66, 230
Lean, David, 6, 15, 55; uncompromis-
    ing approach, 56; the film-maker,
    56–8, 131; and landscapes, 58;
    command and control of, 58–9, 61,
    64; upbringing of, 61–2; efficiency
    of 63–4, on Anthony Asquith, 186
Lee, Jack, 154, 170
Lee, Nora, 148, 150, 153–4, 160, 165,
    166, 170
Lejeune, C. A., 11, 64
Lerner, Alan Jay, 233–4
L'Herbier, Marcel, 114
Life and Death of Colonel Blimp, The, 49
Life of Marlborough, The, 26
Lilacs in Spring, 223
Lindgren, Ernest, 236, 242–3
Lion Has Wings, The, 163
Listen to Britain, 122, 128, 154, 156,
    157, 158, 166, 170
Lloyd, Harold, 123
Lloyds Bank, 37
Lockhart, Sir Robert Bruce, 21, 23
Lockwood, Margaret, 51, 80, 208, 217
Loewe, Frederick, 233–4
London Can Take It, 143, 170
London Film Institute Society, 240
London Films, 145, 165
London Melody, 216
London Town, 26
Long Memory, The, 83
Lonsdale, Frederick, 204
Love Story, 208
Loves of Jeanne Ney, The, 241
Loves of Joanna Godden, The, 107
Lowry, Malcolm, 87
Lucky Jim, 107
Lumière d'Eté, 242
Lye, Len, 119

Macbeth, 39
Mackenzie, Compton, 109
Macphail, Angus, 25–6, 74, 106, 108;

memory of, 89–90, 93–4, 98; writ-
    ing skills, 90, 97–8; eccentricity of,
    90; early life, 90–91; and trivia, 91-
    –2; the screenwriter, 93; old-fash-
    ioned attitudes of, 95–6; contradic-
    tions of, 96; and alcohol, 96, 98–9;
    final years, 96–9
MacQuitty, Bill, 27, 46–7, 52–3, 178–9,
    202, 209
Madness of the Heart, 51
Madonna of the Seven Moons, 212
Magnificent Ambersons, The, 9
Major Barbara, 227
Man in Grey, The, 206
Man of Aran, 103, 104
March of Time, 12
Mason, James, 200, 206, 207, 208
Mass Observation, 151–2
Matter of Life and Death, A, 4
Mayer, Carl, 21, 204
Mayer, Louis B., 102
Maytime in Mayfair, 218
McAllister, Stewart, 152–3, 154–5
McCallum, John, 74, 83
McCrea, John, 143
Melvin, Duncan, 238–9
Mendoza Joe, 122, 124, 126, 143, 144,
    147, 149, 150, 154, 157, 158, 211
Men of Two Worlds, 25
Menuhin, Diana, 186
Menuhin, Yehudi, 186, 195
Meredith, Burgess, 193
MGM, 2, 8, 10, 101–2, 175, 176
Miles, Bernard, 29–30, 31, 38
Miller, Hugh, 92
Milne, A. A., 17
Minerva Films, 17
Ministry of Information, 15, 25, 120,
    121–2, 142, 145, 148, 163–4, 167–8,
    177–84, 193, 194, 204, 228–9
Minney, R. J., 232
Mistress Masham's Repose, 10
Mitchell, Bill, 179
Monsieur Verdoux, 77
Montagu, Ivor, 45, 79, 90, 91, 92–3, 97,
    99, 102, 108, 109, 110
Moore, George, 168
Moore, Kieron, 32
Morgan, Charles, 133
Morgan, Diana, 73–4, 75, 76, 82, 84,
    85, 86, 89, 90, 246
Morgan, Guy, 11, 64
Motion Picture Association of

Index

DH

791.
430
941
090
44
DRA